## ADVANCE PRAISE FOR *THE REAL PROBLEM SOLVERS*

"*The Real Problem Solvers* provides singular insight into the aspirations, challenges, and opportunities of those who are at the front of the social entrepreneurial movement. This is a must-read for the leaders in organizations that seek societal impact at the 'blurred edge' between the non-profit and for-profit worlds."

—*Dominic Barton, Global Managing Partner, McKinsey & Company*

"In this treasure chest of a book, Ruth Shapiro deftly presents and weaves together perspectives from leading thinkers and practitioners in social entrepreneurship. By engaging them in conversations and offering her own well-grounded insights, she deeply enriches our understanding of this important and evolving field."

—*J. Gregory Dees, Center for the Advancement of Social Entrepreneurship,*
*Duke University*

"A wonderful introduction to social entrepreneurship in the United States and the growing ecosystem of organizations committed to supporting it. Ruth Shapiro frames this book with an engaging and insightful account of the critical influences that have spurred social entrepreneurs to take on some of our society's most challenging problems. Regardless of the problems that these pragmatic visionaries seek to address, this book shows that their magic lies in combining innovation, resourcefulness, and opportunity—with an unwillingness to give in to setbacks."

—*Pamela Hartigan, Director, Skoll Centre for Social Entrepreneurship,*
*The University of Oxford*

"In the past ten years, a rich ecosystem has developed around the idea, energy, and success of social entrepreneurs. With years of experience, Ruth Shapiro captures the complexity and complementarity of the men and women whose innovation and drive are changing the way that we solve social problems; it should be required reading for all."

—*Bill Draper, Co-Chair, Draper Richards Kaplan Foundation,*
*General Partner, Draper Richards LLC, and author of* The Start-up Game

"Good leaders inspire, motivate, and create alliances toward attaining lofty goals. This book is full of such people and their stories. A worthwhile read indeed!"

—*Henry R. Kravis, Co-Chief Executive Officer, Kohlberg Kravis Roberts & Co.*

# THE REAL PROBLEM SOLVERS

# THE REAL PROBLEM SOLVERS

## SOLVERS

SOCIAL ENTREPRENEURS IN AMERICA

EDITED BY

# RUTH A. SHAPIRO

STANFORD BUSINESS BOOKS

An Imprint of Stanford University Press

Stanford, California

Stanford University Press
Stanford, California

Special discounts for bulk quantities of Stanford Business Books are available to corporations, professional associations, and other organizations. For details and discount information, contact the special sales department of Stanford University Press. Tel: (650) 736-1782, Fax: (650) 736-1784

Printed in the United States of America on acid-free, archival-quality paper

Library of Congress Cataloging-in-Publication Data

The Real Problem Solvers : Social Entrepreneurs in America / edited by Ruth A. Shapiro.
    pages cm
  Includes bibliographical references and index.
  ISBN 978-0-8047-7440-6 (cloth : alk. paper)—ISBN 978-0-8047-7441-3 (pbk. : alk. paper)
1. Social entrepreneurship—United States.  2. Nonprofit organizations—United States.
3. Businesspeople—United States—Interviews.  4. Philanthropists—United States—
Interviews.  I. Shapiro, Ruth A., editor of compilation.
  HD60.5.U5R42 2012
  338'.040973—dc23
                                                                2012025124

Typeset by Thompson Type in 10/14 Minion

Dedicated to social entrepreneurs around the world.
Live long and thrive!

# CONTENTS

Acknowledgments                                                          xi

List of Contributors                                                     xv

1   Introduction                                                          1

## SECTION 1
## THE ENTREPRENEURS:
## MESSAGE FROM THE FRONT LINES

2   Investing in Microfinance                                           19
    Premal Shah, President, Kiva

3   Dollars, Sense, and Dignity                                         30
    Conchy Bretos, Founder, Mia Senior Living Solutions

4   The Power of an Economic Niche                                      38
    Mary Houghton, President and Co-Founder, ShoreBank Corporation

5   Building on Faith                                                   49
    Louise Burnham Packard, Founder and Executive Director,
    Trinity Boston Foundation

6   The Entrepreneurs: A Conversation                                   59

## SECTION 2
## THE FUNDERS AND INVESTORS:
## WHY WE ARE DIFFERENT FROM TRADITIONAL PHILANTHROPISTS

7   The Power of Social Entrepreneurs                                   69
    Sally Osberg, President and CEO, Skoll Foundation

8    A Hybrid Approach to Supporting Social Entrepreneurs          81
     Matt Bannick, Managing Partner, Omidyar Network

9    Harnessing Entrepreneurial Energy                             92
     William Foote, Founder and CEO, Root Capital

10   The Strength of Business in Sustainable Change                102
     Jacqueline Novogratz, Founder and CEO, The Acumen Fund

11   Funders and Investors: A Conversation                         111

## SECTION 3
## THE THINKERS:
## PROFOUNDLY NEW IDEAS CREATE NEW PARADIGMS FOR CHANGE

12   A Community Committed to Social Entrepreneurship              123
     Christopher Gergen, Founder and CEO, Forward Ventures

13   Social Entrepreneurship and Social Innovation:
     What's New, and Why Is It Important?                          132
     Kriss Deiglmeier, Executive Director, Stanford Center for
     Social Innovation

14   The Blended Value Imperative                                  141
     Jed Emerson, Founder, Blended Value

15   The Thinkers: A Conversation                                  151

## SECTION 4
## THE CHAMPIONS:
## ELEVATING THE DISCOURSE TO GLOBAL DIMENSIONS

16   Collaborative Entrepreneurship: The Way to the "Everyone
     a Change-Maker" Society                                       163
     Bill Drayton, Founder, Chairman, and CEO, Ashoka

17   Building Social Business                                      177
     Muhammad Yunus, Founder, Grameen Bank

18   The Champions: A Conversation                                 187

19   The New Thinking about Social Entrepreneurship                199

Bibliography and Suggested Resources                              215
Index                                                            219

# ACKNOWLEDGMENTS

For a social entrepreneur to be successful, she must find supportive people along the way. Organizations like Ashoka and Draper Richards Kaplan recognize that early support is not only the most critical but the hardest to find. As John Naisbitt famously pointed out, leadership is often the ability to find a parade and march in front of it. Identifying and supporting a person with a new idea takes more skill and more courage.

I have been extremely fortunate to have six such people in my life who supported me when I had an idea that was not yet "proven." I am grateful for the opportunity to thank them and explain why they have been and continue to be so important to me and to the organizations and programs I have built.

Gail McClure, through the W. K. Kellogg Foundation, provided the initial funding for the Asia Business Initiative, the precursor of what was to become the Asia Business Council. By providing early financial support, Gail gave me not only the means to focus on my task but a stamp of approval that was invaluable in securing additional funding. When I came to her years later with the idea for the series that was the basis for this book, she once again provided initial funding, allowing the seed of the project to take root and grow.

Lewis Platt was Chairman and CEO of Hewlett Packard when I met him through a crucial introduction by Susan Packard Orr of the David and Lucile Packard Foundation. Lew was an extraordinary leader, and the world lost a great mind and heart with his early passing in 2005. It was rather intimidating for me to walk into Hewlett Packard in 1997 armed with an idea and a great deal of enthusiasm. Lew did not hesitate. His first words after hearing my presentation were, "Let's do this." After leaving the HP campus, I had to pull the car to the side of the road and have a good cry due to the somewhat unbelievable outcome that someone in his position would affirm and support me.

John C. Whitehead had retired from leading Goldman Sachs when I met him in 1997. I asked him to be on the steering committee of the initiative so that the influence and respect he commanded in the business community could be brought to bear on the project. He said he would on the condition that I go out and find six other business leaders to be on the steering committee as well. After more than a year, I was able to go back to John with the news that Washington Sycip, Lew Platt, Ronnie Chan, David K. P. Li, Dick Shoemate, and Stan Shih had also agreed. Then John said, "Okay, now I want Harvard Business School to be involved." This took a number of trips from San Francisco to Boston, and with the help of Kim Clark, the former Dean of HBS, Mike Yoshino and Dorothy Leonard signed on. I went back to John. He said, "Now we need to involve the Asia Society," whose board he had recently chaired. With his and Ronnie Chan's assistance, I was able to secure help from Nick Platt in New York and Mary Lee Turner in Hong Kong, who provided critical logistical support in setting up our first meetings in Asia. Finally, after I had filled out the steering committee and enlisted the support of Harvard Business School and the Asia Society, John agreed to be on the steering committee. This may have seemed like many hoops to jump through, but John's style of mentoring allowed me to significantly strengthen the organization by creating crucial alliances and types of support. By the time I had accomplished all these tasks, we had a solid foundation to build on.

Ronnie Chan's dual role in the world, one of extremely successful businessman and the other of a believer and leader of social institutions and their value for society, makes him a unique and extraordinary man. After agreeing to be the Asia Business Council's first Chairman, he travelled around Asia with me, building support for the organization. These trips remain a highlight of my professional career.

S. Dhanabalan, Chairman of Temasek, Singapore's sovereign wealth fund, has been a friend and mentor to me since we met in 1999. He became the second Chairman of the Asia Business Council and continues to guide and support its work. Most importantly for me now, he continues to provide priceless support and guidance for my new initiatives.

Gloria C. Duffy is the President and CEO of the Commonwealth Club of California. When I was working on the Asia Business Initiative from my bedroom, she created the Commonwealth Club Fellows program and named me the Inaugural Fellow, thus allowing me to have a desk, a phone, and a computer with which to carry out my work. Years later, after I returned from living abroad, she repeated this generous act by naming me the Social Entrepreneur in Residence at the Commonwealth Club, thus setting the stage for the series at the Club and this book. Gloria remains a great friend and mentor.

This book started out as a speaker series with the generous support of the W. K. Kellogg Foundation, the Skoll Foundation, and the Omidyar Network. The talks took place at the Commonwealth Club in San Francisco. The talented staff of the Club became friends and colleagues. I would especially like to thank Oona Marti, John Zipperer, George Dobbins, and Caroline Moriarity Sacks for all their help. Proceeds from this book will go to the Commonwealth Club of California.

As an edited volume, this book owes its existence and value to its exceptional group of contributors. I could write much about each of the contributors to this volume, but suffice it to say that it was a great honor and privilege to work with each of them and to delve deeper into their work and thoughts regarding social entrepreneurship. I would like to thank each of them from the bottom of my heart. I would especially like to thank Louise Burnham Packard, who helped incubate the idea for the series and the book, and also Kriss Deiglmeier, who throughout this process became a colleague and great friend. I would also like to single out some of the contributors' colleagues who added to the great pleasure and privilege it was for me to be able to work with such a gifted group of people. From Ashoka, I would like to thank Diana Wells whose insights, generous spirit, and thoughtful help are greatly appreciated. Sarah Johnson and Samara Lemke also helped to make Bill's talk at the Commonwealth Club and subsequent chapter so successful. At the Omidyar Network, Susan Philips and Paula Goldman added much to the process and the outcome. At Skoll, Bruce Lowry and Talia Means were very helpful. Todd Bernhardt of the Grameen Foundation was instrumental in connecting with Muhammad Yunus.

I would also like to thank Bill Draper, Christy Chin, Eric Weaver, Regina Ridley, Pamela Hartigan, Trabian Shorters, John Whitman, Jim Thompson, Rick Aubry, Caitlin McShane, Hilary Wilson, Tom Reis, JoAnne Wallace and Margaret Lee of KQED, David Lehr, Amy Bennett, Karen Mundy, Lucy Cummings, Rita Mahoney, Molly White, Pam Joyce, and Chris Thomas. I would also like to thank Katia Madjidi, who provided excellent editing assistance.

I have been extraordinarily fortunate to spend a great deal of my life thinking about and living and working in Asia. Northern California is a place that embraces risk and entrepreneurship, but, increasingly, so does much of Asia.

In both places, it is so much less about where you came from and so much more about where you want to go. In Asia, I would like to thank Washington SyCip, Jaime Zobel, James Go, Tessie Sy-Coson, Azman Mokhtar, Nazir Razak, K. P. Khoo, George Tahija, Koh Boon Hwee, Anthoni Salim, Lim Chee Onn, N. L. Wong, Jamshyd and Pheroza Godrej, Ratan Tata, Anand Mahindra, Narayana Murthy, Mukesh Ambani, Shin Dong Bin, Chey Tae-won, Seung-Yu Kim, David K. P. Li, C. C. Tung, Christine Loh, Winnie Wu, Nancy Hernriech Bowen, Louis Bowen, Neal Horwitz, Jane Horan, Wendy Hong, Mark Clifford, Edward Tian, Zhang Xin, Hong Huang, Qin Xiao, Gao XiQing, Happy Harun, Levin Zhu, Stan Shih, Morris Chang, Daniel Tsai, Douglas Tong Hsu, Matthew Miau, Diane Ying, Vichit Suraphonghchai, Chumpol Nalamlieng, Banthoon Lamsam, Dominic Barton, Nobuyuki Idei, Yoshihiko Miyauchi, Tony Kobayashi, and my dear friends Ann Kildahl and Robyn Meredith. I would also like to include Gerard Kleisterlee, David Coulter, Tom Clausen, and Marcus Wallenberg, with whom I was able to work and build friendships initially due to a shared appreciation of the importance of Asia.

It is not everyone who has the rare opportunity to work with the likes of Margo Beth Fleming and Jessica Walsh at Stanford University Press. Margo sets a high bar, and there is no doubt her keen eye and pen helped elevate this manuscript to a much higher level.

I am extremely blessed to have a wonderful sister, Karen Shapiro, who is my constant cheerleader and dear and cherished friend, and my lovely and talented daughters Shana and Zoe, who are growing up in a world full of complex challenges. They have put up with a peripatetic mother with grace and understanding. They and their generation must master the notion of challenging the status quo and finding real solutions. Lastly, my husband and best friend Michael Gallagher: I could not dream of a better partner to share the adventure of life.

# CONTRIBUTORS

**Premal Shah**
**President, Kiva**
In late 2004, Shah took a three-month leave from his job at PayPal to develop and test the Internet microfinance concept in India. When he returned to Silicon Valley, he met other like-minded dreamers and quit his job to help bring the Kiva concept to life. Today, Kiva raises over $1 million each week for the working poor in over fifty countries and was named a Top 50 Website by *Time Magazine* in 2009. For his work as a social entrepreneur, Shah was named a Young Global Leader by the World Economic Forum and selected as one of *Fortune Magazine*'s "Top 40 under 40" in 2009.

**Conchy Bretos**
**Founder, Mia Senior Living Solutions**
Conchy Bretos saw senior citizens living in decrepit public housing units when she was Florida's Secretary for Aging and Adult Services. In 1996, she convinced the Miami Dade County Housing Authority to let her revamp a run-down building and create The Helen Sawyer Plaza with $1.2 million in Medicaid funding. The project became a national model and has been replicated in twenty-one states serving over 5,000 clients. Bretos received the first Purpose Prize in 2006 and became an Ashoka Fellow in 2010. In 2011, Bretos was named one of the most promising social entrepreneurs by Bloomberg Business Week.

**Mary Houghton**
**President and Co-Founder, ShoreBank Corporation**
Mary Houghton was one of four founders of ShoreBank Corporation, the first regulated commercial bank holding company in the United States with investors

who explicitly combined financial and social objectives. After ShoreBank Corporation began to wind down in 2010, Houghton became a visiting scholar at the School of Advanced International Studies of The Johns Hopkins University in Washington, D.C. She has joined the boards of two other mission-driven regulated financial institutions, one in India and the other in Vancouver.

### Louise Burnham Packard
**Founder and Executive Director, Trinity Boston Foundation**
Louise Burnham Packard is the Founding Executive Director of the Trinity Boston Foundation, a community-based organization focused on urban youth that is a subsidiary of Boston's historic Trinity Church. Earlier in her career, she was Associate Director of Admissions at Yale University and held senior development positions at Trinity Church, Harvard Business School, Stanford Graduate School of Business, and the Central Park Conservancy.

### Sally Osberg
**President and CEO, Skoll Foundation**
As President and CEO of the Skoll Foundation, Sally Osberg partners with Founder and Chairman Jeff Skoll and heads the organization's team in identifying and supporting innovators pioneering scalable solutions to global challenges. She is a well-known proponent of thought leadership, research, and alliances that advance the work of social entrepreneurs solving the world's most pressing problems. Osberg has received the John Gardner Leadership Award from the American Leadership Forum, been inducted into the Junior Achievement Business Hall of Fame, and been named by the *San Jose Mercury News* as one of the "Millennium 100" for her role in shaping and leading Silicon Valley.

### Matt Bannick
**Managing Partner, Omidyar Network**
As Managing Partner of Omidyar Network, Matt Bannick guides the firm's strategy for market-based investments that provide hundreds of millions of people with the opportunity to improve their lives. Prior to joining the Omidyar Network, Bannick served as President of PayPal and of eBay International; he led eBay's expansion from five to twenty-five countries and spearheaded the company's Global Development and Citizenship initiatives. A graduate of Harvard Business School and the University of Washington, Bannick spent early years of his career as a consultant for McKinsey & Company in both North

America and Europe and was a U.S. diplomat in Germany during the time of the fall of the Berlin Wall.

## William Foote
### Founder and CEO, Root Capital

William Foote is Founder and CEO of Root Capital. He has received the Joan Bavaria Innovation Award and the Skoll Award for Social Entrepreneurship and has been named an Ashoka Global Fellow, Young Global Leader, and member of the Young Presidents' Organization (YPO). Foote serves on the executive committee of the Aspen Network of Development Entrepreneurs (ANDE) and is a member of the Council on Foreign Relations.

## Jacqueline Novogratz
### Founder and CEO, The Acumen Fund

Jacqueline Novogratz is the Founder and CEO of Acumen Fund, a nonprofit global venture fund that uses entrepreneurial approaches to solve the problems of poverty. Her best-selling memoir *The Blue Sweater: Bridging the Gap between Rich and Poor in an Interconnected World* chronicles her quest to understand poverty and challenges readers to grant dignity to the poor and to rethink their engagement with the world.

## Christopher Gergen
### Founder and CEO, Forward Ventures

Christopher Gergen is Founder and CEO of Forward Ventures, where he oversees the operations of Bull City Forward and Queen City Forward. Forward Ventures complements Gergen's role as a fellow at the Center for the Advancement of Social Entrepreneurship (CASE) at Duke University's Fuqua School of Business, as well as his position as "Innovator in Residence" at the Center for Creative Leadership. Gergen is also the co-author of the nationally acclaimed book *Life Entrepreneurs: Ordinary People Creating Extraordinary Lives* and currently co-authors a biweekly column on social innovation for the *Raleigh News & Observer* and the *Charlotte Observer* titled "Doing Better at Doing Good."

## Kriss Deiglmeier
### Executive Director, Stanford Center for Social Innovation

Kriss Deiglmeier is the Founding Executive Director for the Center for Social Innovation at the Stanford Graduate School of Business. Deiglmeier is recognized as a pioneer in the emerging field of social innovation and has presented nationally and internationally on social innovation, social entrepreneurship, and public–private partnerships, as well as having guest-lectured at the Stanford Graduate School of Business; University of California, Berkeley; Hitotsubashi University; Kyoto University; Kyushu University; and Nagoya University.

## Jed Emerson
### Founder, Blended Value

Jed Emerson is co-author of the recently published *Impact Investing: Transforming How We Make Money while Making a Difference*. In 2011, he was named to both the Power 25 (*Private Asset Management Magazine*) and Top 100 Thought Leaders of Trust across America. He is Senior Vice President of ImpactAssets, Senior Advisor to the RS Group (Hong Kong), and a Senior Fellow with the University of Heidelberg, Germany. Emerson is the originator of the concept of Blended Value.

## Bill Drayton
### Founder, Chairman, and CEO, Ashoka

As one of the world's leading thinkers on social change and the Founder and CEO of Ashoka, Bill Drayton pioneered the field of social entrepreneurship. Over the past thirty years, Ashoka has elected nearly 3,000 social entrepreneurs as Ashoka Fellows, providing them with stipends, professional support, and access to a global network of peers. In recognition of this achievement, Drayton has received numerous honors, including a MacArthur Fellowship and the Essl Social Prize. He has worked as a management consultant at McKinsey, Assistant Administrator at the EPA, and as a teacher of law and management at Stanford and Harvard.

## Muhammad Yunus
### Founder, Grameen Bank

Recipient of the 2006 Nobel Peace Prize, Muhammad Yunus is internationally recognized for his work in poverty alleviation and the empowerment of poor women. Yunus has successfully melded capitalism with social responsibility to create the Grameen Bank, a microcredit institution committed to providing small amounts of working capital to the poor for self-employment. The innovative approach to poverty alleviation pioneered by Yunus in a small village in

Bangladesh has inspired a global microcredit movement reaching out to millions of poor women from rural South Africa to inner city Chicago. His autobiography, *Banker to the Poor: Microlending and the Battle Against World Poverty*, is a global best seller.

### Ruth A. Shapiro

Ruth A. Shapiro is the Principal of Keyi Strategies, a consulting firm specializing in creating broader networks, understanding, and business ventures between individuals and companies in Asia, Europe, and the United States. She is also Social Entrepreneur in Residence at the Commonwealth Club of California. Shapiro was the Founder of the Asia Business Council and served as its first Executive Director from its inception in 1997. She is now Senior Advisor.

# THE REAL PROBLEM SOLVERS

# INTRODUCTION

The term *social entrepreneur* and the field of "social entrepreneurship" are not universally agreed-upon constructs. In fact, they are complex, contested, and changing, with definitions, methods, and fields of engagement often as unique and varied as the individuals themselves who are innovating in this field.

My own foray into this work began in 1997, the year of the crash of the bhat in Thailand and the start of the Asian economic crisis. During my doctoral work comparing American and Japanese international development assistance, I had become a believer in the power of business in economic development. I did not go so far as to side with the "trade not aid" mantra,[1] but I do believe that business has to be an integral part of any country's economic development strategy and tool kit. During the Asian economic crisis, Asian companies were facing new challenges that had not heretofore been part of their world. Many Asian companies, weaned within the cozy confines of their home economy, had become regional and begun to face new and important competitive challenges, including the need to compete without the support of their home governments, the realities of differing cultural expectations, and, in 1997, exposure to volatile capital markets and currency fluctuations caused by the crisis. Massive downsizing coupled with the lack of a social safety net in many Asian economies increased the political and social turbulence in the region. It became clear that companies needed to think through not only the specific challenges of responding to the crisis but also the larger question of what the role of the corporation was in society.

In response to this need, I felt it was my role to help them with this conversation and ideally to help provide the tools for them to be engaged corporate citizens. I decided to create the Asia Business Council, a membership organization of primarily Asia-based CEOs, to help them think through what the role of the corporation is in society and what it means to be an Asian firm today. I raised all the start-up capital, built the organization, recruited the members and the staff, put into place programs that had never been part of the Asian landscape, and pioneered a new type of CEO membership organization in the region. It was innovative and bold, and the Council became an important player in the nascent world of business–civil society intermediary organizations of Asia.

In the meantime, the emerging field of social entrepreneurship was continuing to grow and develop. The attributes of a social entrepreneur that I read about, such as the ability to see and seize an opportunity, unwillingness to cede defeat, tenacity, and the ability to reconfigure a strategy when approaching a dead end, were all characteristics that had allowed me to successfully create and build the Council. My family and I moved to Hong Kong in 2003 so I could continue to build up and run the Asia Business Council. When I came back to the United States, it was not immediately clear whether I could become a "serial social entrepreneur" as well as build on my own experiences and skills.

I was thinking about this issue while driving and listening to a program on social entrepreneurs airing on NPR. It featured what seemed to me to be very effective nonprofit founders and managers. What was it that made them "social entrepreneurs"? I decided that if I had these questions, surely others did as well. I conducted a small experiment and randomly asked ten people on University Avenue in Palo Alto what they thought the definition of *social entrepreneurship* was. Seven of them thought it was some kind of business on Facebook. Surely, there was a need for more information! So I approached my dear friend Gloria Duffy, president of the Commonwealth Club, and asked if I could create a series on social entrepreneurship in America. I proposed that the series include leading lights in the field, social entrepreneurs themselves, as well as funders, investors, and academics who are doing much to shape the field. She was enthusiastic, as were the W. K. Kellogg Foundation, the Skoll Foundation, and the Omidyar Network, who generously agreed to provide funding for the series. Each of the chapters in this book began as a talk presented as part of the series on social entrepreneurship. The goal of the series and of the book is to provide an introductory overview of the field from a range of perspectives within it. Cumulatively, the voices here present important thinking and views on the field of social entrepreneurship, how it is evolving, and the impact it is having on traditional philanthropy and non-profit management.

This book will allow the reader to answer the following questions:

1. What aspects of social entrepreneurship are particularly compelling and inspirational?
2. How has the field of social entrepreneurship evolved, and what are the implications for traditional philanthropy, nonprofit management, and social change?
3. What barriers are being broken down and through these changes providing social good?

## What Is Social Entrepreneurship?

To create the series, I first had to investigate what the evolution of thinking on the field has been and what the key questions are in the current discourse. What makes someone a social entrepreneur? What are some of the basic assumptions and agreed-upon definitions? What are the key components? What are some of the major debates currently framing the field?

The term *social entrepreneur* was originally coined by Bill Drayton of Ashoka in the early 1980s to refer to someone with the passion and focus of an entrepreneur who tackles a social challenge. Drayton recognized that many of the same attributes that drive traditional entrepreneurs to create new ventures also drive social entrepreneurs. Himself a great social entrepreneur, Drayton built Ashoka to find and fund the most extraordinary of these men and women around the world.

All over the world, individuals with and without resources are crafting new opportunities and finding new ways to approach age-old dilemmas. Greg Dees, a Duke University professor who has been one of the most important academic voices in the field, wrote the following definition in 2001:

Social entrepreneurs play the role of change agents in the social sector, by:
- Adopting a mission to create and sustain social value (not just private value),
- Recognizing and relentlessly pursuing new opportunities to serve that mission,
- Engaging in a process of continuous innovation, adaptation, and learning,

- Acting boldly without being limited by resources currently in hand, and
- Exhibiting heightened accountability to their constituencies.[2]

While Dees's definition still holds, there seem to be new characteristics that are coming into play, characteristics that are breaking from traditional philanthropic and charitable organizational behavior. The goal of these new efforts is the same: making the world a better place. The extraordinary passion that these change-makers are bringing to their life's work has also not changed. What have changed are some of the ways in which this work is getting done. Much of the change in the approach has to do with the application of capitalist tools to bring about social change. In many cases, social entrepreneurship has morphed into much more of a market-based discipline.

How does one apply a business model to social change? While few would argue that one cannot take an entirely capitalist model to carry out social good, many in the field look to facets of profit-seeking behavior and traditional business models to explain and develop the field of social entrepreneurship. Jim Fruchterman, CEO of Benetech, put it this way:

> Entrepreneurs must understand their market. Just about every social question and issue you may address can be recast into market questions, such as: Who is the customer? What is the value proposition? And who is the competition? Understanding your customers, their environment, and their needs is crucial to any social venture.[3]

Elkington and Hartigan write in their book *The Power of Unreasonable People* that "the real measure of social entrepreneurship is a direct action that generates a paradigm shift in the way societal need is met."[4] Within a business context, this is the goal of *creative destruction,* the term rehabilitated by Joseph Schumpeter to mean system change or transformation as a result of an extraordinary innovation.[5] In Schumpeter's theory, new innovations destroy the need for old, as cars replace horses, computers replace typewriters, and so on.

This notion of an innovation changing the status quo has been embraced to a breathtaking degree by those within Silicon Valley. While social entrepreneurship has captured the imagination of people around the world, nowhere is this more true than in Silicon Valley, where many of the most successful men and women devote extraordinary resources to the continued stimulus and support of the field. As we will see throughout the book, there are significant parallels between the goals of a high-tech entrepreneur and those of a social entrepreneur. As Daniel Bornstein wrote in his groundbreaking book on Ashoka and the social entrepreneurial movement, "Everywhere you look, conceptual firewalls that once divided the world into social and economic realms are coming down and people are engaging the world with their whole brains."[6]

Aside from the overarching goal of widespread social change, the transfer of a business mind-set to civil society has brought about strategic and behavioral changes in how individuals and organizations conduct their work. These changes have primarily manifested in three ways: (1) a blurring of the demarcation between for profit and nonprofit activities; (2) an increased emphasis on results and measuring impact; and (3) a focus on scale—how to find successful innovations and cause them to proliferate widely to create the greatest societal change. Throughout this book, these three themes will provide important frameworks within which to look at the field as a whole and how it is changing nonprofit management and strategy.

The first theme, the "nonprofit" versus "for profit" question, and an increased blurring between these two, continues to be a hot topic of debate, as you will read in the various chapters of this book. Nonprofit organizations are still alive and well in the United States. We have a long history of robust civil society organizations, and this continues to gain strength: From 1995 to 2005, the number of nonprofit organizations registered with the IRS grew by 53 percent. However, the traditional definitions of the nonprofit are being challenged. The term *nonprofit organization* implies that the organization, focused on social change and impact, does not make a profit. In the past, this equating of social service work with nonprofit balance sheets was sacrosanct. To do good, common practice and wisdom told us, we could not also do well financially. Now that notion is being turned on its head. Not only do social investors believe that it is possible to do good and do well, but other aspects of an old mind-set are also falling away. Many of these organizations come with skilled and passionate people, innovative funding streams, and new ideas about solutions to our social problems. And many nonprofit organizations are developing profitable income streams to help both their constituencies and the sustainability of their organizations. For example, Juma Ventures, a pioneer in the field of integrating non- and for-profit activities, works holistically with youth at risk by helping them to build job skills, prepare for college, and develop business acumen. Throughout this book, stories of individuals and organizations who blur the distinction between profit and nonprofit will be presented.

The second important theme is an increased focus on and attention to re-sults. Again, this impulse stems from the business world, where measuring results is fairly straightforward. Are we making money? In the world of social change, other measurements need to be put in place. What is success in the nonprofit world? What is the difference between a dreamer and an effective do-gooder? Social entrepreneurs are keenly interested in understanding im-pact. There is great effort to measure efficacy and to seek means of improve-ment. The Acumen Fund has created a management system called Pulse that establishes metrics to determine these very things in delivering social good. Room to Read measures every dollar against the number of schools, libraries, books published and distributed, and the time it takes to accomplish each task.

The third spirited discussion taking place within the field of social entre-preneurship is about scale. While there are numerous examples of extraor-dinary people overcoming obstacles to create and put in place innovative programs, many of these are rather small and confined in scale. How does one take an individual intervention and scale it up to have an impact on larger sets of communities, nations, and even the world? Social equity investors believe that private enterprise must play a role in such a pursuit. Others believe that, within the nonprofit paradigm, scale is achievable.

## Who Are the Players?

There are many who are contributing to the shaping of the field and, by do-ing so, are breaking new ground in the way philanthropy and social change are taking place in the United States and globally. The term *social entrepreneur* can refer to the person who is working directly with the issue or group he or she is seeking to change. It can also be justifiably used to describe the funders who are providing financial support to those on the "front lines." Funders, such as those at Acumen, Skoll, and Omidyar Foundations, are themselves creating new and innovative means by which to find, finance, and support social entre-preneurship. Historically, it was relatively easy to separate out those creating and running nonprofit organizations from those providing the philanthropic resources they needed. Now, the lines are much blurred with individuals and organizations in several roles. Bill Drayton, for example, was the social entre-preneur who first helped to define and identify the field; he became a funder through Ashoka and is a major thinker on the evolution and future of the field. Still, to the extent possible and with the purpose of coherent organization, this book is divided into separate roles and functions with the understanding that it is the community at large that is creating the social entrepreneurship phenomenon.

This book brings together a number of the leading thinkers and doers in the field. Representing different perspectives and roles within the field, their combination of views and experience will offer a wide-ranging picture of the field as it is today and the collective vision of those driving it forward.

At the conclusion of each section, we have included a round robin among those whose talks are part of that section. The round robin format allows the reader to hear, in the speakers' voices, their answers to a number of the most compelling questions and issues in the field.

## ENTREPRENEURS

The first group we are going to highlight within the field of social entrepreneurship is those working on the front lines of social change. These are the most important players in this field. Others can analyze them, fund them, advise them, but without the entrepreneurs, there would be no movement.

As Greg Dees has pointed out, "Social entrepreneurs are reformers and revolutionaries . . . but with a social mission . . . Where others see problems, social entrepreneurs see opportunity."[7] Social entrepreneurs are "can-do" people who are not stymied but are, in fact, invigorated by the knowledge that no one has confronted a particular challenge in exactly the same way that they plan to confront it. For this group, the idea of "starting something" can be exhilarating and motivational.

Social entrepreneurs believe that they have a new idea, product, or process that can benefit a community or a segment of a community in important ways. Social entrepreneurs are often using market tools to make the world a better place. Like for-profit entrepreneurs, they must find a market for their product, new capital to get it going, and ongoing funding or a revenue stream to ensure sustainability.

It was important to identify representative as well as inspirational social entrepreneurs so as to showcase the abundance of issues that are being addressed in innovative ways. The good news is that there are numerous extraordinary people in the United States and around the world doing innovative work. The challenge is that there are so many people to choose from. In the following descriptions, I explain why each of these social entrepreneurs was asked to be part of this effort.

### Premal Shah    President, Kiva

What bummed me out was that microfinance is such a great tool to alleviate poverty and that there is a shortage of capital—but that there is no way for the average guy in the U.S. to invest in microfinance.[8]

Kiva is the world's first person-to-person microlending website, empowering individuals to lend directly to unique entrepreneurs around the globe. Premal Shah and his colleague Matt Flannery are considered the most successful social entrepreneurs for those in their twenties entering the world of social change. Kiva combines technology with social issues in a way that allows mass participation in facilitating solutions. It allows grassroots support for the financing of social alleviation projects and has generated extraordinary excitement and more than $100 million in small online loans that are reimbursed if the donor requests such an outcome.

Shah and Kiva are considered poster children for the field of social entrepreneurship. While Shah joined Matt Flannery and Jessica Jackley after they had been working on Kiva for one year, Shah brings a remarkable sincerity and marvel to his work and the process that he and colleagues embarked on to create Kiva. Kiva's combination of technology and social good epitomizes the belief shared by many in Silicon Valley that there are technological solutions to a number of today's challenges.

### Conchy Bretos    Founder and CEO, Mia Consulting Group

In this nation, we equate success with profit. We wanted to be profitable while also doing something that was right and giving back to the community.[9]

While working as Florida's Secretary for Aging and Adult Services, Conchy Bretos learned of the difficulties that force older people to leave their homes and move into nursing homes for lack of proper care. In response, she started the Mia Consulting Group, a business that advises governments as well as private housing developers on how to bring assisted living services cost effectively to low-income housing communities so that older people can be cared for in their own homes. Bretos presents an excellent example of someone who saw a very present and real social need in her immediate surroundings and innovated in response.

In addition to being named an Ashoka Fellow, Bretos was one of the first recipients of the Purpose Prize, an award for social entrepreneurs who are doing this work as a second career. Bretos's work showcases a number of important characteristics—it's profitable and works with government while addressing an all-too-often overlooked constituency—lower-income elderly. Bretos's organization has found a profitable means to address a complicated and at times seemingly intractable problem of housing for low-income elderly.

### Mary Houghton    President, ShoreBank

We had a high-volume deposit business that was hard to manage because it wasn't very profitable—figuring out the right model was one of our very biggest hurdles. At the same time we used an enormous amount of trial and error to find the market niches on the lending side that would help to rebuild the neighborhood.[10]

ShoreBank is the first community development bank in the United States. Starting on the south side of Chicago in 1973, ShoreBank has expanded to localities around the United States and in emerging markets. Mary Houghton is included in this volume because she was a leader in using private-sector mechanisms to bring about social change before the term *social entrepreneur* was coined. ShoreBank was founded with the goal of using banking resources to revitalize the South Side of Chicago. Houghton provides a longitudinal view of the field, as well as numerous experiences, in her ongoing effort to change banking paradigms.

### Louise Packard    Executive Director, Trinity Boston Foundation

I am a very different person because I do this work. The set of relationships that I have built and that my organization is building across color and class and faith lines in this city changes the fabric of the city even as we change the individual trajectories of the lives of our program participants. Getting black churches and white churches and synagogues and mosques to work together for their mutual benefit is an extremely powerful tool.[11]

The Trinity Boston Foundation is a part of the Trinity Episcopal Church and is the first foundation of its kind within the Episcopalian community. Initially formed as outreach ministries of Trinity Church, it has become the Trinity Boston Foundation, which works with other faith-based organizations in the Boston area to reach out to at-risk youth and struggling populations in low-income areas. Louise Packard's perspective provides an important contribution because she works with a constituency that is traditionally excluded from the conversation—faith-based social delivery programs. Additionally, her work showcases how innovation can take place within faith-based organizations with impressive results. More Americans participate in church-related philanthropy than any other kind of giving. Including this perspective widens the scope and the reach of the book to important and large parts of American society.

## FUNDERS AND INVESTORS

The funders of social entrepreneurs are a unique and pro-active group. To an extraordinary degree, they are driving the field forward. In many cases, the funders are also social entrepreneurs. Many funders have created new types of organizations and mechanisms to get funding to social entrepreneurs operating in the field.

As already discussed, social entrepreneurship often blurs the traditional demarcations between for-profit and nonprofit. Social equity investors are the personification of this gray area. One could argue that they are the most optimistic of all the groups, as they envision and act on two goals rather than one—social change and income generation. Investors differ from funders because they seek a clear return on their investments.

The contributors in this section are committed to wide-scale, transformative change but are not all following the same path to achieve that outcome. This section will provide a view into a debate that will affect the future of the field.

Each of these contributors has been asked to talk about his or her vision and how he or she believes it is reshaping the world of philanthropy. What have been the major roadblocks, and why does each feel that this field is "taking off" as it is now? What would these contributors define as success, and how close do they feel they are to reaching this? What are the criteria they use when identifying and supporting social entrepreneurship?

Investors have been asked to explain how their work complements other funding sources. What are the processes that they employ to find and fund worthy projects, that is, businesses that supply a social good? Do they see increased need in this area and, if so, why? For example, Root Capital often funds businesses that work in partnership with for-profit organizations such as Starbucks and Fair Trade Coffee. What is the learning curve for these types of alliances, and what are their inherent challenges?

### Sally Osberg    CEO, Skoll Foundation
Social entrepreneurs look for opportunities to create social value, uncover the best approaches for realizing those opportunities, and build social "capital." That capital we can pass on as an inheritance rather than a debt to the next generation.[12]

Jeff Skoll created the Skoll Foundation in 1999 after leaving eBay, the company that he founded with Pierre Omidyar. The Skoll Foundation's mission is to drive large-scale change by investing in, connecting, and celebrating social entrepreneurs and other innovators dedicated to solving the world's most pressing problems. The Skoll Foundation has also funded the creation of the Skoll Centre for Social Entrepreneurship at Oxford University. The Skoll Centre is providing academic leadership to understanding, documenting, and promoting the field as a whole. Sally Osberg is Jeff's partner in crafting and carrying out their vision of social entrepreneurship and putting into place a global architecture to support and strengthen the movement.

### Matt Bannick    Managing Partner, Omidyar Network

Imagine what's possible if entrepreneurship flourishes worldwide. Omidyar Network (ON) aims to create opportunity for entrepreneurs to succeed. When they do, so do their families and communities. People living in poverty are often ignored by mainstream businesses. ON prioritizes our support for entrepreneurs providing services and products that can improve quality of life for those most in need.[13]

Omidyar Network was started by Pierre Omidyar, founder of eBay, based on the idea that individuals have the power to make an important difference. The Omidyar Network funds both nonprofit and profitable ventures, as well as several hybrids. Matt Bannick is the managing partner at the Omidyar Network. With a background in consulting and as one of the most senior managers at eBay, Bannick is well positioned to use grant, loan, and hybrid mechanisms to bring about widespread social change. Bannick and the Omidyar Network are included in the series as they are on the cutting edge of hybrid tools and strategies.

### William Foote    Founder, Root Capital

We help harness the existing entrepreneurial energy in isolated rural communities, enabling conservation and encouraging socially responsible business practices.[14]

Willy Foote is the Founder and CEO of Root Capital since its inception in 1999. Root Capital has provided more than $120 million in credit to 235 grassroots enterprises in thirty countries in Latin America and Africa, with a 99 percent repayment rate from their borrowers and a 100 percent repayment rate to investors. One of their trademark investment strategies is to finance agricultural cooperatives. They work closely with Starbucks and coffee cooperatives around the world. Foote was an early adapter and promulgator of social investment and remains an excellent example of using markets to bring about social change.

### Jacqueline Novogratz    Founder and CEO, Acumen Fund

It has been an amazing eight-year journey; and yet, in some ways, we're just getting started. There is a lot of work to do, and we're ready to take on the challenges. We are looking for new and creative ways to raise funds in this difficult economic environment. We are considering questions of talent: more than 600 individuals from top business schools applied for our 10 summer internship spots, and how the world uses this resource is a question we take seriously. We are working on strengthening our performance management as well as bringing our insights from the work in order to influence others more directly.[15]

By creating Acumen Fund in 2001, Jacqueline Novogratz became a trailblazer in the notion that business can be an effective means to bring about social good. Acumen is a global philanthropic venture capital fund that seeks to prove that small amounts of philanthropic capital, combined with business skills, can build thriving enterprises that serve vast numbers of poor people in developing economies. It now has twenty-six investments in a number of developing countries in South Asia and Africa. Novogratz's thoughts on sustainable businesses in the developing world have helped to shape the field of social investment.

### THINKERS

The next section includes those who are changing traditionally held ideas about social entrepreneurship so as to push the field forward. As this field is new, contributions are constantly being made to define it, expand it, and explain it. The thinkers are promulgating groundbreaking ideas that shatter conventional wisdom.

Speakers in this section have been asked to comment on the genesis of their thinking, their arguments as to why it is critical to explore new paradigms, and the resistance they have encountered as they have explained their ideas.

### Christopher Gergen    Founder and CEO, Forward Ventures;
### Lecturer, Duke University

Being an entrepreneur is about proving, again and again, that the impossible is— somehow, someway—possible, plausible, doable. Entrepreneurs find a way to make things work, no matter the obstacles. That's a great lesson for us all, especially now.[16]

Christopher Gergen is a visiting professor at Hart Leadership Program at Duke University. He is also the Founding Executive Director of Bull City Forward, which seeks to establish Durham, North Carolina, as a national model of economic development through social innovation and entrepreneurship. The centerpiece of this effort is a downtown social innovation campus enabling local entrepreneurs to create world-changing solutions. Gergen is included here because of his dual roles of working within an academic setting in promoting social entrepreneurship education and as a practitioner endeavoring to take the ideas he is teaching and roll them out in a community-wide strategy.

### Jed Emerson    Principal, Blended Value

The thing that is striking is what we are really witnessing, I think, is the coming together of different schools. You got folks who are historically in the non-profit sector who are increasingly taking business acumen, skills, and frameworks and applying them toward community ends. You are also seeing a whole set of people who are thinking about value creation in for-profit areas as well.[17]

Jed Emerson began his career leading the Roberts Enterprise Development Fund and was one of the pioneers in the social capital world. He coined the term *blended value* and is recognized as an international leader in the fields of strategic philanthropy, social entrepreneurship, and blended value investing. His work on alternative investing, nonprofit capital markets, foundation strategy, social return on investment frameworks, social purpose business development, and other areas of practice has been viewed as significant in terms of its broad contribution to the field and efforts to support others engaged in the community application of business skills.

### Kriss Deiglmeier    Executive Director, Stanford Center
### for Social Innovation

When I arrived at the Stanford Center for Social Innovation in late 2004, it was a dynamic but unsettling time. While the Center had a lot of excited support, there was also a good deal of confusion over exactly what it was set up to do. Social innovation at the time wasn't a widely accepted construct. To many, the term meant "nonprofit management," to others it meant "social entrepreneurship," and to still others it had to do with "more effective philanthropy." So we set forth a definition of social innovation and a new mission and strategy—and this is key—all clearly grounded in dissolving boundaries and brokering a dialogue between the public, private, and nonprofit sectors.[18]

Kriss Deiglmeier is the Executive Director of the Center for Social Innovation (CSI) at the Stanford Graduate School of Business. She has more than twenty years of management experience spanning the business, social enterprise, nonprofit, and philanthropic sectors. On joining CSI in 2004, Deiglmeier embarked on a strategic planning process that set forth a new mission and strategy focused on breaking down sector boundaries. CSI focuses on understanding and developing expertise on cross-sector solutions and reaches outside the usual silos of the nonprofit, business, and government worlds to educate and connect the best people, organizations, and ideas. Deiglmeier has been at the forefront of understanding the phenomena of social entrepreneurship and social innovation and the ways in which these ideas can best be strengthened and put into practice.

## CHAMPIONS

Our last category of contributors I am calling "champions." Muhammad Yunus and Bill Drayton started off as social entrepreneurs themselves, one in microfinance and the other in creating an institution that finds and supports other social entrepreneurs, but they have moved far beyond their original focus and have succeeded in that elusive goal—scale, and scale beyond imagination. Yunus and Drayton have changed forever our view of the world and the ability on many levels and in many ways of seizing one's destiny.

### Bill Drayton   Founder and Chairman, Ashoka

What is the most powerful force in the world? And I think you would agree that is a big idea if it is in the hands of an entrepreneur who is actually going to make the idea not only happen, but spread all across society. And we understand that in business but we have need for entrepreneurship just as much in education, human rights, health, and the environment as we do in hotels and steel.[19]

Bill Drayton is the Founder of Ashoka, the first organization committed to finding and supporting social entrepreneurs. Bill Drayton is often considered the founder of the social entrepreneurship movement. With the creation of Ashoka: Innovators for the Public in 1981, Drayton put forward the notion that the individual person driving the change is worth supporting rather than the organization itself.

### Mohammad Yunus   Founder, Grameen Bank
### and Grameen America

Grameen has given me an unshakeable faith in human creativity and the firm belief that human beings are not born to suffer the misery of hunger and poverty. Poverty is an artificial, external imposition on a person. And since it is external, it can be removed.[20]

Mohammad Yunus is a Bangladeshi banker and economist. He previously was a professor of economics, where he developed the concept of microcredit, through which loans are given to entrepreneurs too poor to qualify for traditional bank loans. Yunus is also the founder of Grameen Bank. In 2006, Yunus and the bank were jointly awarded the Nobel Peace Prize "for their efforts to create economic and social development from below." He is the author of several books on social banking and a founding board member of Grameen America and Grameen Foundation.

## The Lay of the Land

Through reading through the chapters of these contributors, we will begin to see what makes the field of social entrepreneurship dynamic, vibrant, and incredibly important. Social entrepreneurs are tackling some of the world's most pressing social problems. They are the real problem solvers!

## Notes

1. The term "trade not aid" was originally used by the U.N. Conference on Trade and Development as a slogan for their initiative to promote fair trade with developing nations. Since that time, the term has taken on a larger meaning critiquing international development assistance as a useful tool in economic development in favor of increased trade and private sector growth.

2. J. Gregory Dees, "The Meaning of Social Entrepreneurship." Reformatted and revised edition. (Durham, NC: The Center for Advancement of Social Entrepreneurship, May 30, 2001), p. 4. Retrieved on March 13, 2010, from www.caseatduke.org/.

3. Jim Fruchterman, "For Love or Lucre." *Stanford Social Innovation Review,* Spring 2010. Retrieved on September 15, 2010, from www.ssireview.org/pdf/2011SP_Feature_Fruchterman.pdf.

4. John Elkington and Pamela Hartigan, *The Power of Unreasonable People* (Boston: Harvard Business School Press, 2008), p. 6.

5. Joseph A. Schumpeter, *Capitalism, Socialism and Democracy* (New York: Harper Perennial, 1942).

6. David Bornstein, *How to Change the World: Social Entrepreneurs and the Power of New Ideas* (Oxford, UK: Oxford University Press, 2007), p. x.

7. Dees, "The Meaning of Social Entrepreneurship," p. 4

8. "Christian Fundraising? Kiva's Competitive Lending Teams"; retrieved on October 15, 2009, from www.youtube.com/watch?v=aEC3OwKWgfc.

9. Marci Albohar, "A Social Solution, without Going the Nonprofit Route" *New York Times,* March 5, 2009, B5.

10. "Pioneers in Microfinance: Ron Grzywinski and Mary Houghton of ShoreBank"; retrieved on October 2, 2009, from www.microcapital.org/pioneers-in-microfinance-ron-grzywinski-and-mary-houghton/.

11. E-mail communication, September 20, 2009.

12. Sally Osberg, "Framing the Change and Changing the Frame: A New Role for Social Entrepreneurs," in *Innnovations/Skoll World Forum* 2009, p. 6.

13. "Omidyar Network Commits $30 Million at Clinton Global Initiative to Support Global Entrepreneurship"; retrieved on October 10, 2009, from http://foundationcenter.org/pnd/news/story_print.jhtml;jsessionid=NTWKQJ02HGCOTLAQBQ4CGW15AAAACI2F?id=266600007.

14. "About Root Capital"; retrieved on September 20, 2009, from www.rootcapital.org/newsdocs/pr_20080320.html.

15. "Happy 8th Birthday, Acumen!"; retrieved on September 20, 2009, from http://blog.acumenfund.org/2009/04/01/happy-8th-birthday-acumen/.

16. HBR Blog Network. "Fending off the Recession with 'Adaptive Persistence'"; retrieved on October 5, 2009, from http://blogs.hbr.org/gergen-vanourek/2009/04/fending-off-the-recession-with.html.

17. Jed Emerson in speech at the Commonwealth Club of California, San Francisco, CA, February 23, 2011.

18. "Social Innovation: Off, Running . . . and Still Catching Up"; retrieved on October 10, 2009, from http://csi.gsb.stanford.edu/social-innovation-off-and-running-and-still-catching-up.

19. "Stream of Consciousness: A Quote by Bill Drayton on Ideas, Social Entrepreneurship, Entrepreneurship, and Conscious Capitalism"; retrieved on October 15, 2009, from http://blog.gaiam.com/quotes/authors/bill-drayton.

20. Muhammad Yunus, *Building Social Business* (New York: Public Affairs Press, 2010), p. xiii.

# SECTION 1

# THE ENTREPRENEURS

Message from the Front Lines

# INVESTING IN MICROFINANCE

Premal Shah, President, Kiva

When I was five years old, my parents took me to India. We lived in the suburbs of Minnesota, and right when I stepped off the plane into Mumbai, India, I realized that I was in a very different place. I remember being really overwhelmed with what I was seeing because it was nothing like Minnesota. But it was a common scene for the place that we went, which was Ahmedabad, in the state of Gujarat.

One day I was walking around with my mom, and I was holding onto a one-rupee coin. I had this fascination with just holding onto this coin, as kids do. I must have held it for hours, and while we were walking through a market area, there was an open sewage stream in the market, and accidentally I dropped the coin in that sewage. My mom kind of yanked my hand and said, "Don't pick up that coin, it's dirty." The coin, by the way, was worth less than a penny in value. I remember watching a woman who was older than my mother, in a very ragged sari, coming over within seconds, putting her hand into the sewage, finding the coin, and then looking up at the sky and thanking God for having found that one-rupee coin.

That event, as well as that whole trip to India, probably changed the trajectory of my life, because I saw firsthand the indignity and the injustice that's happening every day on this planet. From that point forward, I always wanted to do something to address that injustice, but I didn't actually know how. I think a lot of us are in this situation right now, where we see an issue that we really care about—global warming, poverty, education reform—but it's often difficult to figure out a simple way to do something about it.

For me, it was on my mind for quite some time until I got to college. That's when I first discovered microfinance, which was filling a gap in the provision of financial services for people who are typically underbanked or underserved. It seemed like such an amazing idea, because it was a business approach to poverty alleviation. The idea that a microcredit loan could help a woman in Uganda buy a cow, and with that small loan she could then start a dairy business and not only repay that loan one day but also have this multiplier effect of being able to provide for her family—it just sounded very sustainable to me. I also really liked the bottom-up nature of it, in contrast to a lot of top-down, large aid projects. It was a way for us here in the north to support the development of leadership in the south, which I found really, really powerful.

So I fell in love with microcredit in college, and then I went on to the corporate world. I was lucky enough to land at PayPal. While I was at PayPal, the great thing was that not only was I learning how to build a product that would allow people to send money from one point to another on the planet but also that PayPal was really popular on eBay. eBay, if you think about it, is kind of a miracle, because twenty-five years ago the idea that you could actually buy a television or radio from a complete stranger and that that person would actually ship it to you was unheard of. But these transactions happen on eBay every single day; people buy *cars* on eBay. I marveled that people were trusting complete strangers and trading directly with them online. PayPal was interesting because it allowed for payment facilitation, but it was what we were doing on eBay and the connections being made between people over commerce inspired by trust that I found revolutionary.

During my time at PayPal, I began to wonder: If people are willing to buy a Beanie Baby or a television or an automobile on eBay, would they be willing to make a microcredit loan? So in 2005 I took a three-month sabbatical and went to India to work at a nongovernmental organization and experiment with this idea. I began by taking a photo of an entrepreneur, and I listed a microcredit loan request in the test category of eBay, to see if anyone would actually hit "buy it now." If anyone actually did, my plan was to get the money out in local rupees using my PayPal ATM card, give it to that person, and then have one of my friends collect that money over time. That's what I was thinking—and that it would just be a small pilot.

I posted the loan request from an Internet café after volunteering one day, went to sleep, and rushed back the next morning to see if anyone had hit the "buy it now" button to make a loan to this first microloan recipient on eBay. No one had actually done it yet, but there's a counter on the bottom of every eBay page that shows you how many people have hit the page, and something like forty-five people had hit the page. I thought, "Wow, at least people are looking at it; that's kind of exciting." That day I was volunteering at a woman's economic empowerment cooperative, and when I came back later that evening to the Internet café to see if anyone had clicked "buy it now" yet, it was missing. I checked my e-mail, and I had gotten an automated e-mail from eBay's legal department saying that requesting loans on eBay is illegal; it's a violation of its terms of service. Now, they had no idea that I was actually an employee of PayPal, which was owned by eBay, and was violating their terms of use—because I had an anonymous handle like SalsaBoy20 or something; they had no way of tracking me down.

That was the end of the pilot, but I got really excited about this idea of putting up microloan requests online for people who just need a little bit of money and connecting them with people who have just a little bit of money and who wouldn't mind making a loan. I came back from India to Palo Alto, California, and I ran into two amazing social entrepreneurs, Matt Flannery and Jessica Jackley, who had started a small website that was still in pilot form called Kiva. It was exactly what I wanted to do, so instead of trying to compete with them, I said, "Hey, can we all work together?"

When we first started it, there were a lot of things we weren't sure about, and there were a lot of naysayers to the idea. I'll get into some of the challenges that we had early on. But for those of you who have never visited the site, let me explain what Kiva is. Kiva is a website run by a 501(c)(3) nonprofit based in San Francisco. This website is similar to eBay, where you can sift through profiles of things that you may want to buy; in this case, you sift through profiles of entrepreneurs in more than fifty countries. These entrepreneurs are looking for microloans from as little as $25 to as large as $10,000 for borrowers here in the United States. You can read their stories, and if you find an entrepreneur who resonates with you—for example, Anne Marie in Benin who wants to purchase condiments and fish for her retail outfit and is looking for $325 from the Internet community—you have the opportunity to lend $25 or more toward this profile.

The way that this profile gets posted on Kiva is that we work with local microfinance institutions—these are banks for the poor. (A microfinance institution, or MFI, is an organization that provides financial services to poor and low-income individuals or to those who do not have access to typical banking services. MFIs range from small nonprofit organizations to large commercial banks. Kiva's work is made possible through a network of MFIs around the world that identify borrowers, create borrower profiles for Kiva.org, and disburse, administer, and collect repayments on each loan.) The most famous one is Grameen Bank in Bangladesh, for which Muhammad Yunus won the Nobel Peace Prize back in 2006. What's really exciting about these organizations is that oftentimes the ones that Kiva works with are not very large. They're small, community-based microfinance organizations that are barely self-sustainable themselves, and the issue they face is that, because they're so small and so unproven, it's very hard for them to attract capital. If they can have access to more capital, they can reach more of the entrepreneurs in their community and help more people. So now the Internet community—all of us—has the opportunity to support these organizations and the entrepreneurs that they serve. Once you hit "lend now" for $25 or something more, essentially over the course of a year, the loan will be repaid. Usually the average loan term on Kiva is about ten months. So if it's $25 that you lend, you'll get $2.50 back every month. Then, when you get all $25 paid back to you, you can turn around and either relend it to another entrepreneur, or you can withdraw that money back to your PayPal account, if you need the money. Not only do you get your money back, but you also get updates on how that business is doing and the progress or lack of progress that it has made.

That's how the Kiva website works. Since its launch five years ago, it has really taken off, though in the beginning it was pretty slow going. We've now hit $177 million in loans, in these $25 chunks. That's come from more than 760,000 individuals on the Internet, in more than 100 countries, not just the United States; we're seeing people all over the world making loans. That money is supported by a network of 135 field workers in fifty-four countries around the planet, and it has touched the lives of 420,000 entrepreneurs. A real testament to the working poor and the entrepreneurs on Kiva is that today there's a 98.9 percent repayment rate on the Kiva marketplace. It's apparent that if the working poor get an opportunity that they can't get elsewhere, they take it very seriously, and the repayment rates can be quite high.

Kiva has had three major challenges since we began. In the beginning, it was keeping the lights on; the second was keeping loans on the website; and the third has been keeping Kiva lenders engaged.

Let me explain the first. After I quit my job and Matt quit his job at TiVo as a computer programmer, Kiva was just a bunch of volunteers, about six of us sitting at the kitchen table in Palo Alto, California, and then we eventually moved up to San Francisco. Literally no one was getting paid, and we needed to put people on health care. If you typed "Kiva" into Google, the top search result was a spa. I couldn't get my closest friends and family to use the website. I looked in the database, and my mom and dad hadn't even used the website. People were being posted up on the website, but the funding wasn't really coming. We went like that for about a year, and after about eight or nine months we finally started putting people onto health care coverage and paying some basic wages. We had about one month of payroll left in the bank as a nonprofit organization, and I was thinking, "I'm not sure if this is really going to make it another year."

Then the miracles of October 2006 happened. First, Muhammad Yunus won the Nobel Peace Prize, which overnight educated the United States and people all over the world about microcredit and microfinance. Second, we were on PBS *Frontline World,* a fifteen-minute documentary on Halloween night, which ended up crashing our website for four days. We were on the $22-a-month server plan, so we couldn't handle that kind of exposure. Luckily, one of our engineers—well, our only engineer—posted a PayPal button on the website and wrote, "Help us buy new servers." Over the four days that we were down, we raised $130,000 from the Internet community to basically get Kiva back online. That was in Silicon Valley terms a series-A financing round for us. It really got us the cash reserves that we needed to pay our staff a living wage, put people on health care, and start scaling our due diligence. From that point on, we decided to run on tips, which means that every time you make a loan on Kiva, we ask you if you'll throw in a tip for Kiva. Last year, those tips covered about 70 percent of our operating budget. Over the next five years, we think it will cover 100 percent of our operating budget. So that's how we're keeping the lights on in addition to keeping our costs really low. That was a really big struggle in the beginning.

The second big struggle was after October 2006, when people started coming to the site. Once our site came back up, people were coming faster than we were ready for, and we kept running out of borrowers for them to support. People would log on to Kiva with a gift certificate, and there would be no loans on the site for people to fund. It's so rare in philanthropy for people to say, "We can't take your money," because, clearly, there are people in the world who could benefit from these loans. But we were not fast enough to actually get loans on the site. The Internet community was hitting us in this exponential, parabolic curve, and we were able to get loans on the site only in this sort of linear curve.

So we did two major things to resolve that problem: First, it came down to incredible people, mainly volunteers; and second, the use of technology. We looked at Wikipedia as a pioneer in the field to learn from. Wikipedia is less than ten years old and is one of the top ten most popular websites on the Internet, and it's a nonprofit. For the longest time, they had only four employees. And what they did was to have many volunteers chipping in, editing articles, reviewing each other's work, and using software to help manage all those people. Similarly, Kiva didn't have that many employees, and we couldn't afford to send people all around the world, so what we did is create a program called the Kiva Fellows Program. Because there's so much interest in microfinance, this program allows a professional to take three months or a year from his or her job to volunteer overseas with us. We train them in the Kiva office and deploy them like a mini–Peace Corps assignment into one of the countries in which we work. They help with a lot of Kiva's presence on the ground, including training the local microfinance organizations on how to use this system and monitoring the organization to make sure that the money being lent is getting to the borrower. Our entire current infrastructure was essentially set up through our volunteer network. The other big part of our volunteer network was created when we realized that a lot of organizations wouldn't come on to Kiva because they couldn't hire someone who spoke English. So we created a huge corps of more than 500 people who every day would log in and review or translate things from Spanish to English or French to English, which allows these organizations to not have to hire an English speaker. Essentially it's through this whole group of volunteers that Kiva was built. There are more than 700 volunteers now in the Kiva ecosystem. For every one staff member, there are ten volunteers who really helped scale the system.

The other thing that helped us get loans on the site is that we realized that by being creative and hiring some great people who understood technology quite well, we could scale things efficiently. For example, we'd see organizations come on to Kiva and start raising money for about fifty entrepreneurs.

Then they were supposed to start reposting payments back to the website. But we saw them stopping. They wouldn't post any repayments. The whole idea of the model is that it's not a donation; it's actually a loan. You're supposed to get your money back, but they've stopped reporting repayments. But what we learned when we actually flew out to East Africa, which is where we first started, is that the Internet connectivity is so slow that loading every single page would take minutes at a time, and then it would just time out sometimes. We realized that in microfinance things go right 95 percent of the time. The repayments usually come in, and only 5 percent of the time do things actually go off-schedule. So we created an exception-based processing system in which, instead of people having to mark every time a repayment came in on our website that was loading so slowly from Tanzania, they now needed to mark only when things were going wrong. That made Kiva much more usable for them. Little technological innovations like that together with the help of all of the volunteers was what allowed us to really start scaling, to the point of getting loans on the site from more than fifty countries.

The final problem that we faced is that when people got repaid a lot of them thought it was a donation, and they wouldn't come back to Kiva. In fact, today we have well over $10 million in loans sitting in Kiva lenders' accounts that are not being put to work in the hands of other people because people don't come back to the website to actually reloan their money. So we've really been thinking hard about how we can keep our lenders engaged. The big innovation that we've stumbled on in the last five years is that we can actually make this site much more fun and social. Facebook, for example, is an incredibly engaging site; some would argue an addictive site. They have more than 500 million people who have registered, and half of us who have registered log on every single day. So one of the things that we decided to do was to create lending teams and groups on Kiva, because social movements are inherently social. On Kiva today you can actually join with other people to form a team. There are over 15,000 teams. The top two teams right now are the atheists and the Christians, and they're competing against each other; they even have message boards and are trash talking. It's all with the right intention of alleviating poverty, but what we want to do is actually make this thing as fun and compelling as possible. One of my favorite lending teams on Kiva is the Women Who Lend to Shirtless Men team. This is a group of women who have come together, and when a man is listed on the website who isn't wearing a shirt, typically from Southeast Asia from what I've seen, they jump right on those loans. We shouldn't underestimate fun. This is, I think, one thing that philanthropy hasn't really thought about historically.

One of the things I've been asked is, "Whom do you view as Kiva's competition?" I actually think that our biggest competition is battling for people's attention. Our challenge is to get people engaged on this platform. Every month, 60 million people are building virtual farms on Farmville, on Facebook, and every month only 60,000 people—0.1 percent of that number—are actually building real farms on Kiva. How do I make building real farms on Kiva as compelling as building virtual farms on Facebook? That's what we want to think about, and that's the kind of Silicon Valley breakthrough we want to bring to the site.

Those are the three challenges and what we're doing to address them.

We see something happening on Kiva that's different from a bank and different from donations. We think that Kiva plays in this middle space that isn't quite a commercial rate of return investment. You're not getting a rate of return, and it's not a donation. What is this middle space? We like to call it *connected capital.* It has a few attributes. One of the things that we're realizing is that when people can see the impact, they're willing to be much more patient with their money. The second thing is that because there are so many people who hit the website every day—90,000 people come to the Kiva website each day—it's a really distributed form of people making bets on different people, and that kind of democratization of who gets to participate in lending is really exciting. That hasn't really happened before. It's been banks up until now. The third thing is that if you can get people who are patient and get them from all over the place, you can actually make sure that money is really catalytic. People are willing to do this only if there's accountability on the other end. I don't think people really value getting paid back; they don't usually want the actual money back. What they like is the *information* of getting paid back, because there's an accountability there that often is lacking with donations. With those attributes of the capital that's flowing on Kiva, we're able to do something that's pretty exciting. I think we can reach places that commercial capital will not reach.

Let's look, for example, at the continent of Africa. There's a familiar story there of civil strife, followed by aid, then the aid drying up, during which time the markets have not yet had a chance to deepen or the institutions to get to a point of strength, and so then the population is left in a place where civil strife can reemerge. We've seen this cycle over and over and over. One of the things that we're learning about microfinance, particularly in sub-Saharan Africa, is that commercial investors are not excited about investing in these places because the country risk appears to be too high or there's not enough information about these organizations on the ground. It just feels too risky. But this is exactly where we feel the Internet community, with their patient, impact-seeking capital, would want to put their money. So we're seeing today that Kiva actually funds more local organizations in post-conflict Africa than any other funder.

I want to give an example about one particular organization that we're working with on the ground in Sierra Leone. This is amazing. A couple years ago, Kiva was their first outside funder. Because they were able to develop a track record of showing how the entrepreneurs in their community have repaid on the Kiva website reliably, other outside funders have now come on board and have started supporting this organization. In essence, the Internet community has been a catalyst, the substance that then creates a chain reaction for this organization to provide inclusive financial services in a place like Sierra Leone, where there are not many points of access for basic financial services. We see loans in Iraq as being one of the most popular loans on the website. It may be more risky, but people are actually seeking those. Loans in Afghanistan are also incredibly exciting to people as well. So this is something that we want to continue to do more and more. I think connected capital as opposed to maybe commercial capital has the potential to be this first-loss, risk-tolerant, catalytic capital that we haven't seen before, and it can be much more abundant than donations.

For the next five years, there are three things that we want to do at Kiva. The first is that today we're at about $180 million in cumulative loans, and we'd like to reach $1 billion in $25 increments from everyday people on the Internet. Not from Bill Gates, but everyday people. The second is that we'd like to break even as an organization, because we'd like to show that nonprofits can actually run as social businesses. No one's going to get rich from Kiva, but we can run in a way that we don't have to ask outside foundations for support. These foundations have been really generous so far—Skoll Foundation has been an incredible supporter of us, Omidyar Network has been a great supporter of us—but ideally it's the tips on the website that will actually help operate this site. Finally, we'd like to innovate in new areas.

Let me touch on two things that we'd like to do. The first is to deepen the connection. We live in an era in which, for the first time, it's going to be possible for every single human being on the planet in the next one hundred years to actually connect with one another. That's a really amazing thing. One way that we see this as possible is through the power of the mobile phone network. If you look at the proliferation of mobile phones in the places where we work, it's incredible. I can imagine one day, in the not even very distant future, where a woman in Kenya who wants to buy that cow to start a dairy business would pull out her mobile phone, because the price of phones has gone down so low. She can take a photo of herself, a photo of the cow, and then basically by punching in a few keys, post that up on the Kiva website. Maybe at that point it won't be 90,000 people coming to the website every day, but maybe millions of people. They can sift through the borrower profiles, and they'll see this woman in Kenya who three minutes ago just posted a loan request for the equivalent of $500. So then they can come in and within hours or maybe even minutes fund that loan. On Kiva today, the average loan request is about $400, and it gets funded in two days—very quickly. So in a matter of minutes, hours, or maybe a couple days, that woman can get her loan fully funded at an interest rate that's lower than she's ever had access to from either the village moneylender or any other source.

Then the question is, How does she get the money out of the system? What's amazing in Kenya right now is that the fastest-growing financial service is actually people using their cell-phone minutes as a form of currency. That Kenyan woman can go to a gas station and cash her cell-phone minutes for local Kenyan shillings. She can take out those Kenyan shillings and buy that cow right there. Then, if she repays that loan, she knows that her future loan from the Internet community that's coming at a very low interest rate will be ensured because she has a great track record of repaying, similar to how credit bureaus work here.

So that's one thing that we can do. We can move to that kind of world where people can participate in each other's stories and ultimately increase access at a much lower cost. We're also hoping to make the world, through technology, a lot smaller. You can imagine a day when there are actually Skype videos or mobile SMS updates on how the cow that you purchased is doing. This is where we want to go with the technology.

The second thing that we've seen is that it's not only about helping entrepreneurs start or grow their own business or helping people smooth their own consumption. We're seeing that there are many different forms where connected capital can go that commercial banks wouldn't go—for example, student lending. Student lending in the developing world doesn't really happen.

The reason why: There's really no repayment track record on student loans; because there's no real repayment track record, banks won't get into it. And because banks won't get into it, there's no repayment track record. So you have this chicken-and-egg issue. Well, that's exactly what the Internet community should be funding. We should be able to take on a little bit more of a risky loan or a longer-term loan—maybe instead of twelve months, it could be three years, or five years, with no payments for several months—to fund a student's college education. Then what if, when you lend to women who get accounting degrees in Peru, they pay back at 96 percent versus men who might get a mechanic's degree in Lebanon, who pay back at 82 percent? If we can show that kind of data on a public website, then I think the banks will start coming in and saying, "Well, here's how we actually think about risk when it comes to student lending." We want to do this not only across student lending but housing, water—you can imagine the different areas that connected capital and patient capital could actually help address a market failure and really make a catalytic difference.

Many people talk about the soul of Kiva being a technology company because we're based in Silicon Valley. But I really don't think that's true. In fact, I think a lot of us are inspired by this quote from Dr. Martin Luther King Jr. He said that, through our technological prowess, the world has become a neighborhood. But, through our spiritual progress, the world can become a brotherhood. If you look at the data right now, it's hard not to be a pessimist. But if you look at what's happening on this website, everyday people connecting through lending to alleviate poverty, it's hard not to be an optimist. I really think that this is a platform that can allow us to share in each other's stories and connect with one another in a beautiful way.

# DOLLARS, SENSE, AND DIGNITY

Conchy Bretos, Founder, Mia Senior Living Solutions

I am writing with a great sense of optimism; it has not always been that way. I want to share with you how I came to this hopeful perspective and to my mission to help provide low-cost, high-quality assisted living solutions for seniors. I will begin by explaining the work I do and why it matters so much to the seniors who are directly affected and to the larger society of which we are all a part. Second, I will tell you my personal story and how I came to understand my part in changing how we care for our poor seniors and disabled adults in this country and, lastly, what that change has meant to me and those I serve.

We know that an aging global population poses challenges to social institutions worldwide and in particular to health care systems. In the United States, very little planning has been done to deal with an increased population of elderly. How we deal with this historical event greatly affects health care systems, retirement, and work. Since 1996 our work has tried to change federal policy by creating a replicable, sustainable service delivery model that has so far been adopted in more than twenty-one states.

Many low-income seniors and disabled adults live in public housing. Public housing regulations require that their residents live independently; when they cannot, they are evicted. Eviction to large nursing homes is not a fate that anyone would wish to have.

In a nutshell, Mia accomplishes three major goals. First and foremost, we create a system that allows elderly who live in subsidized housing to stay in their homes and live out their lives in comfort and with dignity. Second, we create an ecosystem of services that provides numerous jobs, and third, we save the state and federal government a great deal of money.

Integrating low-income seniors and disabled adults into the society as respected contributing members is our major goal. We work to bring about an environment where the elderly can continue to age in place with dignity and in good health. Our model includes changing lifestyles to a more healthy and active one. Our biennial evaluations have revealed a marked improvement in cognitive and physical health, reduction of prescription drugs, number of hospitalizations and emergency room admissions, use of wheelchairs, and incidence of falls. The results are surprising. As a consequence, health care costs have been significantly reduced, as well as the cost of care—a major goal of this nation's health care reform.

A secondary goal of ours has been the generation of new jobs, promotion of economic activity, revitalization of neighborhoods, expansion of the affordable housing stock, preservation of existing buildings, and generation of new revenue streams for our clients. An average of sixty new full-time permanent jobs are created with each new project we do, and those jobs usually go to low-income residents of the area. The positions created include administrators, certified nursing assistants, cooks, assistant cooks, housekeepers, maintenance and security staff, van drivers, activity directors, and administrative staff. In addition to the creation of jobs, the program contracts with vendors for the supply of services and goods, thus furthering economic activity. We started retrofitting old buildings that were in disrepair and in danger of being shut down, and they are now functional and welcoming sites. New revenues that our projects generate cover most of these capital expenses.

All of our projects are totally self-sustainable and replicable and generate good operating margins. Many private sector investors are motivated by these revenues. Our projects have proven to drastically cut Medicare and Medicaid costs. We have used these results to convince state and federal governments and legislators to properly fund community care and in the end effect policy change at the federal level.

In 2003, after working at the individual level by creating successful projects, we approached two federal agencies, the departments of Housing and Urban Development and of Health and Human Services. We wanted to change existing federal policy and facilitate the provision of services to residents of public and subsidized housing. It took eight years, but in 2011 both agencies agreed to contract with each other to establish the Community First

Option Program, providing access to $3.7 billion in increased federal funding and rental subsidy vouchers to transition seniors and disabled adults back to their communities.

Our model is unique in two ways. First, the client receives twenty-four-hour services where he or she lives, avoiding the need to relocate. Second, we stack subsidies to make the program self-sustainable. In other words, we have created a model of providing services to residents of public and subsidized housing by layering federal and state funds and providing services to enable them to stay in their homes at a considerable savings to taxpayers. Our ability to have access to government funding to create this new affordable model is unique, and our firm is the only one in the nation with the expertise to make it work. Our facilities are open to everyone regardless of ability to pay. We do more with less as we service three times as many residents with the funding provided by the government.

Our business has focused on public housing authorities, due to the high concentrations of poor, disabled seniors and adults living there. We have found that most of the public housing buildings are subsidized and regulated and have in place safety and accessibility features that make licensing possible with little or no retrofitting.

Before our model, residents of public and subsidized housing were evicted from their units when they could no longer live independently. With few, if any, options, these residents became homeless or moved to costly and depressing nursing home care, prematurely taxing the states' Medicaid budgets.

Considerable research proves the cost effectiveness of keeping seniors and disabled adults in their homes with quality services and proper care. Yet convincing state and federal governments to shift emphasis from institutionalization was difficult, partly because of the inability of policymakers to be pro-active and responsive to individual's needs and preferences. Another factor has been the lobbying strength of nursing homes that see this shift as a threat to their livelihoods.

As recognition for the innovative approach of our model and the accompanying social impact, we have received two prestigious national and international awards. In 2006 we were awarded the first Civic Ventures Purpose Prize, funded through Atlantic Philanthropies and The John Templeton Foundation. The award gave us broad recognition and exposure in all major media, including being featured in CBS News, CNN, and NPR. In 2010 we were awarded the Ashoka Fellowship, given to international social entrepreneurs who have created and implemented unique solutions to critical social issues. Both Civic Ventures and Ashoka conducted considerable research to determine if this was indeed an innovative program. They consulted federal agencies and consumer groups, among others. Determining this fact was essential in granting the award.

This year we were selected by *Bloomberg Businessweek* as one of the most promising entrepreneurs in 2011.

CBS news presented the case for my work extremely well. The research showed that, for every person we provide services, we were saving the Medicaid budget $18,000 per year. If you multiply that by the 5,000 people who are currently being served at home, we are cutting the Medicaid program, which is a big budgetary issue in every state in this country, by millions of dollars. That's why our program gets so much attention. It has little to do with doing the right thing, with altruism. It is a matter of budgetary concerns. Our program helps state and federal governments save money and cut spending.

Working to change government agencies is like working against the wind. Every time I go to a state, I negotiate Medicaid waivers. I have been doing this for sixteen years, first in Tallahasee, Florida, and now in many states. There are very few individuals who can claim to be able to do that effectively. In addition to the federal regulations, each state has hundreds of pages of regulations and categorical funding. Our model tries to bring all the funding and regulations together into one package so that our clients and residents do not have to deal with this complexity. We help them live their lives and not worry about how they are going to pay for their room, board, and services. Our program allows the elderly to spend down their assets, qualify for government subsidy, and not be forced out of their homes.

We have created new Medicaid waiver programs in Pennsylvania, Tennessee, Ohio, and West Virginia. We also created a new program in Florida, a state that, surprisingly, did not have appropriate funding in place. We have found a way to rely on government subsidies but at the same time change the systems that provide them.

I have come to this work through my own life choices and those that were made for me. I was born in a culture that highly respects and values its elders, but I was still a difficult and irreverent child, according to my ninety-one-year-old mother. At the age of fourteen, I was flown to Miami as one of the 14,000 unaccompanied children who came into the United States from Cuba during the first years of the 1960s. This exodus of children was the result of a pronouncement made by the new military government that children should be taken away from their families and put into collective schools and communities. My parents were terrified of the possibility that my brother and I would be taken to one of these schools, which they believed were effectively military camps where children were being indoctrinated and brainwashed. So in 1962, my mother put both of us—me at age fourteen and my brother at ten—on a plane bound for the United States. We ended up in an orphanage in Lincoln, Nebraska.

Living in an orphanage taught me to identify with those less fortunate, with their plight and needs. Ever since, I have not been able to face injustice and remain uninvolved.

Most people would probably feel that they had lost everything at that point, but I felt a great sense of liberation, of freedom. I was away from the protective arms of my mother and was able to do whatever I chose. It was exhilarating, and I took full advantage of this door that had opened. I did well in school, and in 1973 I was admitted to Oberlin College. Oberlin was a wonderful experience for me. It is an institution that focuses on instilling in its students a desire to give back and, more important, an appreciation of one's own abilities and knowledge.

Thinking back, my roots as a Cuban may have instilled in me a revolutionary spirit and a worldview that has led me to the work I do today. For example, I often wonder if we live in a just society, with the number of people who are systematically disadvantaged, including the poor, the seniors, and the disabled; and, given these injustices, what kind of change is required today? That was my thought on one pivotal afternoon in November 1994. At the time, I was working in Tallahassee as Florida's secretary for aging and adult services, and I had been asked to travel to Fort Lauderdale to visit an elderly housing building, subsidized by public funding, where there had been a fire. Five people had died, and eleven more had continued living in the building, which had been totally destroyed, because they had no place to go. When I arrived there, I saw things that put me to shame. I saw rat-infested apartments, rotten food, and people lying on beds of feces, surrounded by worms. And I said to myself, "The world must not know about this, and I must be here for a reason. I think that I am the right person to change this. I need to tell everybody what is going on." I had really no option but to act; this is a mind-set that has gotten me into a lot of trouble throughout my life. I like projects that are difficult and have little chance of success. I also believe that the best innovations have no basis in logical thought; they happen when you are confronted with a pressing issue, as I was that day. In those cases, I don't stop and think; I act out of moral obligation.

This was again the case in 1996 when I lost my job in Tallahassee because of a change in administration. I went home to Miami and was determined to speak out about the plight of older seniors and disabled adults. I immediately went to see the Miami housing authority director. I thought I would have the greatest impact there because, after all, most of the older poor live in public housing or in subsidized housing. I found a lot of nonbelievers in public housing, people who were not ready to change or see things differently or who said there was no money to take on these kinds of projects. But, as has been the case with me over and over again, the timing was just right.

The day I arrived at the public housing office in Miami, the director was trying to sell a building because it had totally deteriorated and they had no funds to retrofit it. He was going to give it away for almost nothing. I asked him to give me the building and promised him, without knowing what it was going to take, that I would produce enough income by the end of one year to retrofit it. I was able to negotiate with the Florida legislature $2.8 million in service funding—Medicaid waivers. Six months later, we opened that building and started providing services, with 101 units full and fifty-six people on the waiting list. At the end of that first year, we were producing half a million dollars in revenue. The Helen Sawyer Plaza building in Miami became the model for the nation in 1998. Many newspapers and magazines published stories about it, and the project won four national awards.

I have been more successful with Mia than I would have thought possible, but I want to share with you that my life has been full of failures, and I have learned more from those failures than from my success. You might ask, "Why?" It's because when you fail you realize how much you need to do to succeed. I have never been afraid to fail, and in fact I suggested to the president of Ashoka that they should start recognizing people for their failures and not their accomplishments. It shows the true caliber of people when they fail and come back. I have tried and failed many times, but I have never failed to try.

I feel most fortunate to be recognized for my work. Many others have done much more and remain unknown. The award of the Purpose Prize was a turning point in my life. The Purpose Prize awards up to $100,000 each to five people annually who are more than sixty years old and who are creating new ways to solve tough social problems.

It was the first time that I heard that I was a social entrepreneur. I thought I was just simply a troublemaker, a stubborn person who was really concerned about issues in my community. I was so inspired when I walked into the room on the day of the award ceremony to find over 200 people, most of them much older than I was, tackling and succeeding in some of the most difficult problems confronting our community. They are like me, and they wanted to leave some evidence that they existed.

Being named an Ashoka Fellow again surprised me. It has renewed my sense of responsibility and my resolve to continue my work. Up until now, I've felt that my work has effectively changed behavior at the individual level. I have given a voice to those who did not have one and have created forty or more successful projects in twenty-three states. This, combined with the decision by two federal agencies to work together, will be my and Mia's legacy.

It seems that timing has been on my side, as the mistrust toward government has prompted more awareness and responsiveness to the communities that government agencies serve. I often think that government is afraid to deal with social and moral issues. I call it the spiritual blind side. They also have a human capital crisis. I have met people who work for government and are almost ashamed to admit this. Our country today has a problem enticing talented people into government and a huge need to bring committed individuals with public interest—the definition of a social entrepreneur—to provide new ideas and new solutions.

The public also mistrusts corporate America. The good news about this has been an increased motivation on the part of corporations to engage with social service organizations and show their commitment toward the communities in which they operate.

Our firm has benefited from corporations seeking to engage with civil society. We have also benefited from the housing crisis currently facing our country. Guess what some of those private investors are doing with all those distressed properties? They're not building luxury condominiums or hotels because that market is saturated. Instead, for the first time, they are taking those properties and creating service-enriched, midmarket affordable housing units. We have started several partnerships with tax credit developers and private investors with plans to implement our model in other parts of Florida, Pennsylvania, the District of Columbia, and Colorado, among others. In addition, and under the auspices of Ashoka, we now have an advisory board comprised of members of the local Young Presidents' Organization that has opened doors to the private investment world and from whom we have learned much about how to expand our business in partnership with the private sector.

There is no doubt in my mind that timing has been in our favor and that what others call a *crisis* has offered us great opportunities. We are benefiting from the aging of America and ironically from the profound housing crisis our country is experiencing. Today is the beginning of what I can only describe as a demographic tsunami, the enormous impact of the aging baby boomers' generation. For the first time in the history of this country, older people will outnumber teenagers two to one. Life expectancy and quality of life while aging, in America and elsewhere, continue to be influenced directly by the class divide. Those who are educated and affluent are healthier and live longer; those who are poor don't have the same destiny. We segregate old people to be neither seen nor heard. They suffer in resignation and silence. We know so little about them and preclude our children from seeing them as role models and from learning through their experiences and wisdom. I was fortunate to spend time with my grandmother while growing up, and I learned a great deal from her guidance and wisdom. It is a shame that in the United States we don't value the contributions of old people the way many other cultures do.

I will never forget that big innovations have always been created on the basis of rejection. Think back in history, and you will see that this is true. I think it's the right time to do the right thing. I believe that those who have initiated change, as I and millions of others have done, are in a better position today to manage that change. I have always believed that altruism is part of us, that as social beings we are inherently compassionate. We have shown it in every crisis or catastrophe around the world. Given that we live in a global society where we are all interconnected we are now coming to the realization that to survive, as human beings, we need to connect with others and be more sympathetic. Most of our problems would be over if we had an array of people committed to serving others.

We would not have elders in nursing homes anymore. They would be living at home and dying with dignity. We need to replace apathy with empathy because apathy remains a major obstacle to change. Many of us believe that we can no longer afford to remain uninvolved. At last the age of indifference seems to be over.

# THE POWER OF AN ECONOMIC NICHE

Mary Houghton, President and Co-Founder, ShoreBank Corporation

In this chapter, I want to explain banking on values and banking as a growing form of social enterprise. I will spend some time explaining community-development banking in the United States and how social banking and microfinance are taking place internationally. I will then share my thoughts about two different niche businesses that I really care about but that are much tougher to do and don't happen so often. Finally, I have a possible declaration of independence for investors in social enterprises, which I'd like to urge you to think about. But before doing all of that, I want to tell the story of Shore-Bank, my major foray into the world of values-based banking.

It was a different world in the 1960s in this country. There was no bank credit in African-American neighborhoods at all. There was a panic among white people to sell their homes and move out of neighborhoods. So the neighborhoods in the Northeast and Midwest were just consigned to go down once they changed racially; it's what life was. After starting a successful city-wide minority small business lending department at the Hyde Park Bank in Chicago in 1968, a group of bankers, myself included, decided to develop a more ambitious business strategy to deal with the absence of bank credit in minority U.S. neighborhoods. The genesis of ShoreBank was saying that it couldn't possibly be the case that if a neighborhood had African-Americans living in it, it was no longer a decent neighborhood. Let's prove that that's not the case. Let's prove that you can have a nice neighborhood that African-Americans live in, and that African-Americans will pay back loans as well as white people. That's the genesis of ShoreBank. Our idea was to acquire an existing neighborhood bank and combine it with something like a real estate development firm and a nonprofit organization to provide job training. We would then use this combination of entities to restore normal market activity in the neighborhood by attracting additional outside public and private resources to the neighborhood.

By 1973 we had succeeded in raising adequate private capital from eight investors and had secured a bank loan. On August 23 we acquired South Shore National Bank of Chicago, with just under $40 million in assets.

We spent the first decade stabilizing the bank's products, operations, and staffing and then began to expand. In 1988, ShoreBank opened a second office on the West Side of Chicago and created a rural development bank holding company in Arkansas called Southern Development Bancorporation, in connection with the Winthrop Rockefeller Foundation's rural development strategy. In the 1990s, in response to local requests, ShoreBank added operations in Cleveland, Detroit, and the Pacific Northwest, and it partnered with Northern Michigan University to create a rural small business support organization. The group also took advantage of other opportunities. A one-off invitation to help the Founder of Grameen Bank launch a microcredit bank ultimately evolved into an international advisory business that helped banks set up profitable small business loan departments, initially in the former Soviet Union but then globally. This led to ShoreBank's sponsorship of an investment fund that could provide capital to small banks that specialized in self-employment and small business in Africa and Asia. Today, the advisory firm is deeply involved in the development of mobile banking innovations in Bangladesh, India, and Pakistan. Two nationwide U.S. programs were also developed: the National Community Investment Fund (NCIF), which invests in and supports community development banks in the United States; and the Center for Financial Services Innovation (CFSI), which primarily advises large, mainstream financial service companies on ways to serve "underbanked" consumer markets.

ShoreBank's lead bank in Chicago specialized in developing profitable lending niches to finance rehab entrepreneurs, churches, and nonprofit organizations. The rehab entrepreneur niche was among the most important for the bank's ability to make a profit, grow, and have an impact on the neighborhoods where we were operating. It involved identifying small investors and contractors who had the skills and drive to purchase six- to twelve-unit apartment buildings that were in serious disrepair. The rehab entrepreneurs would borrow from ShoreBank to fund the cost-effective renovation of the buildings. The repaired buildings could attract paying tenants, which would bring about profitability for the investor and improve the neighborhood more broadly. The bank's lending helped to restore the multifamily rental market on the southeast side of Chicago, but it did not have a measurable impact on obsolete commercial strips or in building a strong small business sector. The bank funded its growth, which peaked at $2 billion in assets in 2008, by attracting socially motivated investors who could obtain market-rate, FDIC-insured deposit accounts. Our annual net loan losses averaged about 30 basis points (0.30 percent) and were within 10 basis points (0.10 percent) of all banks of similar size across the country for the ten years prior to 2008.

ShoreBank also founded four nonprofit organizations (in Detroit, Cleveland, the Upper Peninsula of Michigan, and Washington state), each focused on supporting young small businesses by making loans that a commercial, regulated bank would be unable to make. Prior to the recession of 2008–2010, these loan funds experienced annual net losses in the 2 to 3 percent range, a level that can be absorbed as a cost of business charging normal rates of return and in normal times. During the recession, losses were higher but should have returned to the former level if conditions normalized. These nonprofits continued to provide local small businesses with nonfinancial services, such as marketing advice, which are equally needed but more difficult to provide sustainably.

Our general counsel at ShoreBank was fond of saying that if we ever woke up one morning and found that ShoreBank was not on the edge, we would move there immediately. Well, ShoreBank definitely found itself on the edge in 2010. Rising loan losses and declining real estate values linked to the deep recession wiped out the capital of the bank as well as the parent holding company. Thankfully, all of the component parts of ShoreBank have survived, even if under different ownership, but the corporate structure did not. All eleven former ShoreBank operating units (four for-profit subsidiaries, six nonprofit units, and one corporate division) began independent operations in the fourth quarter of 2010 or first quarter of 2011.

The lead bank is now owned by the investor group originally assembled to recapitalize ShoreBank Corporation and is managed by the new management group recruited by the holding company in early 2010. The holding company raised $148 million from this investor group to rebuild the capital base required by the government to operate a bank. The recapitalization funds had the condition that the U.S. Treasury approve a Troubled Asset Relief Program (TARP) investment of $71 million. When Treasury did not act on the TARP application by July 2010, the investor group reconvened and agreed to buy the bank directly from the FDIC after the FDIC closed the bank in late August. These investors are a consortium of major U.S. financial services companies and a few charitable foundations that are committed to the mission of neighborhood and small business growth.

The $175 million–asset ShoreBank Pacific bank subsidiary that focuses on environmental lending was sold to One California Bank in December 2010. The new investors have run an urban reinvestment strategy in California for several years and will broaden this to include an environmental mission with the help of this investment. It can now operate in California, Oregon, and Washington. ShoreBank sold the international advisory firm in January 2011 to an anchor investor, a subsidiary of Triodos Bank in the Netherlands. This company has grown steadily over the last few years, focusing on inclusive finance in emerging markets and in particular on small business, microcredit, and housing. It currently is managing major projects in Bangladesh, India, and Pakistan to rapidly accelerate savings products. Some of their work is also funded by the Gates Foundation.

The four regionally based nonprofit organizations are continuing to operate, supporting small business growth. There are also two national nonprofits: CFSI and NCIF. CFSI works with major corporate financial services firms, technology companies, and nonprofits on innovation in product development for financial services that will encourage savings among the underbanked in this country. NCIF provides capital and other financial and nonfinancial services to regulated banks and credit unions that have focused on low-income markets in this country.

Finally, ShoreBank sponsored two equity funds that invest in small banks in Asia and Africa serving either microbusinesses or small businesses. After a successful initial round of raising funds from investors, the second fund's initial closing at $50.5 million in 2011 will fund more investments in small banks. In 2010, federal regulators required that the fund management company at ShoreBank be spun out as an employee-owned firm called Equator Capital Partners, and the affiliated nonprofit, now known as Capital Plus Exchange, also became an independent entity. So, going forward, all of the twelve companies of ShoreBank are well managed, they are social enterprises, five are profitable businesses, and seven are healthy not-for-profits. Independently, we expect that they are going to continue to try to change the world.

Now I want to shift gears and ask you to think about the meaning of three commonly used terms in this field: *triple bottom line, inclusive finance,* and *capital plus.* When people say triple bottom line, what do they really mean? When Triodos Bank in the Netherlands says so eloquently that lending can create value other than financial value, what does it mean? Well, it means very different things to different people. In Europe it might mean organic agriculture. To a bank in Bangladesh it might mean they're going to branch into small business funding and start looking at cash flow and market analysis as opposed to just character. For ShoreBank, which aspired to change a neighborhood on the South Side of Chicago, it meant finding what ended up being hundreds of African-American rehab entrepreneurs who were able every twenty-four months or so to buy another building, fix it up, manage it, and ultimately change a neighborhood. But the key is the idea that you can create value beyond merely financial value.

I like the term *inclusive finance,* which we increasingly are using. In the old days we used to call it *access to capital* or *access to credit.* But if you think about it, inclusive finance really plays on the idea that we live in societies where there are many people with entrepreneurial energy or investment energy and that if we figured out a way to include them in the system, the society would be better off. This is one of our primary focuses through ShoreBank—to include those people in the market who according to "normal" banking procedures would be excluded from receiving loans or seed capital but who were really based in the community and had great potential as entrepreneurs.

Capital plus is a simple notion. A bank loan is not the beginning and the end of success for anybody. Capital is on some level a commodity, and people who are going to succeed need access to knowledge, not just capital. So at ShoreBank we managed a difficult combination of twelve companies to be more than a bank, to be able to offer services or take actions that are well beyond what a regulated bank could do. It's not an easy strategy to implement. It does mean that you have the advantage of having a sustainable banking activity at your core, and then you can try over the long term to implement other strategies that would be integrated with the bank and that would maybe get you closer to your goal—in our case, that of poverty alleviation.

In the fall of 2010, we were all reminded that we now live in a country that has 43.6 million people living in poverty, the largest number in the fifty years that statistics have been kept, up from just under 40 million last year; 26 percent of all African-Americans live in poverty, 25 percent of Hispanics, and 9 percent of whites. Where I worked, on the South Side of Chicago, the official unemployment rate in the last year was greater than 20 percent. Generally, in African-American communities, the unofficial rate would double those figures. There are very distressed communities all around the country these days. So we sorely need this idea of social banking, or more modern banking, or value-added, long-term banking, now.

Banks today prioritize loans to their best customers, and *best* usually means substantial personal and business net worth. But if there's no flow of credit in a market, think of all the things that will happen if that market is not affluent. Homes can't change hands, businesses can't finance growth, and investors can't do new things. Consumer needs are not specifically addressed. So community development banks exist to be anchor investment companies in communities, using the power of the regulated banking system to use government-insured deposits and keep a flow of capital moving through the community. There was a Social Capital Markets (SOCAP) conference in October 2010, and I'm told that 1,300 people came. They describe their work as "at the intersection of money and meaning." So there's growing enthusiasm for this idea of social capital investment and social enterprise.

The four people who founded ShoreBank were almost as young as some of the SOCAP attendees when we started. We were all in our thirties. We were biracial. We had a very big idea: Why couldn't a community bank be a community development institution? At that point in time, bank credit was unavailable in our market. It was as unavailable in 1973 as it is completely unavailable today. And then racial discrimination and preference for affluent customers dominated all bankers and all credit decisions. So we bought a failing $40 million institution, and we ran it sustainably with losses no higher than our peers for thirty-five years. We were not as profitable as some banks, and, in lieu of dividends to investors, we used some of the bank's earnings over time to staff the launch of the affiliates I described earlier. But we supported a very large number of minority entrepreneurs, often through this business of housing rehab. Each year we were able to lend three to four times our average capital in the form of new loans on the street. We also created an incubator culture, which supported the growth of twelve companies that will now continue to innovate independently.

I'm going to give you a picture now of the landscape for values-based banking in the United States. Today there are eighty-one commercial banks and thrifts that specialize in banking in low-income markets. Each of them has taken the trouble to get certified by the U.S. Treasury, and those eighty-one banks collectively have $27 billion in assets. We also did some research at the National Community Investment Fund to see what other cases of this kind of banking we could find among all 8,000 banks in the country. We identified 500 banks with the highest percentage of their loan portfolio in residential real estate loans and the highest percentage of their branch offices in low-income markets. We would have preferred to have been able to look at small business lending as well as housing, but we were dealing with public data. So we found 500 banks that were high performers, and that tells you that there are not just eighty banks that could do this work but maybe 500 that are already doing this work. We're going to try to coin a new term and call them *community development banking institutions.*

In addition to these 500 banks, there are 230 community development credit unions in the United States, with total assets of $11 billion. If you deposited your insured savings resources in these banks or thrifts or credit unions, you would add to their funds, which could be loaned out to improve neighborhoods and people's lives. They really need to be supported now because the large banks have fled these markets. The large banks are hardly lending in affluent markets, much less poor markets.

Today all of the banks in those categories that I just described hold assets totaling about $240 billion. We live in a society that has banking assets of $14 trillion; however, this pathetic little group of banks has the ability to advance about $40 billion in loans annually—which means they are putting out $120 million of new loans every working day of the year. It's not peanuts. It's not $14 trillion, but it's more than a lot of efforts. In addition to these regulated institutions, there are another 600 loan funds, community development financial institutions, and community development loan funds. They account for another $5 or $6 billion in assets. They do a lot of highly innovative work, and they don't keep everything on their balance sheets, so they're bigger than that $5 billion.

Now there's a growing group of environmentally oriented banks. We were able to help start up the first one in 1997. Today there are six or seven green banks around the country. Two of them are in California, New Resource Bank and First California Bank. First California Bank has just bought ShoreBank Pacific in Washington State, so it's going to expand up the coast. That's the landscape in the United States.

I'm going to shift now to the international landscape. The most exciting thing I know about internationally is a very small but wonderful effort called the Global Alliance for Banking on Values. It was spearheaded by Triodos Bank in the Netherlands and cosponsored by ShoreBank and the BRAC in Bangladesh. In the wake of the financial crisis, Peter Blom, the CEO of Triodos, decided it was time to take a stand and say, "You know, there is a better form of banking than the one that we have just experienced. It's long term; it sees value creation as more than financial value." He's done the work to put together what is today a group of ten banks. They have together $12 billion in assets and a million customers on four continents around the world. They intend to keep growing, persuading banks to join this idea. Their goal is to get to a billion customers on every continent by 2020, and they're serious. They're going to create an equity fund to invest capital in this group of banks.

In addition to those kinds of social banks, there is of course the microfinance movement internationally. It has turned the world of foreign aid upside down. All of a sudden we make investments, not grants; loans, not handouts. We have scale, not anecdotes. It's a very exciting field and has been a wonder to watch. You can make small loans to very poor people for working capital. You can do it profitably, and you can do it at scale. There are today more than 200 microfinance organizations around the world that each has more than 30,000 customers. If we look at the big players, there are maybe a dozen microfinance organizations that have more than a million customers, some of them as many as 5 or 6 million.

I was lucky to be in Bangladesh the day after Grameen Bank got its bank charter in 1983. I was spurred on by the experience to learn how to use one of those newfangled things called a PC. I learned how to use software called VisiCalc, and we did the long-term financial projections for the Grameen Bank that year and for the next decade. It was a great window on the beginning of microfinance. Since then I have found many extraordinarily talented entrepreneurs who have attached themselves to microfinance. I've had the chance to be on the board of the Women's World Banking, Accion Texas, and now the Calvert Foundation.

In general, microfinance has not done as well in the United States. There are only 25 million businesses in this country that have from zero up to five employees. This is a huge category of the self-employed that are very hard to serve here. But globally, microfinance is much bigger and more exciting, really, than what's going on in the United States. Overseas we are seeing visionary leadership, lots of money, and the ability to manage an institution that can grow 30 to 40 percent a year, every year, for ten years. One of the reasons they do well is that they just do one thing. They make small loans; they haven't until now even been trying to mobilize savings. But now some of them are expanding. So there's a German organization called Pro-Credit that is now only doing small business loans; SewaBank in India is succeeding with insurance; BRAC Bank in Bangladesh is about to start a very big-time mobile banking activity, helped by our affiliate, ShoreBank International. So it's going to be very interesting to keep watching these organizations and to try to replicate this level of ambition and determination to affect what is happening in one's society

Now the big banks are really large. I think that you should look to the large banks in this area mainly for mass-market products for consumers, for product innovation, and for wholesaling services. Historically, they have been too large to do some of the work that is needed when you're dealing with relatively uneducated borrowers. Now, however, there's a lot of activity in this area, and with technology, and with the per-unit cost of a lot of transactions having gone way down, it may be much more possible to deliver products that poor people actually need and can use. You can look at what Key Bank has done by creating a whole suite of profitable services for low-income people. So the large banks in part are also very serious, and that's where the money is. So we really need to collaborate.

I'd like to share three lessons from the Great Recession, two of which are about ShoreBank. First, like the rest of the global banking industry, with twenty-twenty hindsight we should have kept higher capital levels. We were always classified by the regulators as well-capitalized, but we were lulled by the profitability and the low loan losses that we experienced. We put our emphasis on getting more money out on the street every year, which would create jobs and improve communities. We probably should have raised enough capital many years earlier so that we would have had longer to withstand the tumult that occurred in our market.

Second, we had a very specific strategy of targeting a local market. We were going to restore normal markets on the South Side of Chicago. We had this fabulous niche of real estate rehabbing that was profitable. It had huge impact. We should've tried harder to have a second and third profitable niche.

We were not diversified enough away from real estate lending. So that's an important lesson for other people who follow ShoreBank.

Third, I'd like to share a thought about the regulators. When we were in the period of the real estate bubble, regulation of nonbank lenders was non-existent. Profit-seeking money poured into these new niches, often in highly inappropriate and unsustainable ways, like the predatory home mortgage product. Nobody could compete with those players for equity or for share of market. We tried to compete responsibly and ethically in our market, and there was no way. They could beat us in speed and product every day of the week. Then, even though some people may have benefited temporarily from this huge opening up of credit, most people ultimately lost out. When a bust comes, the regulators become very tough. Again, credit is not available, because the regulators want banks to have more capital, governments are stretched, and equity flows to the big banks that are too big to fail.

Lastly, there are these two niches that I think are worth focusing on that are not as easy as microfinance. It's much easier to run a sustainable business that makes a loan than to run one that delivers a knowledge service. The borrowers are really pleased to pay for capital; they're not at all pleased to pay for knowledge because knowledge is a kind of public good.

I have a good friend in India who is the founder of Selco, which sells solar cooking and business products to poor women. He's found he must provide highly customized products and post-acquisition maintenance, and he has to do a lot of relationship building to get these products developed. It's a great example of why a social enterprise might not be fully self-supporting. It's covering a lot of activity for which nobody will pay. So we need softer forms of capital; we need patience; we probably need for many of these activities to be based in a lending activity or some activity that is financially sustainable.

Then we come up against all of the people who say, "Yes, social enterprise is fabulous; you can maximize both profit and social returns, and you can have it all. And if you don't get it all, it's really not very good. If you can't get 18 percent returns on equity and have a documented excellent social return, you haven't done anything." But who says that all investors want to maximize their return? Can't you choose to take a lower percentage return because you're happy if it's complemented by a specific social return? I, for my part, would much rather work to increase the pool of investor money that would sometimes accept a lower market return rather than to work to generate pools in which the profits are coming from the interest rate, which hurts the borrowers.

It's not that profit is bad, because it's not. It's important to fuel a growing business and to pay a return. But we live in a world in which there is sort of one best way; there's either real business or there's charity, there's for-profit or there's not-for-profit.

To conclude, I would like to suggest that maybe you could participate in believing that there's a hybrid space and challenge those dichotomies or truisms or mantras. Many segments could evolve in the space between charity and profit maximization. There might be ten separate segments. Wouldn't it be interesting to say, "Let's not have any more silver bullets; let's just see what works and see how it evolves, and use our brains and our ability to innovate to solve some of the problems that we have here in this country, and overseas." That's my proposed declaration of independence for you. *You* choose the combination of financial and social return in which you want to invest, and don't let anybody tell you that it's 15 percent or nothing, or 15 percent or a grant. It's what you choose. Let's see what happens.

# BUILDING ON FAITH

Louise Burnham Packard, Founder and Executive Director,

Trinity Boston Foundation

The Trinity Boston Foundation probably needs a new name. We don't have an endowment, and we don't give away money. We're a subsidiary of Trinity Church in Boston, with a mission of changing the odds for Boston youth, particularly around educational achievement, violence, and incarceration. We pursue that mission in three ways. We run direct-service programs, we work to improve community health and cohesion across Boston through effective collaboration with other organizations, and we work for social change at the systems level to improve the lives of those we would never be able to reach through our direct-service programs.

I'm going to explain why we created the foundation, why we've chosen this multipronged approach, and why I believe that the nonprofit sector's disparate efforts to address poverty and social inequality leave many assets untapped or underleveraged. I'm going to suggest that the best way to discover and deploy those assets is through building and strengthening community, not just within city neighborhoods but across neighborhoods and out to the suburbs. It is also by creating not just a web of individual relationships but also organizational partnerships and networks that weave together the faith-based organizations, social enterprises, and traditional nonprofits that make up our social sector.

Four years ago a pastor in Boston who chaired the board of our community foundation told me that Boston was resource rich and coordination poor. I think that is less true today because our sector has worked hard to build relationships and get connected. At the Trinity Boston Foundation, we've brought organizations together for advocacy, for our annual collaborative fund-raising dinner, to participate in Bostonians for Youth, and to strengthen our public schools.

But, first, what is a faith-based organization? The many forms of faith-based organizations defy a quick summary. Entrepreneurs who are people of faith have created extraordinary organizations that reflect their faith perspective and priorities. Various denominations have formed large social-service organizations in the United States and abroad. Then there are all of the faith communities and congregations that provide social services to members and nonmembers.

You may think that congregation-based social services are a small part of the social-service sector. Not so. One study in Philadelphia showed that the replacement value of the social services provided by congregations in that city was $250 million, and the total investment by the city of Philadelphia in social services was $522 million. That's a lot of social services, but note that the statistic is about replacement value, not direct expenditures. Congregations have significant assets to leverage, such as buildings that might otherwise be empty during the week, a volunteer labor pool ready to put their faith into practice, and a history and connection to their community that can make them informed and effective players. All of these assets enable congregations to deliver significant services on frugal budgets. There is a lot of value embedded in America's congregations, and the geographic density of those congregations is unsurpassed.

When we created the Trinity Boston Foundation, we talked a lot about the assets of Trinity Church and how the Foundation's organizational structure could help us leverage them on behalf of the community. But I believe that the most valuable asset that congregations and other faith-based organizations can leverage is faith. The core of this faith is the belief that there is great love at work in the universe that seeks justice, mercy, peace, and joy. Our various faith traditions and practices teach us how to stay open to that love, tap into it, align ourselves with it, and be empowered by it.

What does faith look like in an organization? Despite great diversity in form and focus, there are common values that I typically see in organizations in which the leadership is intentional about putting faith into practice. First, there is a focus on relationships and community. There is an emphasis on building relationships and partnerships and accruing a deep understanding of the surrounding community. Second, there is an emphasis on today's needs. In response to critical needs, there is a bias for today versus tomorrow. Third, there is a tendency toward action versus caution, spending versus saving. Fourth, we have flexibility. The ability to respond nimbly to opportunities or changing circumstances is prized over disciplined adherence to a multiyear plan. There's a willingness to pursue promising but risky ideas without paralysis due to fear of failure. Fifth, we have a holistic approach. The emphasis on relationship and community inspires the leadership to see the needs of the whole person and want to help. And finally, we have big dreams. Often the approach is accompanied by a "whatever it takes" determination. The organization has the courage to make leaps of faith, to tackle big challenges or pursue big ideas despite a lack of resources.

Now, this is not the list that typically headlines a social enterprise conference. So let me give you an example of these values in action. It's a story I'm pretty sure you've heard before.

The feeding of the 5,000, also called the miracle of the loaves and fishes, is one of only two miracles included in all four Christian gospels. The other is the resurrection of Jesus. As a busy executive director and as a parent, I love how this story begins. Jesus is tired. He's been teaching and healing nonstop, and all he wants to do is go off by himself somewhere to pray. But the crowd follows him. They are hungry for spiritual food, for healing, for a message of hope, and now they are physically hungry, too. The disciples come to Jesus and say, "Send the crowd away so that they may go into the surrounding villages and countryside to lodge and get provisions, for we are here in a deserted place." But Jesus says to the disciples, "You give them something to eat." Note the big idea with no visible resources to execute on it. Also note the holistic approach. He does not say, "Well, my job is healing and teaching, but food distribution is not in my business model." In response, the disciples say exactly what any good CFO or board treasurer would say: "It's not in the budget. It would cost 200 denarii. All we have are five loaves and two fish."

So Jesus does two things. First he says, "Make them sit down in groups of about fifty each." Here's the focus on relationships and community. Let's imagine for a moment that we are in that crowd. We've been watching Jesus, hanging on his every word, and now we sit down in smaller groups. We take our eyes off the leader, and we start looking at each other. We say, "Oh, you're from my village. Oh, you have a child about my child's age. Oh, you're older and might need some help sitting down on the ground." We look at each other and form relationships, we see each other as individuals, and we begin to care. The second thing that Jesus did was to take the five loaves and two fish, bless them, and give them to the disciples to set before the crowd. You know how this story ends. All ate and were filled. What was left over was gathered up: twelve baskets of broken pieces. Now, my understanding of this miracle is this: Jesus forms communities and models generosity, which in turn inspires the crowd to be generous. They open up their knapsacks and share what they have, and it was more than enough.

What did each of us in the crowd have to do to create that miracle? We had to look at the loaf of bread or piece of fruit in our knapsack and override our impulse to save it for later, maybe for breakfast tomorrow. The tensions were between our own needs and the needs of others, between the present need and a future need. Inspired by the power of community, the generosity of Jesus, and the connection we felt to each other, we shared, and not only were our physical needs met, our spiritual needs were met, too. We were part of a miracle. Five loaves, two fish, 5,000 people fed, no denarii changing hands, no government contract, no fund-raising, no earned revenue. Don't we want to analyze that process, replicate it, take it to scale? I would argue that faith communities replicate that miracle in small ways all year round. The question then is one of scale.

Let me name four things in this story that we've tried to put into practice at the Trinity Boston Foundation. One is to leverage existing assets. The food was already in the knapsacks. We need to get as good at deploying what already exists as we are at creating something new. Two is building relationships and community. We need to focus on building relationships both within our enterprises and with external partners. At Trinity we're taking this one step further by working to strengthen institutions, specifically churches and schools, that themselves have the capacity to be engines of community. Three is to model generosity. Jesus gave all he had to the crowd. We need to not be so focused on our own plan and our own bottom line that we miss significant opportunities to collaborate and leverage our assets in partnership with others. Finally, recognize that our hunger for connection, meaning, and purpose is the most powerful asset in our knapsack. My own theological framework links spiritual hunger to the power of divine love. The two are always seeking each other. When connected, they can make the seemingly impossible possible. I think the point holds up without the theology, and let me state it that way, too. The world is teeming with people who are feeling that something is missing in their lives. To the extent that we can offer connection and meaning, we can create public appetite and will for social change.

I joined the staff of Trinity Church in 2001 to help this Episcopal parish achieve an audacious goal: raising $53 million to put its building, a masterpiece of American architecture, to work supporting its church community and the greater Boston community. The goal was too high. One rule of thumb for a capital campaign is to raise ten times annual giving. That would have set the bar at about $30 million, and we were going for $53 million. I'm not sure how Jesus knew there was a sufficient amount of food in the knapsacks. As campaign director, I had research methods at my disposal to determine that in fact there was $53 million in the knapsacks of the Trinity congregation. But I don't mean there was $53 million in the discretionary budgets of the Trinity congregation—far from it. It would take a reordering of priorities, a shift in the way each of us thought about our money, about self and other, today versus tomorrow, for that $53 million to be offered up. But it was there.

Trinity was blessed with a great teacher in its rector, Sam Lloyd. His core message was about stewardship, about recognizing the abundance of our lives, feeling grateful and giving back in gratitude, and saying "yes" to the divine love at the center of the universe. But preaching just gets the words in the air. It is in the development of community that the words are put into practice. That was what the capital campaign was all about. It wasn't ultimately about our national historic landmark building or even about our need for gathering space. It was about the process of building a community and putting our faith into practice. We read scripture, we talked about generosity, and we worked toward tithing. As we made our gifts, we modeled generosity for each other and inspired ourselves to dare to give more. In December 2004, the Trinity congregation achieved that $53 million goal. I believe that, at that point, it was the second largest congregation-based campaign in the country, with the two others in the top three being evangelical megachurches, Willow Creek in Illinois at $84 million, and Rick Warren's Saddleback in Southern California at $50 million.

There's a coda to the capital campaign story. Well, it seemed like a coda at the time, but it turned out to be the beginning of the next chapter. In November 2004, right at the end of Trinity's campaign, I met the Reverend Hurmon Hamilton. His African-American congregation in Roxbury was in the midst of its own building renovation, and, though they had met their initial fundraising goal, in the demolition phase of the construction project they found some very expensive surprises.

Now, it was not in Trinity Church's strategic plan to raise money for another church. But the project tugged on me for a couple months, and eventually I dove in. We hosted a breakfast meeting at Trinity. We invited members of Trinity's congregation and philanthropic partners. Reverend Hamilton invited pastors from the Black Ministerial Alliance and friends from suburban congregations. We had liberal, progressive Christians, and conservative evangelical Christians, and the head of the Jewish Community Relations Council all there together. At the breakfast, Reverend Hamilton told the story of the campaign, including the fact that he and his wife had given the down payment they had saved to buy a house to renovate the church instead. A column in *The Boston Globe* told the story of the breakfast and the pastor's gift, and within a month we had raised nearly $1 million.

In the years since then, it has become clear to me and to Reverend Hamilton that the most important outcome of the breakfast and the Roxbury Presbyterian campaign was the set of relationships we formed. Reverend Hamilton leveraged those relationships with extraordinary impact when he later became a driving force in the successful passage of health care reform in Massachusetts. The relationships I formed, particularly the working partnership with Reverend Hamilton, set the stage for the creation of the Trinity Boston Foundation.

In 2006, Trinity's assets included a historic building in the heart of Boston's Back Bay neighborhood with beautiful new program space. We had a large regional congregation with significant financial and social capital. We were a Boston brand that had been around for more than 270 years. The exterior of our building is often the backdrop for the nightly news. We had robust administrative infrastructure, including a very capable finance office. We also had two strong outreach programs with annual operating budgets of about $250,000 each. As evidenced by the Roxbury Presbyterian breakfast, we also had convening power. That's a lot of assets in one knapsack.

I found myself saying two things. One, there are enough resources in Boston to solve Boston's problems. Two, if we all got to know each other, this would be a different city. So we started thinking about how we could open up Trinity's knapsack and leverage our assets on behalf of the city and how we could model a generous and collaborative approach to addressing Boston's social issues that would inspire others to join in.

In January 2007, the Trinity Boston Foundation took its current form. We worked out a governance structure that assured Trinity's vestry a measure of control. The church committed a start-up grant of $150,000 a year for two years. We assumed the management and expense of the two outreach programs, and we set a budget that first year of about $900,000. Where would the revenue come from? Remember that part I mentioned about big ideas and no visible resources? It was a leap of faith. Thankfully, the resources continue to appear, and we've seen four years of steady growth.

You may be wondering how this approach I've been describing makes the Trinity Boston Foundation a new, innovative form of social enterprise. Lots of faith communities deliver community services, and many have created 501(c) (3) organizations as a way to attract resources and manage initiatives.

What is innovative about our foundation is its three-pronged strategy. Most organizations choose to develop a particular program or set of programs that will have a defined social impact. We do that through our Trinity Education for Excellence Program (TEEP) and our Counseling Center. But we do not stop, for example, with TEEP's mission goal of empowering youth to achieve excellence. We then use the knowledge and relationships built through delivering the program to increase coordination and effectiveness within the social sector and to build the public will to create social change.

Let me say a word about our programs. TEEP is a year-round program that engages students from seventh grade all the way through high school and beyond. We excel at taking students who are in the bottom half of their sixth grade class and ensuring that they get to and through college. One hundred percent of the students who complete the six-year program go to college and graduate on time. Seventy percent of them are the first in their families to do this. The program produces leaders, and many of our college graduates are choosing careers working for social change, including Juan David Lozano, who recently joined our staff as the assistant director of TEEP. Last fall, Root Cause recognized TEEP as one of the top seven college access programs in Massachusetts.

Our other youth-focused program, Street Potential, serves young men caught in the juvenile justice system. Street Potential is part of our counseling center, which targets the epidemic of untreated trauma in distressed neighborhoods, both through individual counseling and work with partner organizations. Like TEEP, Street Potential and the counseling center build our knowledge of social issues and our network of relationships in the city. That knowledge and those relationships enable us to be effective agents for systemic change.

Here's one example drawn from Street Potential, where participants in the program are reentering the community after being locked up for an extended period of time, maybe six to eighteen months. In metro Boston, there were five community reentry centers to which these youth had to report after school. This was very convenient for the case managers, having the kids come to them, but it wasn't so great for the youth because, instead of being engaged in positive activities in the community, they came back together again every day after school to be with the people with whom they'd been locked up. So we convened a series of meetings with faith partners, nonprofits, and the staff of the relevant government agency, and it turned out that everyone thought the reentry model was a bad idea. A year later the system changed.

Here's another example. When we realized that we needed to hold an annual dinner to raise funds for our programs, we thought about how it could reflect our three-pronged strategy of delivering programs, building community cohesion and coordination, and working for social change. The result is Bostonians for Youth. Unlike most fund-raising dinners, the purpose is not to market the effectiveness of a single program. Instead, the purpose is to shine a spotlight on a critical social issue and show how different organizations are working together to address the problem. As was true for its first event in 2009, Bostonians for Youth 2011 is focused on youth violence. We are partnering with a small community organization that provides direct services to the families of victims and a very large agency that is known for its expertise in treating trauma. Our values of collaboration and generosity lead us to split the net proceeds evenly with the two partner organizations. We hope to send each a check for $100,000.

The 450 people who attend Bostonians for Youth this year will hear two key messages. The first is that violence—the number-two cause of death for youth nationally and a seemingly intractable product of educational failure, untreated trauma, and a lack of economic opportunity—is not a neighborhood issue but a Boston issue. The youths on both ends of the guns belong to all of us. The second message is that we can't end violence without deep coordination and collaboration within the social sector.

It's not your typical gala. We try hard, as our youth would say, to keep it real. Noted filmmaker Topper Carew produces an original film for the events. You can watch his past films at *Bostoniansforyouth.org*. They're edgy, provocative, and not easy to stomach. In the 2009 film, we meet the Odom family and learn that Steven Odom was murdered at age thirteen as he walked home from school. We also meet Raychand, a Street Potential participant. Four months after that film premiered at our dinner, I went to Raychand's funeral. We work hard to use the event to raise money, but even more important than that is our effort to develop the public will to address the issues. We want to affect people on a deep level so that something will shift inside. We hope that a connection will form, an awareness perhaps of the full humanity of the young people who are caught up in violence, both the victims and the survivors. Then we want to empower the guests to get involved. Our approach inspires individuals to give, and it builds relationships among the organizations that lead to programmatic partnerships. Those partnerships in turn help us leverage each other's assets for greater impact.

So what's next? In neighborhoods that are fragmented and suffer from high rates of poverty, violence, and despair, the two institutions most able to generate community are congregations and schools. So if our theory of change involves leveraging existing assets to strengthen communities, it would make sense to focus our investment there. We continue to have a close working partnership with Roxbury Presbyterian Church. I sit on the board of its 501(3)(c), the Social Impact Center, and Reverend Hamilton sits on the Trinity Boston Foundation board. Our newest collaboration is around Roxbury Presbyterian's Dream Again campaign. The big idea is that the Roxbury community has lost its capacity to dream, and it's time to help the community dream again. After extensive interviews conducted by going door to door in the neighborhood, Reverend Hamilton's congregation decided that the best way to reach a large number of neighbors would be to adopt a nearby public school in danger of being shut down.

One reason that inner-city schools may not generate community is that the parents and guardians are focused on daily survival needs and lack discretionary time, or English-language fluency, and/or the comfort or soft skills needed to get involved. So if the families can't create community at the schools, can a faith community adopt a school, wrap it in love, and inspire and empower parents, students, and teachers to find new hope? Roxbury Presbyterian is developing the model, and Trinity has become a secondary partner at the Dearborn Middle School, which is now dreaming of becoming a six-through-twelve early college science, technology, engineering, and math school. A failing school dreams of becoming a model school for the whole state. With the help of Roxbury Presbyterian, the Greater Boston Interfaith Organization, and Trinity, that dream has already garnered a $40 million commitment from the state to renovate the building. Having learned the partnership model from Roxbury Presbyterian, Trinity hopes to adopt our own public school and to inspire other communities to do the same.

I hope I'm not making this sound too easy. It is really hard work, and the tension between faith calling and best business practice runs high. Serving on the board of the Social Impact Center requires either a lot of faith or a huge appetite for risk. Its expense budget is less than $150,000 a year, it has no operating reserves, and the balance in its checking account is rarely more than $10,000. Yet, as Reverend Hamilton says, if we based our actions on our checking account, the Dearborn would not have a $40 million commitment from the state. Faith prompts action, and a lack of cash can necessitate partnerships and leveraging existing assets.

Over at Trinity, the numbers are not quite as daunting, but nevertheless, the tension persists. In January, the foundation board looked hard at two numbers. The first was our $20,000 deficit for 2010, which we needed to cover from our meager operating reserves. The second was the fact that we had given $135,000 to other organizations, $55,000 each to our Bostonians for Youth partners and $25,000 we had raised in response to the earthquake in Haiti and used to inspire a much larger citywide faith offering. So on a $1.3 million expense budget, we had both run a deficit and tithed. Best business practice? I am not sure. Faith calling? I hope so.

Four-plus years into the experiment of the Trinity Boston Foundation, we have created something that I hope will be as enduring as our 278-year-old parish. We've raised more than $5 million, delivered successful programs, developed ways to increase collaboration and coordination within our sector, and built significant citywide partnerships and coalitions to create systemic change. Nevertheless, the dropout rate in Boston schools is still too high, and the graduation rate too low. College entrance and completion statistics describe a generation of young men and women with very little chance of social mobility. An African-American boy in the ninth grade in the Boston public schools has a 7 percent chance of graduating from college. There were seventy murders in Boston last year and many more nonfatal shootings. It is tempting to think that the problems are too great and too difficult. It is tempting to think, as the disciples did, that we need to send the crowd away so that it can fend for itself. But I hear what Jesus said when the task seemed impossible, and there were no visible resources in sight: "You give them something to eat." So we press on, forming relationships and community, modeling generosity, and giving what we have so that all will be fed. Our tagline at the Trinity Boston Foundation is "Together, let's change the odds." But unless we get the "together" right, there's no way we will succeed.

# THE ENTREPRENEURS

## A Conversation

Shapiro: The word *entrepreneur* often means "an individual who is driven and passionate." What do you think of this term *social entrepreneurship,* and can it be applied to a team?

Packard: I don't like the focus on the individual because I think that, for any enterprise to get off the ground, there has to be a team. But I do understand why we think about it that way because somebody has to embody the vision and be the driving force. I know that I've had a big team at Trinity, but certainly the entrepreneurial pain of the first few years has been mine to carry and bear. We have to resist the star system of lone entrepreneurs taking on the world, because (a) I don't think it's healthy, and (b) it makes it so much harder to collaborate when someone has staked their whole identity on an organization. If you have done that, why would you partner? You'd think, "I'm going to prove my model and attract my funding." It doesn't work to say, "Well, actually, there are sixteen organizations that all have to do this to really make the change." You have to be saying, "My organization is going to make the change." That's worth resisting.

Houghton: I agree. It had better be able to be applied to a team because very few enterprises make it because of one person. We had a run-in with one of the foundations that focuses on social entrepreneurship a couple of years ago because we were looking for capital from them. They said, "You're not a social entrepreneur; you're this ancient institution. We finance young social entrepreneurs." I think there's kind of a cult of the individual hero, and anybody who's really tried to make something happen knows that you're really trying to build an institution, and it relies on many, many people.

Bretos: There is little to add except to say that we have to learn to work together. The role of the entrepreneur may be more to create alliances and galvanize people than to do the work by him- or herself.

Shapiro: It seems that there is agreement that while the focus is at times on the social entrepreneur, success ultimately depends on the team. Let me ask you about another key focus within the social entrepreneurship discourse, and that is the notion of scale. Is there a difference between scale and social change, and what are your aspirations in this regard?

Shah: One of the debates in microfinance right now is, "To what degree is microfinance actually alleviating poverty?" One way that I think about it is that I'm stepping back from "Does it actually affect poverty?" to "Is access to financial service a basic right?" If you're living on two dollars a day, the ability to turn small payments into a large lump sum to capture an opportunity, whether it's buying that cow or paying for a medical expense, is a valuable thing. Other financial services, such as savings and insurance, are incredibly valuable, as well. Does that actually result in you getting out of poverty? Not always. Does that just help you cope with poverty? Oftentimes that's the value of these loans. Now, just like education or health care, those two things don't exactly get that person out of poverty, but we're seeing that it's one step in many different things that need to happen to create the conditions of choice, so that people can have the opportunity, the dignity, to live a life up to their most potential. I think what we could see, though, is that the more patient the members of the Internet community are with their loans, the more social impact we're going to see. What I'd like to see is expanding into things like micromortgages. Today, this really does not exist, the idea of a thirty-year fixed mortgage in the developing world. They really are living in short cash-flow cycles. But would the Internet community be willing to finance someone for ten years or fifteen years with no payments, or minimal payments, until an income stream is generated? This is the kind of experimentation I like to see so that people who are being told "no" today about getting access to credit are being told "yes" in the future.

Packard: We think about scale a lot, because one of the models that seems to be out there in the social enterprise conversation, particularly about youth development programs, is that as soon as you get multicity, then you're a national organization, and then you can attract a whole lot of funding because people like that you're going to scale. You can have pretty small programs in a number of cities, but that puts you a whole category ahead. To my way of thinking, the deeper you get in the community, the more you can change the community. So if you're focused on replicating in four other cities, how do you go deep in those cities? You end up being very focused on your program model and how you replicate your program model, but you're not developing the kind of ties that do all the things I talked about. We've thought about TEEP; should we start having TEEPs in other cities? Actually, it started in New Orleans, so it already is multicity. But I think where to go with TEEP is to figure out how to build leadership academies within public schools in Boston, so you're serving a whole lot more people. But that doesn't get you the same attention as if we went to multiple cities. I do think it's replicable in other cities—not by me, but by other institutions.

By the way, I think if you took our lens of saying, "What are our assets?" you could replicate that. In fact, I've mentioned to the dean of Harvard Business School that there should just be a little group inside the Harvard Business School trying to figure out how to leverage the assets of the business school on behalf of Cambridge and Boston. In other words, what's replicable is the practice of looking up from your business plan and trying to figure out what's going on around you and how you can connect.

What are characteristics of Boston? It's a small city. It is not impossible for us to all get to know each other. We have had a bad history of segregation. We have a big wound in our collective psyche about busing. There is a lot that divides us, but I've really seen a movement toward building more connection and trying to come together. I think we're even beginning to have public conversations about the busing crisis. That just shows you that people are trying collectively to heal the city.

Shapiro: Which brings me to another question. The role of government is often absent in discussions on social entrepreneurship. To affect wide-scale change, do governments have to be involved?

Houghton: Certainly for big banks, government involvement helps. The last time that the large banks got really excited about community investment was when the Clinton administration put a lot of guts into the enforcement of the Community Reinvestment Act. The large banks knew that they would be stopped from merger activity if they didn't have an excellent record of community reinvestment. They all got religion at the same time, and they got really interested in community reinvestment, so that was a stick. Then, in the Bush administration, that went away. In the Obama administration, there has been interest in this field but no pressure on the large banks to focus.

The fact that eighteen large financial institutions became the investors in ShoreBank has got to be way up there in terms of financial commitment to community banking; $130 million from the large banks into one bank on the South Side of Chicago. They really cared about preserving the institution. So there are people inside those institutions who understand that if the society deteriorates, nobody wins.

Shah: There most certainly is a role for government. One change I would love to see is the expansion globally of local credit bureaus. In southern India today, what's happening is a problem called overindebtedness. A borrower—and this happens here in the United States—will get one loan from one microfinance organization and another one and another one and start basically repaying one loan with another loan. One of the things that's happening is that these microfinance organizations do not check with each other before making a loan. In the United States, we are able to check the indebtedness of a borrower through a credit check. But in most countries, there is not a credit bureau to say, "Wow, this person is pretty significantly in debt." So one of the things that precipitated this crisis in India is that the local government-run self-help group—microfinance provider, essentially—because they were more flexible, when people started getting loans from multiple sources, they were being paid last. That, combined with suicides of about forty farmers who were basically in over their heads, is absolutely tragic. It got a lot of media attention, and the government in southern India actually shut down the microfinance sector. Now, in southern India, there's nothing short of a crisis. But this crisis is good because, like the mortgage bubble here in the United States, it's an opportunity for us to learn, to do things in a way that's in line with our values and the original reasons why microfinance first started. I think through better regulation, through credit bureaus, and then basically through more responsible players, including the people who are investing, I think we can make sure there's minimal damage as we try to expand access to the poor.

Bretos: I believe that my effectiveness in achieving social change has to do with my ability to work with rather than against any given system, including government. Our goal from the beginning was to change the way we care for low-income seniors and disabled adults, and to do that we had to change federal policy, which we did this year. So it was impossible for me to achieve that by excluding government. That does not mean that I rely exclusively on government, rather that I used the private sector and even government pilot programs to come up with remedies for things that were wrong and used that proof to convince government to support and fund our programs.

Many among us start from the position that government does not work because they do not want it to work. For so many years we have been hearing that government is the problem, and some of our leaders have set out to prove it by relaxing standards, appointing mediocre managers, and allowing performance to deteriorate. It was a self-fulfilling prophecy. I believe that we need to help government perform better the important task of creating value for the public. We have done that by bringing new ideas to them, understanding how the system works, respecting some of the people who work within government, and leverage resources; in other words, redirecting their efforts. It is hard for me to understand how social change can be achieved without some government involvement.

Shapiro: Do you feel that there is an appropriate emphasis on utilizing business tools and strategies in your work today?

Packard: The most innovative aspect of Trinity is not a business skill but our three-pronged strategy and the way we model generosity. We are focused on strengthening the community that supports Boston youth, not just building a particular intervention. Sometimes that strategy is in tension with business practice—for example, when we write checks to Bostonians for Youth partner organizations even as we are facing a budget deficit or deciding that we should ask our donors to give money to Haiti when we also need them to give to us. When you think of year-end fundraising and the pressure of that, business rigor would say that this is a bad idea. We're also generous with my time and my staff's time, giving advice and helping others launch ventures and collaborate.

Having said that, however, I apply as much business rigor as I can at any time to what we're doing. I think to the extent that we're innovative and we are pushing the envelope, I feel as if we fall in that social enterprise category. We're still in start-up mode. It's been four years. I think what happens is you kind of go out and do, and then when you get a little bit bigger you can stop and invest more in your business infrastructure. Then you get a little bigger, and you need to stop and invest more. We're in one of those second-round stages now, where we're going back and trying to put in the whole next level of management infrastructure. My first hire was an MBA, because I knew I needed that discipline and that practice. In our field, business rigor is also used interchangeably with the word *metrics*. You hear a lot about metrics in the social enterprise conversation, but sometimes the most powerful impact is the hardest to capture in a set of numbers. It's really important, but there are some things that we haven't figured out how to capture yet. So why exactly do all our TEEP students go to college? How can you measure how empowered someone is? Or how much hope do they have? If one of our Street Potential participants is murdered, did our intervention matter? What was the value of the fact that while he lived, he experienced unconditional love and support? Even my whole point about community connection and cohesion—what's a good metric for that? How do you know you've strengthened the social fabric of the city? I'd love to figure that out.

Bretos: I understand both how the market and government work. Very few people understand both. When people tell me a story about whether it can or cannot be done, I understand the system; I know how to work it. So I think, in a nutshell, that we do things other people—or at least the private service organizations—don't want to do because it's unpredictable, it's difficult, there are too many regulations, there's too much supervision. We go to their homes. I sell my program to the policymakers in the federal and state government. For every person for whom I provide services in his or her home, I'm saving the Medicaid budget $18,000 a year. Now you multiply that by the 5,000 people who are already today being served at home, we are cutting the Medicaid program, which is a big budgetary issue in every state in this country, by millions of dollars. That's why they give us the money. Altruism is not already there; they want to cut spending in the Medicaid program, and we have the way to do it.

Shapiro: Premal, we know that for-profit microfinance is quite controversial. Can you just talk a minute about the difference between for-profit and nonprofit microfinance and what you think the rationale is for your approach?

Shah: Let me walk through the lifecycle of microfinance organization. Just like Dr. Yunus, who started with a small group of people, or maybe that pastor who starts lending to people in his congregation and will then form an organization, usually, it's a nonprofit organization. Today on Kiva, more than 80 percent of the organizations on that platform are nonprofit. The average profitability rate of the organizations on Kiva, if you combine them, is negative. So they're not yet sustainable. But of course what we all want at the end of the day on our deathbeds is the idea that, if I live in rural Sierra Leone, I can actually walk into an organization that will be around for a long time because they're now accepting my deposits as well and you can trust that they'll be sustainable. Kiva's view on this is that sustainability is a good thing; hitting profitability or the ability to cover your costs, this is exactly why I love microcredit and microfinance. It can be abused, and, like a lot of great things, there are some bad apples, and there's need for things like regulation and a lot more self-restraint. For example, Kiva will not work in southern India, because we feel as if the microfinance industry there is very competitive, and there are a lot of big microfinance institutions. One of them just had an initial public offering that made investors tens of millions of dollars, including Silicon Valley investors like Sequoia Capital. It's not a bad thing, because they're expanding to be an institution, but it's not the role of the Internet community, we believe, to provide subsidized capital. What we'd like to see are a couple of things that you've seen here in the United States: more regulation, once the microfinance industry actually matures. For example, in the United States, they have the Truth in Lending Act. Transparency on pricing is key—the idea that there's an APR (annual percentage rate) or nutrition facts box when you apply for a credit card. It still wasn't good enough. People had to introduce more regulation because people still didn't understand with credit cards what they were getting into. You can imagine right now, with populations that don't have literacy or numeracy, that there's a lot of confusion around what the interest rate is and which loan is actually the best loan for me. So what's needed is regulation around pricing transparency and a lot of actual monitoring, which is what Kiva and a lot of other social funders want to do. That's a really key issue.

Shapiro: Okay. Kiva is right in the middle of this space that challenges the notion of for-profit and nonprofit. Obviously, Kiva is a nonprofit organization, but you're engaged in business in a very significant way. One of the themes of social entrepreneurship is the blurring of the lines between profit and nonprofit. What's your stand on that? Is there a particular formula? Is there a right way? Is there something that you're excited about in terms of the blurring of that demarcation?

Shah: You know, what I love about social entrepreneurship is that people are really focusing on what works, and they're bringing a business rigor to it, no matter what your tax status is. To be a nonprofit or for-profit is really just a tax status, and for Kiva it's completely a pragmatic decision to be a 501(c)(3) nonprofit. Here's why: It's a lot like Wikipedia. Wikipedia's a nonprofit. I often point to this example. I think if any small group of people were making profit off Wikipedia, a lot of the people who contribute to that Internet public good would not feel so good about contributing all their free time. But because no one is really profiting from it and it truly is an Internet public good, a lot of people are contributing to it. This is why it has grown to the heights that it has. In fact, right now, only one out of three articles is in English. It literally is a global Internet public good, and it's less than ten years old. Similarly, Kiva likes to think of itself as an Internet public good. The only reason we can scale after five years to fifty-four countries and do this at a low cost structure is because no one person is trying to make a profit, and we're all trying to achieve good. Basically, it's not the currency of money, it's the currency of meaning. It's a very powerful currency. So I think it's not fair to think in this old paradigm that if it isn't for-profit, it won't scale. Look at Wikipedia. I point to that as a nonprofit that's now scaled to huge heights, and I look at Kiva's trajectory; it's another nonprofit that's scaling. It's more of a pragmatic thing that in our case, we felt like this is the way we could scale, by being a nonprofit, and make the most impact.

Bretos: When we formed Mia back in 1995, I was of the opinion that success was measured by the profits you generated and that our firm needed to be fueled by profit in order to grow more rapidly. I am more inclined today to measure success by making more with less, which is what we do in how we use public funding to serve low-income seniors. We did realize back in 1995 that philanthropic funding would not be available to us. However, we did have enough clients willing to pay for our services. In fact, we did get our first contract without having a company. So time was of the essence. This is not to say that we have not had cash flow problems in the past, and we have become experts in keeping our organization very lean and mean.

This year, however, we formed a not-for-profit entity to access grants and provide pro bono work. We realized that you need a track record of results to compete for this funding, and back in 1995 we did not have it. So in essence it was the right decision to go the for-profit way. I would conclude by saying that you utilize the tools you can to make the situation work.

# THE FUNDERS AND INVESTORS

Why We Are Different from Traditional Philanthropists

# THE POWER OF SOCIAL ENTREPRENEURS

Sally Osberg, President and CEO, Skoll Foundation

Before we go to the subject of social entrepreneurship as a field, I'd like first to take you down a sidetrack; not just any sidetrack, mind you, but a flat track, the kind preferred by serious motorcycle racers like Barry and Andrea Coleman. Just last week these two iconic bikers, who also happen to be iconic social entrepreneurs as the founders of Riders for Health, visited with us in our offices in Palo Alto, where they explained just what flat-track racing has to do with social entrepreneurship.

Now I suspect that, like me, few people have ever heard of flat-track racing. To serious bikers, though, it's the most primal, authentic, and thrilling form of competition, harkening back to the origins of the sport at the turn of the twentieth century. The track itself is dirt, it encompasses that classic oval shape, and the motorcycles make twenty or so laps around during the course of the race. As they roar around the track, the bikes gradually wear a groove where you'd expect to find it: near the center and hugging the inside. Along the outside, the kicked-up dirt and dust form what's known as "the cushion," a far riskier place to ride for obvious reasons: the dirt is soft and traction, therefore, uncertain.

Social entrepreneurs, as Barry explained to us, ride in that cushion: no grooves, plenty of potential to slip and slide out of control, plenty of guts and determination required. In case you might be thinking social entrepreneurs like the Colemans are daredevils, let me assure you that they are as disciplined as they are determined. Taking to the cushion requires confidence in your experience, your skill, and the condition of your motorcycle, which must be impeccably maintained: oil, gas, gears, engine, down to knowing the depths of the treads in your tires to the millimeter.

I want to stress that social entrepreneurs are *entrepreneurs*; they are every bit as focused, disciplined, creative, courageous, and hard driving as, yes, Bill Gates or Steve Jobs—even more so. To underscore the point, think about that famous dancing duo, Fred Astaire and Ginger Rogers. (I know: "What's she doing now? First motorcycling, and now ballroom dancing?" Stay with me!) To me, the social entrepreneur is to the entrepreneur what Ginger Rogers is to Fred Astaire because social entrepreneurs have to do everything that entrepreneurs do but backwards and in high heels. Social entrepreneurs see and seize opportunities just as entrepreneurs do, but they must plan each step forward without financial services or venture capitalists to back them. Social entrepreneurs, like all successful entrepreneurs, combine a predisposition to action with rigorous business planning. Even though they can't aim at anything as definitive as a liquidity event, they must convincingly articulate where they're headed and the social impact they'll achieve. Most also will carry out their strategies just as entrepreneurs do, by building ventures that require boards to govern, cash to pay the bills, and organizations of talented, highly motivated folks to do the heavy lifting. The difference is that social entrepreneurs can't pitch profit or stock options, so they must tap into "psychic equity" to attract the funding and the talent they need to be credible.

In what follows, I'm going to share how the Skoll Foundation came to focus on social entrepreneurs, what we've done over our first decade of work to help them scale their impact, a bit about what we've learned along the way, and where we're headed.

Ten years ago, I'd never heard the term *social entrepreneur,* and neither had Jeff Skoll. When Jeff invited me to serve as his foundation's first CEO in late 2000, he knew that he wanted us to seek out and back a certain kind of leader, people with entrepreneurial solutions to social and environmental problems. As I met and got to know Jeff, what I saw was someone of that same stripe: an entrepreneur prepared to bring his creativity, his business savvy, his razor-sharp mind, and his driving determination to address societal challenges with his philanthropy.

A serial entrepreneur, Jeff had himself already started two companies by the time he joined Pierre Omidyar as eBay's first president. Jeff's first real foray into philanthropy was his creation of the eBay Foundation, which he did in a decidedly entrepreneurial way: dedicating pre-IPO shares of eBay stock to seed an endowment that soared to $35 million after the company went public in 1997. Jeff then ran the eBay Foundation, so that by the time he launched the Skoll Foundation two years later, he'd developed a real bias for folks with exciting visions, proven track records, and compelling plans for making big dents on big issues. Shortly after joining Jeff, I arranged for us to meet together with one of my mentors, John Gardner. John was advisor to five U.S. presidents, architect of Lyndon Johnson's Great Society, founder of Common Cause, and, fairly early in his career, head of the Carnegie Corporation, where among other accomplishments he commissioned a report that led to the creation of the Public Broadcasting Service. I could think of no one wiser to counsel us, so I held my breath as Jeff asked John how to make as much of a difference with his foundation as possible. John's answer was as unforgettable as it was deceptively simple: "Bet on good people doing good things," he told us, advice that affirmed we were on the right track.

Our first mission was "to invest in those with the greatest potential to make lasting positive change to their communities and the world." However, we needed to get clear about who those good people were and how to evaluate the good they proposed to do! We were attracted to and already supporting people like Bill Strickland and his Manchester Craftsmen's Guild and Nick Moon and Martin Fisher of ApproTEC (now KickStart).

Once we learned there was a neater description for these sorts of people, that they could be called "social entrepreneurs," and that organizations like Ashoka had been at work identifying them for some time, we knew the responsible thing to do was to look at what was needed in the larger space—the field, if you will—and how we could contribute. That led us to undertake a process of market analysis with Noah Manduke, now chief strategy officer for the Jeff Skoll Group, but then head of a well-known branding organization called Siegel Gale. What Noah helped us figure out was that Ashoka was focused on early-stage social entrepreneurs working globally, Echoing Green focused on emerging social entrepreneurs working in the United States, and Acumen Fund focused on potentially profitable social enterprises, but scant attention was focused on social entrepreneurs at the mezzanine stage, when, arguably, leverage could be greatest. We also discovered that social entrepreneurship was very much a niche in the larger space of societal change-making and not really yet on the policy, media, or philanthropic radar. Putting all of this together, we saw a great opportunity to go deep, by seeking out and backing the highest-potential social entrepreneurs we could find, and to go broad by building the field of social entrepreneurship. Thinking more like social entrepreneurs, which was no accident given our founder's DNA, we crafted the strategy that, with tweaks and upgrades, continues to serve us today: to help bring about change where change is most needed by investing in, connecting with, and celebrating social entrepreneurs dedicated to solving the world's most pressing problems.

Many people want us to define a *social entrepreneur,* and I'm not going to disappoint in this chapter. I actually hope to convince you that social entrepreneurs play a catalytic role in driving societal progress, that they are to social change what business entrepreneurs are to economic development. Both the concept and the practice of entrepreneurship have been around for hundreds of years, long before those paradigmatic Silicon Valley entrepreneurs came onto the scene. As early as the sixteenth century, the term was used to describe someone who undertakes a business venture; by the eighteenth century, an Irishman who's considered the first economic theorist, Richard Cantillon, characterized entrepreneurs as those who bear the risk of bringing an idea or an innovation to the marketplace. Social entrepreneurs, like entrepreneurs, are game changers. Joseph Schumpeter's famous paradox defines entrepreneurs as forces of creative destruction. We define social entrepreneurs as pioneers of innovations whose purpose is to benefit humanity. They're out to change the status quo, what Roger Martin, dean of the Rotman School of Business at the University of Toronto, and I have characterized as unjust societal equilibriae— those that sustain human suffering, marginalization, and oppression and hold people back from realizing decent lives and their full potential.

Social entrepreneurs see opportunities where others see intractable problems. Fueled by the power of their visions, they assume the risk of building social ventures, generally in the form of organizations, to drive those innovations forward. In their ways of working and their zeal to effect equilibrium change, social entrepreneurs are different from social service providers and social activists, though some get started as providers or activists, and many integrate advocacy strategies in targeting specific policy reforms. I suspect most of the people reading this book are worried about one or more problems out there. Some proportion of us may even have ideas about how to address them, but it's the rare human being who actually translates that idea into an innovation and builds the mechanism for a venture to carry it forward.

The social entrepreneur's journey almost always begins with identifying an opportunity to make a significant difference. The idea may germinate for some time, but eventually the social entrepreneur arrives at a personal tipping point, that existential moment when she puts to herself the big questions: "If not me, who? If not now, when?" She then tasks herself with the business of designing the innovation and venture, often in the face of enormous skepticism, and summons inexhaustible stores of fortitude to drive into serious headwinds. The social entrepreneurs we invest in at the Skoll Foundation are of this breed, and they're well on their way, having proven their models and arrived at an inflection point where they're poised to significantly scale their solutions. We select them, we provide core support to them in the form of an initial multiyear grant, and we connect them to their peers, media, funders, and others with the power to help.

To build the field of social entrepreneurship, though, we had to go beyond grant making and partnering with existing organizations. If we were to make the kind of impact on the enabling environment that we hoped to make, there would be nothing to do but roll up our sleeves and build some new ventures ourselves. Today, those ventures have played a significant role in bringing social entrepreneurship from the margins and into the mainstream. They include the Skoll Center for Social Entrepreneurship, at Oxford University's Saïd Business School; Social Edge, our online community for social entrepreneurs; The Skoll World Forum, dubbed by its third year "the Davos of social entrepreneurship"; and a suite of media products and partnerships with entities like Sundance, "Frontline World," "The PBS NewsHour," and the BBC. These media partnerships alone have led to seventy-nine broadcast stories, 181 news reports for radio and podcast, and twelve feature-length documentary film projects. Our work has also helped spawn more than 200 university and college programs around the world dedicated to social entrepreneurship. It has contributed to a steady increase in interest, references, and action among influencers in the media and policy realms, including the Obama administration's new Office of Social Innovation. It also has led to dramatic increases in awareness and funding from the philanthropic community. All of these accomplishments have made us proud, even as we acknowledge how much more there is to be done and tip our hats to new players carrying this agenda forward.

As for our direct engagement with social entrepreneurs, we've been on a remarkable journey over our first decade, learning a great deal about their strengths and flaws, the design and stages of their ventures, and the habits of mind and strategies that are likely over time to make them successful. Along the way we've kept faith with Jeff's vision to bring about a more peaceful, prosperous, and sustainable world and with our mandate to go beyond grant making in our work by connecting social entrepreneurs with opportunities and resources and celebrating who they are and the difference they make.

To illustrate how this strategy has played out, let's go back to those two motorcyclists, Andrea and Barry Coleman. Their story begins in Donington Park, home of Britain's motorcycle grand prix. Barry, whose academic degree is in philosophy, was working as a motorcycle correspondent and feature writer for *The Guardian*. Andrea, a former professional rider and granddaughter of a race organizer, was the public relations manager for American motorcycle race champion Randy Mamola. At the time, Randy had decided to use his prestige to help initiate fund-raising to support children in developing-world countries, and together Mamola and the Colemans contacted Save the Children to see how they could help. Save the Children offered to sponsor them to travel to Africa to view the conditions for themselves, so, together with Mamola, Barry and Andrea took their first trip to Somalia in 1986. What they experienced shocked them. They heard from nurses unable to deliver heath care to villages within twenty kilometers of a clinic. They saw women hemorrhaging from childbirth transported in wheelbarrows, and they counted by the hundreds the rusted vehicles abandoned on roadsides and the motorcycles piled up at clinics for want of an oil change. For people who knew about engines, none of this made any sense. For people who were raising funds to benefit suffering children, it was, in a word, unacceptable.

For several years following the trip, Barry worked with Save the Children to develop a system to manage and maintain vehicles in harsh environments, testing and proving the model in partnership with Africans in Uganda, Lesotho, and Zimbabwe. Andrea focused on expanding global support in the motorcycling community for Africa's children. Over the ten years between 1986 and 1996, they demonstrated the brilliance of Barry's transportation resource management (TRM) approach. TRM contributed to increasing the efficiency of African health workers by more than 300 percent, dramatically reducing infectious disease incidents and mortality rates, and significantly strengthening African health ministry capacity and accountability.

By the mid-1990s, the Colemans were ready for independence, craving the autonomy and focus that is the entrepreneur's differentiator. Going back to my "backwards and in high heels" analogy, though Barry and Andrea were successful, well-educated people, they were by no means wealthy. To capitalize their venture and secure its autonomy, they couldn't just reach into their own pockets, tap a circle of rich friends, or get a bank loan; so they mortgaged their house. In 1996, Riders for Health became a registered charitable organization in the UK. In 2005, we undertook due diligence on Riders, assessing it against our criteria: evaluating its entrepreneur founders, the significance of the issue, its track record, its inflection point, whether it was poised to scale its impact, and its readiness for what we had to offer. They passed with flying colors, and we brought the Colemans and Riders into our portfolio, honoring them with the Skoll Award for Social Entrepreneurship in early 2006 and granting them $765,000 over three years for core support.

So far so good, but thus far this is still just good, albeit somewhat progressive, grant making. The story gets more interesting as we get to know Barry and Andrea, and they get to know us. In 2008 they approached us with a plan to expand their work by transforming their model. Instead of managing an effective but modestly scaled program in The Gambia, they were prepared to contract directly with the Gambian minister of health to meet 100 percent of its transportation service needs. But, to do so, they would have to amass the capital necessary to purchase outright their fleet of vehicles. We could have just made a grant, but Barry and Andrea were advancing a business model and sought financing. We could have made a program-related investment (PRI) directly with Riders. A PRI is a tool available to a private foundation. It's not a grant but a market-based investment, usually debt or equity, made in support of a U.S. foundation's charitable purpose. But that would have missed another opportunity, which was to help strengthen The Gambia's institutional lending capacity. So what we did was deposit $2.2 million in a Gambian bank in Banjul to serve as a guarantee, thereby securing the deal. Guarantee Trust Bank Gambia then lent Riders the money to buy its fleet, and the health ministry signed the contract, thereby providing the revenue needed to underwrite service delivery and debt payment. The real excitement here, though, is that this deal is securing health care for the entire Gambian population, more than 2 million people, and proving that last-mile health delivery can be achieved consistently and sustainably over time.

Last year when we were approached by an organization to develop a series for distribution on the BBC, we naturally wanted to include Riders, and happily the producers agreed. Supported by Rockhopper TV and entitled "Alvin's

Guide to Good Business," the series aired in April 2010. Because Andrea and Barry are as strategic as they are telegenic, they seized on the opportunity to use their star power to turn on the BBC to influence their position with the Gambian Ministry of Health. Nine months into working in The Gambia, they were still in the early stages of negotiating. The customary and usual negotiation with a new African country takes upwards of two years. After screening the episode with ministry officials, they inked a memorandum of understanding in an unprecedented nine days. And I'm still not done with this story. At the Skoll World Forum in April 2010, senior representatives of OPIC, the Overseas Private Investment Corporation, were in the delegate audience for a session during which Andrea spoke. Hearing about Riders and its model, OPIC officials went straight up to her following the session and offered financing support.

Another story that's fun to tell, and that shows just how fraught with risk the social entrepreneur's path can be, is about Premal Shah and Kiva, also featured in this book. Kiva is a big success today, but it almost didn't make it through year one. The organization's bank account was heading toward empty in the fall of 2006 when "Frontline World," with Skoll Foundation's support, did a story on Kiva as part of a report on social entrepreneurs. The night it aired, the organization's servers crashed due to traffic overload. Three days later, when Kiva got back up, it was able to process more than $250,000 in new loans. Without the right intervention at the right moment, Kiva might not have made it and certainly wouldn't have passed the $100 million mark, as it did in 2010.

I tell you these stories not as an exercise in self-promotion. As a friend of mine liked to quip, self-congratulation can be habit forming, and most organizations are long gone in addiction! I tell them to bring our "invest, connect, and celebrate" mission to life. You might have noticed by now that I haven't once referenced that "going to scale" shibboleth so common in this sector. For us, as for most of the organizations with which we work closely and for thought leaders in this field—people like Greg Dees of Duke's Center for the Advancement of Social Entrepreneurship—the only scale that matters is that of impact. Elsewhere, I've argued that our concern with scale shouldn't focus on an organization's size or budget but on its ability to transform systems, right injustices, and demonstrate that it can solve seemingly intractable problems. This isn't to say that social entrepreneurs shouldn't expand their organizations but only to restate my thesis: that how big you are is in no way a measure, or even a proxy, of how good you are at driving change.

Inevitably, though, questions of scale force us to consider numbers, what to count and what that information tells us. At the risk of voicing yet another earnest caution about the role of metrics, let me admit straight out that numbers only get us so far on the proof-of-impact imperative. To make this point, I invite you to consider one of the most famous acts of philanthropy ever: Andrew Carnegie's initiative to build public libraries, carried out between 1886 and 1919 through a matching grant program. More than 2,500 libraries were built as a result of this effort, the first in Scotland, most in the United States, but also across England, Canada, and even Fiji. Now, library buildings are easy to count, as are the books that fill them. Circulation data, such as how many people are checking out books and how many books they're taking home with them, give us a bit more information about people using libraries and what they're reading. What's harder to measure is the arguably more important impact of those libraries on communities, whether their citizens are better educated and more informed due to the libraries in their backyard. Common sense tells us they are. Common sense also tells us that Carnegie's philanthropic intent was not simply to dot the landscape with libraries but to ensure that the people he believed to be society's most industrious and ambitious and most capable of helping themselves were afforded the means to improve their lives and their communities.

Doing the work we do, either as social investors or social entrepreneurs, requires not just accountability systems but what I'd call unapologetically commonsense leaps of faith. For great philanthropists such as Andrew Carnegie and Jeff Skoll, as for the great social entrepreneurs in the Skoll Foundation portfolio, empowering those with the greatest stake in improving themselves, their societies, and the larger world is fundamental to achieving large-scale impact. It may seem an obvious point, but it's not trivial. Enlisting, engaging, enrolling, and fully empowering individuals in local communities, especially those who are written off by markets, ignored or marginalized by governments, and patronized as beneficiaries by nongovernmental organizations (NGOs), is the very oxygen social entrepreneurs breathe.

Beyond working in respectful partnership with those they serve, social entrepreneurs are more likely to be successful in driving large-scale impact when they can clearly articulate an innovative solution to a pressing problem, when they punch above their weight by engaging strategic partners to scale their impact, when they align their revenue generation models with their missions, and when they build sound, sustainable organizations.

Within the Skoll Foundation's portfolio, Amitabha Sadangi provides a great example. International Development Enterprises India, IDEI, helps turn subsistence farmers into income-generating producers of base-of-the-pyramid market products. Over the organization's twenty-year history, its line of pumps and customizable Krishik Bandhu (KB) drip irrigation units have generated more than $1 billion in wealth, leading in turn to significant increases in health, education, and dignity for rural farm families. Adding to these direct impacts, Amitabha's work has also helped counter two inter-related and increasingly threatening trends: groundwater depletion and climate change. IDEI's products are 50 to 70 percent more efficient in their use of water than their competitors' offerings, while simultaneously boosting crop yields by an impressive 50 percent. In addition, because IDEI's hand-powered pumps have displaced gas-driven models, they reduce carbon emissions. Typically for a social entrepreneur, Amitabha has seized on this measurable benefit to obtain carbon credits under the European Union's cap-and-trade system, bringing in additional revenues to support his work. We believe IDEI is doing for poor rural producers what Grameen did for poor borrowers: literally design-building the field of micro-irrigation. The Gates Foundation's recent decision to invest $27 million in IDEI to bring its model to Africa is just one more sign of the organization's growing impact.

The examples continue. Mitch Besser and Gene Falk have led Mothers to Mothers (M2M), which works to halt pediatric AIDS transmission, on a growth-of-impact trajectory that has the organization now reaching one in five pregnant women with HIV worldwide. Now, a 20 percent global market share of a target audience is a phenomenal achievement for any company, the more impressive in this case for being a market of expectant HIV positive mothers who, when given the opportunity to be educated by their M2M-trained peers, can protect their babies from AIDS. Soraya Salti of INJAZ al-Arab now reaches hundreds of thousands of students across the Middle East with life skills and entrepreneurship training because she's been able to get entire public school systems to embrace her program. Anne Cotton's CAMFED, the Campaign for Female Education in Africa, has developed a community-based power-sharing model so powerful that the hugely influential Linklaters International Law Firm is documenting its governance principles and strategies to influence aid deployment in the developing world. You get the picture! Amitabha, Gene and Mitch, Soraya, and Anne are well on their way to achieving big impact, and in that process they've taught us what it takes: legions of empowered stake-holders, well-designed and effectively deployed models, evidence-based systems that track results, aligned resource engines, strategic partnerships that scale impact, and organizations built to last.

Many people believe that we at Skoll have this work nailed, that all we have to do is let those social entrepreneurs get to it, but, let me assure you, it's early innings, and the game is far from over. Definite victory on any major front, the kind declared and justly celebrated in the twentieth century for defeating scourges like yellow fever and smallpox, is uncertain.

Heading toward our tenth anniversary at the Skoll Foundation, with Jeff's and the board's encouragement, we held up the mirror and asked ourselves whether we were doing enough, whether we were doing it well enough, and whether social entrepreneurs were up to the formidable challenges confronting humanity and the planet. Just looking around, big problems like climate change or extremism seem to be getting worse, more complex, their implications far more frightening. But, as a good friend of ours, Paul Hawken, has said, "When asked if I am pessimistic or optimistic about the future, my answer is always the same. If you look at the science about what is happening on the Earth and aren't pessimistic, you don't understand the data. But if you meet the people who are working to restore this Earth and the lives of the poor, and you aren't optimistic, you haven't got a pulse." At the Skoll Foundation, we felt for that pulse, and it came up strong. Optimistic? No question about it—not the flaccid wide-eyed kind, but rather the sinewy, steely-eyed kind, what Arctic explorer Ernest Shackleton meant when he defined optimism as courage. Preparing to go the distance with social entrepreneurs who are tackling the big issues of our time—poverty, food security, human rights, health, climate change—requires more than reaffirming our commitment to social entrepreneurs. We have to raise our game.

So instead of seeing social entrepreneurs and their organizations as the "be-all and end-all" of change making, we've taken to heart three of the lessons they've taught us. First, strategic partners in business, civil society, and government are not nice-to-haves, but absolutely key to driving impact at scale. Second, though vested interests will always resist the forces of disruption, every ecosystem is fizzing with allies, ready to help, but they need connecting and celebrating, too. Finally, to be a serious partner, we need to get off the sidelines and into the fray. In the near term, we've set ourselves the goals of getting a lot smarter about a set of priority issues, better networked with players in those issues, and clear about what we can do to help influence the needed changes in behavior, policy, and systems. Some of our partners are already in the Skoll family: our colleagues at the Skoll Global Threats Fund, Participant Media, Capricorn Investment Group, and the Jeff Skoll Group. This is the remarkable community of organizations Jeff has created to help bring about a better world. Believe me, we're seizing opportunities to unleash our collective impact. We're making sure Skoll social entrepreneurs focused on public education know about Participant Media's documentary *Waiting for Superman,* that others know about documentaries on water or other subjects in the pipeline. We're tapping the Global Threats team and our knowledge networks as we build out each year's program for the Skoll World Forum, referring social entrepreneurs with paradigm-shifting energy or other business ventures to Capricorn and much more.

I don't think John Gardner knew the Colemans, but he might have had them and other great social entrepreneurs in mind when he wrote, "Life isn't a train ride, where you choose your destination, pay your fare, and settle back for a nap. It's a cycle ride, around uncertain terrain, with you in the cyclist seat constantly correcting your balance and determining the direction of your progress" (Gardner 1981, xii). To Andrea and Barry Coleman, the direction of their life's work has everything to do with making darn sure their motorcycles are also in fighting trim: oil topped, tires on tight, engines firing on all cylinders. Andrea and Barry, like Partners in Health co-founder Paul Farmer, Amitabha Sadanghi, Anne Cotton, and all great social entrepreneurs, are not just on any old joy ride, tooling along in the groove. They're on that cushion, braving the dust and the dirt, because risk is worth it when you mean to win. Make no mistake about it, they're out to win: to transform health care delivery in Africa, to save millions of lives, and to prove what's possible.

# A HYBRID APPROACH TO SUPPORTING SOCIAL ENTREPRENEURS

Matt Bannick, Managing Partner, Omidyar Network

We live in a world in which technology and innovation are breaking down barriers and drawing us closer like never before. Yet, at the same time, there are old divisions and rivalries rooted in static thinking and ideology that are inhibiting us from making the most of these historic opportunities. This is true in the world of philanthropy, where disagreement and confusion over the appropriate roles of for-profit and not-for-profit enterprises are constraining our ability to drive positive social change. I would like to highlight how businesses and not-for-profits each offer valuable solutions; indeed, when used in concert, how they can be complementary tools for creating opportunity, innovation, and social progress, particularly for those who are less fortunate.

I'd like to start with a story about how Pierre Omidyar's experiences at eBay inspired him to embrace this sort of hybrid thinking in the first place. Pierre is known best for starting the online marketplace eBay. The corporate history of eBay is well known, but an equally important story is what we learned about creating opportunity and positive social change in the process of building a thriving global enterprise. Pierre often remarks that if he had been asked to create a million jobs with a nonprofit or a governmental organization, he wouldn't have known where to start. eBay not only generated more than a million jobs; it also brought livelihoods to people excluded from similar entrepreneurial possibilities.

Today, an army of more than a million entrepreneurs forms the backbone of eBay, generating more than $60 billion of annual economic activity. These are people like Brandi Tolley from Springfield, Illinois. In 2001, Brandi was a twenty-six-year-old single mom and Army veteran whose son had recently been diagnosed with autism. Brandi couldn't hold down a regular job, because she had too many medical appointments to go to with her son. eBay gave Brandi an opportunity to start a successful online business selling oversized men's clothing while staying at home to take care of her family. Through eBay, Brandi found customers in sixty-seven countries and in the process made lots of friends and became part of a vibrant, supportive virtual community.

After eBay went public in 1998, Pierre and his wife Pam decided to commit much of their wealth to the betterment of society. They first established a traditional foundation focused on distributing money to worthy not-for-profits. But Pierre soon felt he was being asked to participate in a fight with one hand tied behind his back. eBay had taught him how the private sector could create social benefit. Yet the very definition and legal structure of foundations seemed to be built on the assumption that for-profits were of no use in driving positive social change. So, in 2004, Pierre and Pam established Omidyar Network as a new type of philanthropy, a philanthropic investment firm that would marry the social good focus of the not-for-profit sector with the market incentives and drive for scale of the for-profit sector.

Today, as you emerge from the elevator at the offices of Omidyar Network, you are greeted by a quotation painted in large letters on the wall that reads, "Every individual has the power to make a difference." This core belief is the cornerstone of our work. What we learned at eBay from people like Brandi inspires and informs the Omidyar Network. Our work is founded on a belief that people are inherently capable; that, when given access to opportunity, people frequently develop innovative solutions to their own problems; that entrepreneurship in the private sector can be a powerful tool for positive change; and that technology is a great way to foster social connections and quickly spread innovation. We invest in and help scale up entrepreneurial ventures that each has the potential to create opportunity for hundreds of thousands if not millions of people. We believe that creating opportunity for individuals enables them to improve the quality of their lives, the lives of their families, and those of their communities and ultimately creates a more fair and prosperous society.

At the very heart of our strategy is a flexible approach to philanthropy. We embrace whatever tools are necessary, including not-for-profit grants and for-profit investments, to support high-impact social entrepreneurs and the broader environments in which they work. Our hybrid investment approach is supported by a hybrid organizational structure. We operate both the foundation and a for-profit investment fund under one roof.

My goal, however, is not actually to focus on the specifics of our particular model; it's rather to convince you of a broader point. I aim to illustrate the importance of finding hybrid solutions to pressing social problems.

In the past, we've witnessed a counterproductive and sometimes bitter debate among social change practitioners. In one corner of this intellectual boxing ring are those who boldly assert that the private sector and unfettered markets will solve all our problems and that grants merely breed inefficiency and dependence. In the other corner are those who argue that the profit motive itself is a root of many of society's ills and that the private sector does not have viable solutions. Charitable grants untarnished by the profit motive, they insist, are the morally acceptable way to address society's ills. If there's any message I'd like to leave with you, it's that we need to avoid the straightjacket of this *either-or* thinking and embrace the power of *and*. Grants and investments are both critical for progress.

To make these arguments real and tangible, I'll highlight a few stories that demonstrate the value of for-profit social ventures. I'll then share similar stories that illustrate the value of not-for-profit social ventures. Finally, I'll bring these threads together and show how the two approaches can be complementary and how for-profits and not-for-profits can work side-by-side to create, nurture, and scale up entire new sectors that improve the lives of millions.

Let's start with one cross-section of the billions of people who can benefit from more access to opportunity: schoolchildren in Kenya. The Kenyan public school system is in shambles. Illiteracy is off the charts. Teachers show up only about half the time and, even then, rarely hold class. In an entire day, by some accounts, the average time dedicated to instruction is ninety minutes. Also, "free" public school education is actually not free. Parents pay for school uniforms, books and supplies, and lunch. Worse, they're often forced to bribe officials and schoolteachers just to get them to do their jobs.

In response to this challenge, a few years ago Omidyar Network invested in Bridge International Academies, an ultra-low-cost chain of primary schools that we think can transform the education sector in Kenya. Bridge was founded by Jay Kimmelman, Shannon May, and Phil Frei. Jay is a technology entrepreneur from the Bay Area who started and sold a successful educational software company called Edusoft. Motivated to put his business skills to work for social good, Jay and his team spent several years researching scalable solutions to poverty. It was in the slums of Nairobi that Jay and his team began to implement the idea of a school in a box—essentially, a franchise model of schools providing standardized, high-quality education services that could be easily and quickly replicated for poor communities.

Notably, Bridge International is a for-profit company. Yet, because it's been able to create economies of scale, Bridge offers its students a vastly superior education for less than four dollars a month. Wouldn't we all love to have tuition like that? This is about the same cost as a public school. Bridge students get about forty-five hours of instruction per week, compared to fewer than ten hours a week at a public school. Despite living in incredibly tough environments, Bridge students are dramatically outperforming their peers from much wealthier neighborhoods.

Jay's model is getting great traction. Bridge already serves 2,700 students in twenty-two schools, making it perhaps the largest chain of private schools in Africa. They expect to have 100 schools at this time next year, and by 2018 they expect to have more than 3,000 schools serving more than 2.5 million students. Jay's vision is nothing short of transforming education, not only in Kenya but in the entire developing world. I've been to a Bridge School, and I think Jay has a good shot at realizing his vision.

Another inspiring example of one of our for-profit investees delivering great social impact is d.light, a business that manufactures and distributes ultra-low-cost solar lamps designed for people living in extreme poverty. Many people don't know that one out of four families lives without electricity. Schoolchildren in these families can't do their homework at night because they don't have any light. Or, if they do have light, they use kerosene lamps, which are expensive and dangerous. Every time a child uses a kerosene lamp, it releases fumes equivalent to two packs of cigarettes. Kerosene lamps also cause accidental fires. It's estimated that 2.5 million people in the developing world suffer from severe burns every year, and most of those burns are the result of overturned kerosene lamps.

Solar lamps from d.light are much cheaper than kerosene, don't emit toxins, and virtually eliminate the chance of fire. With these lights, thirteen-year-olds like Monika Singh in Uttar Pradesh, India, are able to make simple but really important decisions that you and I and our children take for granted. Monika may think, "It's late, I'm tired; maybe I'll go to sleep now, but I'll wake up really early, turn on the light, and do my homework then." These decisions can have enormous consequences; it's the difference that allows a driven student like Monika to study longer, improve her grades, and maybe go to university. It's the difference that might mean Monika can become a scientist, a doctor, or even—why not?—a head of state. d.light has already illuminated more than 3 million lives and is poised for exponential growth.

Both d.light and Bridge are for-profit businesses, but don't get the wrong idea. At Omidyar Network, our goal is to marry the best of the for-profit and not-for-profit worlds. That means we use grants as well as commercial investments to support innovative social entrepreneurs. In fact, of the $400 million of philanthropic capital to date that we've deployed, about 44 percent has supported equity investments, but 56 percent, the majority, has actually supported grants.

Here's how we think about the different roles of for-profit investments and grants. For-profit investments leverage the power of markets to generate positive social impact. By definition, for-profit companies such as Bridge and d.light have to offer a product or service that people are willing to pay for at a price above the company's costs. In essence, the success of a business is determined by its ability to cost-effectively deliver value to the individual and therefore offer value to society. If unable to do this, a business will simply fail. If successful, however, a business can generate an income stream that enables it to become sustainable over time. These profits and access to financing from capital markets, debt, and equity help businesses grow fast and scale up, potentially delivering valuable products and services to millions. This is just the kind of scale that we need to address today's most pressing problems. To give you a sense of the ability of companies to scale, since 1970 tens of thousands of for-profit businesses have grown from zero to more than $50 million in annual revenue. In that same period, only 144 not-for-profits have gone from zero to $50 million.

Of course, while efficient, markets and for-profit companies have obvious limitations in this social change game. Most important, people need to understand that what's profitable is not always what's fair and most beneficial to society. Though investments in for-profit companies leverage the power of markets to achieve impact, grants to not-for-profits achieve impact by addressing the weaknesses of markets. Whereas businesses deliver value to people who can afford their products and services, grants frequently help disadvantaged populations. Grants also can help fund public goods, such as clean air or libraries. Grants are effective tools in subsidizing the creation of goods and services, such as vaccines, that benefit both society and the individual—goods that have what economists call *positive externalities*. Also, grants can kick-start entire new markets, where early-stage business ventures are just too risky for profit-seeking investors.

Grant-based philanthropy has done tremendous good in the world. Thank goodness for Andrew Carnegie and the public libraries he funded, bringing books and enlightenment to millions. Thank goodness for the Rockefeller Foundation and its contributions to the green revolution, which benefited hundreds of millions through dramatic improvements in agricultural productivity in the developing world. And thank goodness for the pioneering work on vaccines spearheaded by the Gates Foundation and others.

Ory Okolloh, one of the co-founders of the not-for-profit Ushahidi, is a great example of the inspiring social entrepreneurs whom we have supported with grants. Ory grew up in a poor family in Kenya. Her parents could barely afford to send her to primary school. Her father died when she was a young adult. Through sheer determination, Ory gained entrance to college and later to Harvard Law School, after which she returned to Kenya to contribute to the development of that country's young democracy. In 2007, the contested presidential election in Kenya precipitated widespread violence, as you may recall. In response, Ory helped create Ushahidi, which is the Swahili word for *testimony*.

Ushahidi is a crowd-sourcing website that collected and recorded eyewitness reports of violence during the elections, using text messages combined with Google Maps. Virtually overnight, the website was used by more than 45,000 people to track negative incidents and create effective interventions. This Ushahidi technology has since been used more than 15,000 times in dozens of applications around the world. Just hours after the recent devastating earthquake and tsunami in Japan, activists used Ushahidi to map and better coordinate relief efforts. In Libya, Ushahidi has been critical in helping the United Nations, the Red Cross, and others to more effectively help embattled citizens. Indeed, Ushahidi is at the very cutting edge of a wave of tech-based innovations that are shaping social and political interactions around the world.

Ushahidi is but one of a number of high-impact not-for-profit entrepreneurial ventures that we've supported. Other examples include Janaagraha and Refugees United. Janaagraha is an Indian organization that seeks to reduce petty corruption by encouraging individuals to draw attention to bribe-paying incidents through a public site called Ipaidabribe.com. Refugees United is an online search tool that allows refugees to trace missing family members and reunite with loved ones. Sometimes we forget that there are more than 45 million people in this world who are displaced persons, a lot of them divided from their families. Refugees United has developed this wonderful tool to enable them to find each other.

For all of our diverse grant recipients—whether the goal is enhancing government transparency, reuniting families, or creating public goods—they are helping disadvantaged populations, or they are catalyzing new markets. But grants, too, have limitations. As I've noted, they don't scale as quickly as for-profit enterprises. For-profit enterprises know they are delivering value based on a customer's willingness to pay. No such mechanisms exist for not-for-profits; in fact, they tend to charge far less than it costs for them to produce a product, or more likely they don't charge at all. As a result, it's difficult for a not-for-profit to assess what value it's delivering to its customers or to society.

I've given examples to describe the merits of both for-profit investments and grants in driving positive social change. So what is exactly new here? Philanthropists have been making grants to nonprofit organizations for centuries. There is also an increasing number of so-called impact investors, who are investing in businesses they believe can generate both financial and social returns. What is highly unusual is that we do both, nonprofit and for-profit investments in the same house, with the same staff, and we dedicate nearly equal resources to both. We're organized that way because we know that effective social change is not an either/or proposition. Sometimes for-profit solutions are the answer; sometimes nonprofit solutions are the answer. Very often, the most effective solution is actually the right combination of both.

This assertion that for-profit and not-for-profit investments can be complementary is not just some abstract theory. It's playing out in important ways around the world today. A recent study by the Monitor Group, for example, concluded that most of the organizations that have had the biggest positive impact on the poor in India are actually for-profit companies. It also noted, however, that most if not all of those for-profit companies received grants or other forms of soft funding in their early start-up phases. So again, it's not an *either-or*, it's an *and*.

Perhaps more exciting, moving even beyond the Monitor work, is what we see when we zoom out and focus on the bigger picture. Specifically, we're discovering that a thoughtful and complementary blend of early-stage for-profit and not-for-profit investments can move forward entire sectors. To us, this is the Holy Grail; not only is this approach supporting high-impact social entrepreneurs who can touch thousands of lives, but it is nurturing and growing entire sectors that can touch hundreds of millions or even billions of lives in a positive way.

The field of microfinance is perhaps the best illustration of how hybrid approaches can achieve such large-scale impact. The microfinance industry is built on the premise that the poor are indeed credit worthy and should have access to capital, just as we do, to improve the quality of their lives. You've heard the wonderful stories of poor women who borrow modest sums to buy a cow and start a dairy and are able to generate the income to send their children to school and change the trajectory of their children's lives. The phenomenal growth of microfinance really illustrates how a complementary mix of grants and for-profit investments can first nurture and then accelerate market growth.

For example, in the 1980s and 1990s, most microfinance institutions (MFIs) were grant-funded NGOs. As the size and commercial viability of the microfinance sector became apparent, commercial investors, many of whom had a strong social motivation, invested heavily in rapidly growing MFIs. Commercial MFIs that had access to capital expanded much more rapidly than their capital-constrained nonprofit brethren. As recently as 1998, only 22 percent of the fifty largest MFIs were registered for-profit banks. Ten years later, by 2008, 62 percent were for-profit registered banks. In other words, grant capital sparked and nurtured microfinance, and for-profit capital helped take it to scale.

Omidyar Network has consistently applied a flexible philanthropy approach to microfinance. We've been very active in this space for many years, and we've sought to catalyze the sector with a mix of for-profit and not-for-profit investments. Since 2004, we've invested more than $100 million in microfinance across twenty-eight organizations: fifteen not-for-profits and thirteen for-profits. We recognize, of course, that microfinance has come under increasing scrutiny. Among other things, it appears that MFIs have paid insufficient attention to consumer protection and consumer education. Government oversight has sometimes been inadequate and other times simply been overbearing. Competition has not always been sufficient to drive up quality and drive down costs. But it's critical not to forget how much good microfinance has accomplished. Because of microfinance, 150 million people who otherwise would not have had access to capital now have it. One hundred and fifty million people, most of whom live on less than a dollar a day, can now decide to start dairy farms or corner stores, generating the income necessary to send their children to school and eventually break the cycle of poverty.

The success of a hybrid approach in creating markets particularly in microfinance raises a question: Is the microfinance experience unique? Is this just a one-off, or can it be replicated? Can we really use hybrid approaches to develop other market sectors that benefit the underprivileged? Well, as you might suspect, we believe the answer to this last question is "yes."

Late last year, we commissioned the management consulting firm McKinsey & Company to look at new solutions for improving the lives of the poor in India through innovations in medical technology and clean energy. The potential for social impact, it appears, is absolutely enormous—in the hundreds of millions of lives for both sectors. The market opportunity, which is in the billions of dollars, is also quite promising. After a thorough examination, McKinsey concluded that the best path toward developing these sectors is similar to what we saw in microfinance: a thoughtful mix of grant capital (to create required industry infrastructure and reduce risks) and large-scale commercial capital (to bring potential life-changing innovations to scale).

Though incredibly impactful, this mixing of grant capital and investments raises really important questions with which we continue to wrestle, such as: How does one determine which sectors should receive this scarce grant capital? Why microfinance, why clean energy? How does one ensure that grant capital does not constrain the creation of a viable for-profit business? If you are subsidizing, are you subsidizing the right things, or are you subsidizing in a way that will hold back the market? Is it appropriate for businesses to benefit financially from early grant funding coming from philanthropists or others? Perhaps most pressing, where can we find socially motivated investors who are willing to make high-risk bets early on early-stage businesses?

On this last question, it's worth noting that a giant pool of capital that cares deeply about social change can be found at U.S. foundations, and mostly it is sitting on the sidelines of the early-stage investment game. It's a little-known fact, for example, that U.S. foundations are allowed to make investments in for-profit businesses that serve a social mission. Currently, a few pioneering foundations, such as Skoll, Rockefeller, and Gates, are beginning to take advantage of this capability. The vast majority, however, are not. In fact, of the $44 billion in capital deployed by foundations in 2007, 99 percent went to grants. Only 0.05 percent, or a mere $20 million out of that $44 billion, went to equity-based for-profit investments. Scratch beneath the surface here, and you'll discover that part of the obstacle is simply perception. Equity investments are seen as too risky, because you may actually lose some of your principal. It's important to remember, however, that when you make a grant, you are giving the money away. In other words, you will lose 100 percent of your principal—guaranteed.

This is just one example of how reexamining our assumptions in favor of flexible philanthropy could make a tremendous difference. Another really interesting statistic for you: If U.S. foundations invested just 5 percent of their endowment, which is about $560 billion, into for-profit social businesses that aim to serve the underprivileged, they would free up a pool of capital that amounts to $29 billion. This sum, to put it into perspective, is larger than what the entire U.S. venture capital industry invests in start-up businesses in a typical year. Now, let's pause to think about this for just a moment. In just a few decades, the U.S. venture capital market has spurred technological innovations that have dramatically changed the lives of billions around the world. A full 21 percent of U.S. GDP is created by early-stage venture-backed start-ups. Imagine what we could do with a similar sum of capital deployed for the purpose of positive social change.

It's easy to get lost in the details here and lose sight of the bigger picture. I've described Omidyar Network's approach to social change, but this is actually not about Omidyar Network. Indeed, we're still early in our journey, and we have a lot to learn from our peers in the philanthropic sector. What we're really talking about is something much larger than Omidyar Network and much larger than any of these stories that I've shared with you. Ultimately, it's about the movement to break down artificial and unnecessary boundaries between nonprofit and for-profit sectors so we can get more quickly to effective solutions. It's a vision for a new kind of philanthropy that's not just supporting charities and not just supporting businesses but supporting what really works.

We have so much to gain by looking beyond our own silos to find hybrid solutions with the biggest impact. But overcoming the prejudices that divide the for-profit and nonprofit sectors won't be easy. Just recently a woman working in the social sector described to me the attitude she encountered when trying to make a career move from the private sector to the social sector. The first question she was asked when interviewing for a job at a very prominent foundation was, "Why have you decided to move from the greed side to the good side?" These stereotypes work both ways. When I run into former colleagues and tell them that I work in philanthropy, I occasionally get asked if this means that I have retired. These prejudices suggest that we're focusing on the wrong questions. Instead of arguing about which side is better or has the right solution, we should be carefully examining when and how to capitalize on our respective strengths.

There is much urgent work to be done, but I for one am very optimistic. I'm optimistic because of people like Jay Kimmelman and his team in Kenya, who are managing a network of schools that allow young people to take control of their own future. I'm optimistic because of the millions of people we haven't named, such as the courageous mothers in Bangladesh who take out loans to start corner stores that can change their children's future. We've seen, time and time again, that when you give people access to opportunity, you unlock their drive and creativity to find their own solutions. The answers they come up with are often incredibly inspiring.

Our job is to harness this entrepreneurial talent for social good. When we're able to use all of the resources we have available—for-profit, nonprofit, and every possible combination of the two—it is then that we have the chance to create opportunity for millions and to solve the world's most intractable problems.

# HARNESSING ENTREPRENEURIAL ENERGY

## William Foote, Founder and CEO, Root Capital

I'd like to start with a story from Tanzania, where we, Root Capital, began working in 2006. Shiwahiade Munuo is a thirty-eight-year-old farmer who was born and raised in the lush rain forests that are sandwiched between the snow-capped peak of Kilimanjaro and the cultivated grasslands of the savannah below. That grassland is home to elephants and leopards and about one million small-scale farmers, many of whom are coffee growers.

When I met Shiwahiade last year, she had a machete in hand and was pruning the coffee bushes on her tiny plot of land. During our conversation, Shiwahiade told me how her life had changed in recent years. She and her two sons had been living on $2 a day. Her children stayed home for much of the year to work on the farm, but it still wasn't enough. Market prices for coffee had plummeted, and she was considering cutting down her coffee bushes to sell the wood for charcoal.

She decided to stick with coffee when a new farmers association was created in the village nearby. Hundreds of growers were organizing to collectively market their crop and try to tap into new markets. An association or cooperative typically involves farmers coming together for mutual benefit, to fulfill common economic and social needs. The farmers are both suppliers to and owners of the cooperative. Shiwahiade and other farmers hoped that by joining together, they could better market their crops, get better prices, and improve their standard of living. Cooperatives are a very common method of organizing agricultural production and primary processing, especially in Latin America. However, though the region is an ideal climate for growing high-quality coffee, Shiwahiade and the members of her association relied on old-fashioned equipment to manually depulp the beans, which breaks them and lowers their quality. Poor quality control prevented the farmers from exporting to premium markets in North America and Europe. Roughly 400,000 small-scale coffee growers across Tanzania still rely on manual home-processing methods.

In 2006, Root Capital made a loan to Shiwahiade's association to finance the purchase of water-efficient processing equipment and a centralized milling facility. Over the next three years, the new equipment greatly improved the quality of their coffee, which attracted Starbucks, among others, to buy one container in the first year and dramatically more in subsequent years. Hundreds of families in the association have now benefited from access to that new market.

Meanwhile, Shiwahiade doubled her income and reinvested part of her earnings in four cows, six goats, and a new chicken coop, with which she now runs her micropoultry business. Perhaps most important, Shiwahiade's children no longer work on the farm because their mother can afford to pay for school fees, books, and uniforms.

In just three years, Shiwahiade went from subsistence farmer to agricultural entrepreneur. There are literally millions of people like Shiwahiade with the potential to improve their standard of living dramatically. But, too often, this potential is unrealized because they lack access to capital, technology, managerial talent, and markets. It is because of individuals like Shiwahiade that we started Root Capital, and it's because of people like her that we continue to grow.

Ten years ago, I founded Root Capital, a nonprofit organization that grows rural prosperity in poor, environmentally vulnerable places in Africa and Latin America by providing capital, delivering financial training, and strengthening market connections for small and growing agricultural businesses. Root Capital clients are associations and private businesses that bring together small-scale rural producers. These enterprises help build sustainable livelihoods in sectors such as agriculture, wild-harvested forest products, and handicrafts.

Across the developing world, the rural poor—approximately 75 percent of the 2.6 billion people living on less than $2 a day—are practically excluded from the formal economy. Most of these people depend on agriculture as their primary source of income. Without access to capital and viable markets for their crops, small-scale farmers in the developing world are trapped in a cycle of poverty. Rural poverty often takes an environmental toll, as survival tactics such as illegal logging and slash-and-burn agriculture degrade the ecosystems on which farmers depend.

So Root Capital is investing in small and growing businesses, like farmer cooperatives, artisan associations, and a new generation of agricultural entrepreneurs. These are businesses that often aggregate hundreds and sometimes thousands of farmers and artisans, can move rural populations out of poverty, and become engines for sustainable development. In places such as Rwanda, Bolivia, and Haiti, they create alternatives to short-term survival tactics, like slash-and-burn agriculture and illegal logging and fuel wood collection, all of which trigger environmental degradation and actually worsen poverty over the long term.

Here's the challenge: Those businesses are stuck in the gap, the "missing middle," between microfinance and traditional banking. They're too large for the $500 loan to the street vendor or the bike mechanic, but they're still seen as too small or too risky and too remote to attract commercial financial institutions.

I saw this gap early on in my career. I was on Wall Street in the first half of the 1990s, and then I traded that job for a business journalism fellowship that sent my wife and me on a two-year journey across rural Mexico. That's where I saw firsthand that capital—access to credit—was not reaching the communities that needed it the most.

Here's what I suppose qualifies as my "lightbulb" story, the genesis of what became Root Capital. About a dozen years ago, I was sitting in a vanilla field in southern Mexico. I could hear parrots squawking and the rushing of a river nearby. Many hours' travel by pickup truck had landed me in the heart of the Chimalapas jungle, which is one of Mexico's last remaining cloud forests. Underneath the jungle canopy, 100 or so vanilla growers from an association of Zoque indigenous farmers had gathered to hear their leader. He stood atop a large tree stump.

"We organized ourselves," he said. "We kicked out the narco-ranchers and took back our land and forest. It hasn't been easy for us, but we're organized now. We have our cooperatives. We will reach the markets. We will have money for our families and this community."

As I watched him rally the farmers, my mind returned to Manhattan. Before leaving New York City, I had met with a development practitioner who had lived for years in rural Latin America. He said, "Mark my words, Willy, you will encounter leaders in very remote places who have just as much poise, sense of purpose, and leadership talent as a congressman or CEO." Sitting in the Chimalapas jungle that day, I did a mental scan of all the leaders in grassroots businesses I had come to know across Mexico. Most lacked formal business training, but they had passionately dedicated their lives to building competitive enterprises in the countryside. If they could pull it off, even where drug traffickers ruled the jungle, what would keep thousands of other agricultural entrepreneurs from doing the same?

In the end, sadly, the vanilla cooperative failed. Without access to credit or the financial skills to manage a business, the organization couldn't overcome the odds. As I traveled across rural Mexico in the ensuing months, I started thinking about how to bridge the gap between microfinance and corporate banking, so that the vanilla co-op and others like it in Mexico and beyond could build a better future. I knew it was going to be an uphill battle, that building the needed market connections, for example, might be too challenging. Yet I had seen how grassroots businesses across Mexico were starting to supply natural products to North America and to Europe.

Ten years later, the good news is that there are lots of companies that want products from farmers like Shiwahiade in Tanzania. Consumers are looking for products that are sustainably grown and ethically sourced, like fair-trade-certified cocoa, organic cotton, and natural-fiber handicrafts. We now see green seals and social labels in virtually every supermarket and department store. Global demand is booming, even in the recession, for products that are good for people and good for the planet. But because those businesses, in places like Guatemala and Uganda, are stuck in the "missing middle"—unable to access capital to grow their operation, to invest in productive infrastructure, or merely to pay the farmers on time—they're missing out on good business opportunities and the rising demand for their products.

That's where Root Capital steps in. Over the past decade, we have developed a three-pronged strategy—finance, advise, and catalyze—to help fill the missing middle in rural financial markets. First, finance: Provide capital to businesses that are locked out of the banking system for lack of traditional collateral and other constraints. Second, advise: Build local capacity and talent through financial education and training, so that people with little to no formal education can better compete in world markets. Think of it as an MBA in finance for rural business leaders. Third, catalyze: We aim to spur the development of a whole new industry to fill the missing middle by including in local financial institutions and encouraging them to recognize market opportunities in the countryside and join us in our work.

Let me focus on our lending, through which we enable businesses to scale quickly and, in doing so, transform rural communities. Most of our loans support working capital needs, in particular the cash that small and growing businesses need to pay the farmers or artisans on time. We also issue loans for long-term investments in equipment and productive infrastructure, such as the loan to Shiwahiade's coffee association for purchase of the milling equipment, which increases quality and reduces water usage by 80 percent.

An example from South America: Quinacho is a cooperative of 550 cocoa farmers located in a region of northern Peru, mired in a struggle against drug production. In 2006, no local bank would finance them, but we did. That year, we made a $50,000 loan for them to purchase, process, and export high-quality cocoa to Europe. Four years later, Quinacho's revenues had soared from $500,000 to $4 million, and our loan had grown to $1 million. The co-op is now accessing several different sources of financing. Meanwhile, farmer income grew to $7,000 per capita. Now cocoa production is offering a legitimate alternative to the drug trade.

Quinacho is representative of most of our clients. There are a number of good reasons why local banks didn't want to lend to Quinacho. First, Quinacho is located in an unstable region that's prone to violence and roadblocks. That is not ideal for a business that needs to transport its products from the mountains down to the port. Second, Quinacho is a seven-hour drive from the regional capital, where all the banks are. That's a big effort for a loan officer, when less risky businesses are down the street, and you can stop at Starbucks on your way home. Third, Quinacho has little in the way of traditional collateral to offer. Fourth, Quinacho is an agricultural business, and many banks are simply afraid to lend in agriculture because of both real and perceived risks. Finally, Quinacho's manager didn't study at one of the country's elite universities and therefore can't call in a favor from a friend when he needs money.

How did we make the loan? Our Peruvian loan officer, Daniel Rivera, traveled by bus to the community and spent the entire day with the board of directors and the cooperative manager. He saw in Quinacho what we see in scores of small and growing businesses across Latin America and Africa: committed membership, trustworthy leadership, and market demand for high-quality product. Quinacho's buyers in Europe wanted a reliable supply of cocoa and were eager to work with us. Their purchase agreement with Quinacho would, in effect, replace the need for traditional collateral because it represents a discrete future revenue stream pledged to repay our loan. When the product shipped, the buyer repaid Root Capital the principal and interest due.

We've employed this triangulation model with hundreds of loans with more than 100 buyers, ranging from specialty importers to global buyers such as Green Mountain Coffee Roasters, Starbucks, Home Depot, and Whole Foods.

Of course, none of this would be possible without the steadfast support of our donors and investors, even from the very beginning. We made our first loan in 1999 for $50,000 to a cardamom cooperative in Guatemala. But first we had to raise the capital for it. So I rolled up my sleeves and managed to borrow the money from religious investors, like the Sisters of the Sorrowful Mother from my hometown of St. Louis, and angel investors in the Boston area, where I now live. I remember taking one potential investor and his family to southern Costa Rica and going on a hike in the cocoa country. His kids happened to wear sandals that day, and along the path I remember spotting about five poisonous snakes. The sisters must have been praying for us, because if the kids have been bitten, Root Capital wouldn't be here today.

I like to sing and play the guitar to welcome new colleagues to Root Capital or to celebrate an accomplishment, and it sometimes helps with the fundraising as well. One time, I was with Green Mountain Coffee Roasters in Rwanda, before they had become a partner and made an investment in Root. We were in the back country traveling with Rwanda's minister of agriculture, who was there to speak with Green Mountain's coffee buyer, not me.

It turned out that some of the farmers we visited had Nicaraguan flag pins on their lapels, thanks to an exchange program they had been on to learn how Central American coffee farmers organize themselves. Someone mentioned that I played lots of Nicaraguan revolutionary folk songs, and the next thing I knew, the TV cameras were rolling, and I was playing the guitar and singing "Pobre la Maria," beside the minister and with a drum team behind me. Next day in Kigali, a stranger ran up to me in the street and said, "I saw you on national television yesterday!" That was my fifteen seconds of fame, and Green Mountain ended up investing. Whatever it takes, right?

We've come a long way. In 2011, we made more than 200 loans, totaling nearly $130 million in disbursements, to small and growing businesses representing more than 250,000 farm households. Over the past ten years, we've made more than 1,000 loans, totaling more than $350 million in credit, and we maintain a 98 percent repayment rate from our borrowers and 100 percent repayment rate to our investors.

I should highlight that the more lending we've done over the years, the more we have recognized that capital is not enough, that rural businesses often lack the technical skills to manage and grow their businesses efficiently. That's why we have developed financial training, focused on bookkeeping, financial management, inventory management, and other skills that prepare a business to gain access to credit from Root Capital or other financial institutions. This pairing of capital and capacity enables us to reach more businesses at an earlier stage in their development.

One such business is Ankole Coffee Producers Co-operative Union (ACPCU). It's a cooperative located in southwestern Uganda that represents 3,700 coffee farmers. For years the cooperative sold at very low prices to local buyers, largely because it lacked direct access to financing. In 2008, it approached Root Capital for a loan. At that time, the organization had a three-person staff and an entirely manual accounting system. Our Ugandan investment officer based in Kampala, Richard Tugume, was concerned about the ACPCU's ability to manage the loan and its cash flow. Rather than walk away from the need, Richard spent five days on-site with the co-op staff, training them how to reconcile accounts, how to do stocks management, and how to create and maintain reliable cash flow statements.

Several months later we approved a loan of $113,000, which financed its first direct exports and generated $450,000 in revenue for the business. A year later, ACPCU had repaid the loan, hired a qualified financial accountant, purchased computers, and taken out a new loan. Last year, the co-op's sales more than tripled. ACPCU has a long way to go, but there is a real sense of possibility in the organization. ACPCU's manager has told us that Root Capital's first loan marked the turning point for the organization and the community it serves.

Since 2006, we have successfully strengthened the financial management capacity of nearly 100 producer associations. Going forward, we are integrating our financial advisory services even more tightly with lending, using preinvestment technical assistance to help enterprises qualify for loans and post-investment technical assistance to help them overcome roadblocks, grow, and gain access to new financial products. This work creates tremendous mutual benefit for our clients and for our own portfolio, but, because the enterprises that need financial assistance the most are precisely the enterprises that can't afford to pay for it, it is a part of our model that relies most heavily on grant funding.

Every loan we make, every business we train, brings us closer to our objective. But ultimately, we're looking to have impact at scale. Part of that will be scaling Root Capital as a direct provider of capital and financial training. But an even bigger part of that impact is the catalyze piece of our mission, spurring other organizations to begin addressing the missing middle. Beyond our direct lending and financial training, we seek to do for the missing middle what Muhammad Yunus did for microfinance: to build a global movement for financial inclusion, to catalyze a new asset class that unlocks billions of dollars to build better livelihoods through small and growing businesses worldwide.

One of our proudest achievements is being a founding board member of the Aspen Network of Development Entrepreneurs, or ANDE, which was launched in 2008 and has quickly become the leader in building the industry infrastructure that will enable small and growing businesses to thrive in developing countries. We are also a founding member of the Global Impact Investing Network, or GIIN, which convenes investors such as J. P. Morgan and TIAA-CREF together with practitioners such as Acumen Fund, the Calvert Foundation, and Root Capital, all united in a common belief that capital is a critical tool for solving the world's social and environmental challenges. Through ANDE, GIIN, SOCAP, and many other alliances that have emerged in recent years, would-be competitors come together to forge collaboration, develop common metrics, and build an advocacy platform that's much greater than the sum of the parts.

One of the critical objectives for any social enterprise is to move beyond the original innovation to become an innovation-driven enterprise. In our case, the original innovation was basically trade and finance in sustainable agriculture. We have recently launched Root Lab, which is a way for us to increase our research and development efforts. In addition to our Sustainable Trade Fund, which includes our core lending in established value-chain markets such as coffee and cocoa, we now have a Frontier Fund to support lending in new sectors and geographies and with new financial products. We want to continue financing cocoa, coffee, mango, and the more than twenty-five other natural products we are now working with but also to move into adjacent markets that contribute to food security and post-conflict reconstruction.

Some of these possibilities include seed companies, agroprocessors, producers of millet and sorghum, local millers of fortified flour, and producers of ready-to-use therapeutic foods for severe acute malnutrition. For example, we loaned $150,000 to a Tanzanian company called Tanseed so it could buy

300 metric tons of hybrid, high-yielding, drought-resistant maize seed. Tan-seed sells this seed through an agrodealer network to 60,000 one-acre farmers across Tanzania and more than doubles their yields.

Root Capital also invests in businesses in countries that have recently experienced conflict or disaster, such as Rwanda, Uganda, Columbia, Guatemala, Haiti, and Liberia. There is a strong interconnectivity among economic development, peace, and security. Though poverty can lead to conflict, economic reconstruction can contribute to peace and recovery. Not surprisingly, private investment is slow to enter post-conflict or post-disaster regions; yet, because the majority of people in these regions are farmers and because the industrial base takes longer to rebuild, agriculture is one of the few sectors that can rapidly absorb large amounts of labor and rebuild rural livelihoods.

For example, we recently got a million-dollar investment from the Clinton Bush Haiti Fund to support our growing portfolio in Haiti. We are working with the mango sector, the coffee sector, and artisan cooperatives. I was in Haiti in August. We drove from Port-au-Prince through beautiful but totally denuded mountains down to the town of Jacmel, which is about three hours south. Jacmel had been the epicenter of papier-mâché production in Haiti. It was just leveled by the earthquake, much like Port-au-Prince. Most of the ateliers—the workshops—collapsed. But when we arrived, more than 100 artisans who had survived the earthquake were working overtime to deliver on the biggest purchase order they've ever had—not for cheap souvenirs but for high-value home décor going to Macy's Anthropologie. We're helping to finance this production.

What struck me is that in the midst of destruction, it was just amazing to see how excited everybody was. I think that's the key. There's this hope and this optimism around unleashing the power of enterprise, even in a devastating situation like that.

By the end of 2011, we had loaned close to $1 million in the mango, coffee, and artisan sectors in Haiti and put into place a full-time loan officer and financial literacy trainer. Both hires are local Haitian Creole speakers. This has helped us reach more businesses there and serve those businesses more effectively.

In closing, as I mentioned earlier, music is a big deal for me personally and also for Root Capital's organizational culture. I found in communities from Guatemala to Liberia to Rwanda that there are few things that you can do to connect people more directly and build bonds more quickly than to sing together. So I'd like to close by sharing a story about music.

It was about two years ago, and I was traveling with colleagues in the jungles of northern Nicaragua. We had spent almost all day with farmer cooperatives, and we were pretty much ready to call it a day, when the manager we were traveling with said, "No, we've got to make one more stop." So we got back in the truck and went over the potholes and through the mud and into the forest, and we came to a warehouse on the side of a mountain. By this time it was pouring rain, and we sprinted out of the truck to take shelter under the eaves of the warehouse. I was pretty exhausted and not that psyched about going and seeing yet another coffee milling facility.

So I opened the door and walked in. There were twenty-five children, ages five to twelve, with the most beaten-up horns, trumpets, and trombones you've ever seen, and there was the music teacher at the front of the class. He raised his arms, and the kids began to play "Jingle Bells." Meanwhile, I look out the window of the warehouse, and there in the downpour I saw the proud, smiling faces of two dozen beaming parents, parents who took part of their earnings from sales of specialty coffee to pay for a music teacher to come from the nearest town, two hours away, to teach their children how to play in the brass ensemble. The future of these children, and their hopes and their dreams, depends in large measure on the success of their parents' business.

At the end of the day, this is why we feel this great sense of urgency to provide access to capital, knowledge, and markets so those businesses can succeed.

# THE STRENGTH OF BUSINESS IN
# SUSTAINABLE CHANGE

Jacqueline Novogratz, Founder and CEO, The Acumen Fund

When I was twelve years old, my uncle Ed gave me a beautiful blue sweater. It had fuzzy zebras walking across the stomach, and Mount Kilimanjaro was right across the chest. I wore it all the time until one day in ninth grade, when my adolescent curves were shifting the contours of the sweater, my high school nemesis said in a loud and booming voice that the boys no longer had to go to the mountains, they could all just ski on the mountains on my chest. I was so humiliated that I immediately ran home to my mother, chastised her for ever letting me wear the hideous sweater, and demanded she drive me to Goodwill, where we somewhat ceremoniously got rid of it. The idea was that I would never again have to think about the sweater.

Fast-forward about ten years and 5,000 miles: I had left my career on Wall Street and was working in Kigali, Rwanda, with a small group of women in an effort to start the country's first microfinance bank and make small loans to poor women. I was twenty-five years old, jogging the steep slopes of Kigali when I saw a little boy about ten feet in front of me wearing my sweater. I ran up to the child, grabbed him by the collar, and turned it over; there was *my* name. I tell this story because it has served—and continues to serve—as a metaphor for how interconnected we all are. We too easily forget that our actions (and our inactions) can affect the lives of people we may never see and may never know all around the world. In many ways, finding that blue sweater was the beginning of my journey, a journey that included the microfinance bank in Rwanda, Stanford Business School, the Rockefeller Foundation, and the founding of Acumen Fund in 2001.

I arrived at Stanford as a student of the class of 1991. I had left the microfi-nance bank in Kigali and walked onto a campus of Patagonia shorts and Ray-Ban sunglasses wondering how I landed there in the first place. But I learned very quickly that Stanford would have a huge impact on me. My professors taught me the importance of crafting a life and how you must find purpose in everything that you do.

There was no individual who affected me then, and still does today, like John Gardner. I remember meeting him as if it were yesterday. I was sitting and listening to the professors tell us about the classes for the upcoming se-mester. They were talking about financial analysis and vector analysis, and then an elderly man walked up dressed in a houndstooth jacket and a fedora, and with a wave of his hand he said, "Why do civilizations rise and fall? Why do some of us throughout our whole lives renew ourselves with a sense of childlike curiosity well into our eighties and nineties, while others sit on the couch through our thirties and never get off again?" I was hooked. I marched up to his office that same day and told him I wanted him to be my mentor, and he somehow wildly agreed.

It was only afterward that I discovered he'd served as the secretary of Health, Education and Welfare under President Johnson and had worked with every president since then. Speaking to him was often like sitting with a guru. He would use aphorisms all the time. Once I was offered a job with a political figure, and he asked, "Will taking the job make you more interesting, or will it give you the opportunity to be interested in other people, in other things?" I didn't take the job, and it was a hard decision, but he was right. On other oc-casions, he would say, "Jacqueline, don't worry about what other people think about *you*, because frankly they're too worried thinking about themselves. What you need to do is commit to something bigger than yourself and focus on it, because commitment will set you free."

John would talk about big problems. He would say, "If you look around the world, there are all of these extraordinary opportunities, but they're disguised as insoluble problems. Your job is to find those problems. Don't be afraid of them; just go after them. But take small steps, because it's the only way it ever gets done." Every day I think about John, even today.

I also learned a lot from him about legacy. Oftentimes people think legacy is about their name, their ego. John understood that the real legacy is the way we have an impact on people, the way we touch them. I've understood since then as well, not only because he lives inside of me and I feel him, but because there are thousands of people just like me who consider John their mentor, and many more in the next generation who feel his words flow through them. We must be carriers of John's life, too.

On graduating from Stanford, I planned to go abroad again, because it's my passion; but John said, "You shouldn't go into other countries until you understand your own." So I took a job at the Rockefeller Foundation, where I worked on issues of leadership and philanthropy in the United States for several years.

Then one day in 1994 I was riding the New York City subway downtown and opened the paper to find that genocide was happening in Rwanda. I wondered what happened to the microfinance institution I helped start. What happened to the women? So in 1996, when the refugees went back, I also went back to Rwanda and discovered that the women I'd gotten to know had filled every conceivable role in the genocide. They had been killed in the first hour, they'd watched their families get killed, and at least one of them had been a major perpetrator. In fact, our first executive director was one of the planners of the genocide that ultimately killed 800,000 people.

Every summer, for one month, I would travel back to Rwanda to sit on the floors of the prisons, talk to the women, and try to understand what it means to be human, *really*. What I discovered was that monsters *do* exist, but they don't look the way we think they do; rather, monsters live inside all of us, and they are the broken parts, the fragments of us. In times of great anxiety, it is easy for demagogues to prey on those broken parts and sometimes make us do really terrible things. With my experiences in banking, microfinance, and philanthropy, I learned that dignity is more important to the human spirit than wealth. Too often we focus on whether someone makes $1 per day or $2 a day, but that is not the right metric. I also learned that the markets themselves are not going to solve the problems of poverty, and neither is traditional aid, government, or charity. We need new models.

So in 2001, with a cohort at Rockefeller, I focused on what kind of model might work and the idea of a third way. We started with this idea of "patient capital" and the notion that capital exists on a spectrum. If we could be more ecumenical about that capital, rather than disperse it as handouts, we could invest in entrepreneurs who see the poor as full-bodied human beings who want to make their own choices, their own decisions. Maybe then we could do a better job of getting basic goods and services to them.

That year I started Acumen Fund, and today we exist to create a world beyond poverty by investing in social enterprises, emerging leaders, and breakthrough ideas. We take philanthropic money and invest it as patient capital in increments ranging from several hundred thousand dollars to $2 million to support entrepreneurs who are focused on the basics: health care, water, housing, alternative energy, agricultural inputs, and education. We leave in the money for a long time, because these are entrepreneurs who aren't just starting companies that will go viral; they are working to ensure that tens of millions of people have access to affordable goods and services they never had before.

For example, in parts of the world where people believe that water comes from God, it's difficult to convince people that it's in their interest to pay for water—especially when government officials say we give water for free, elites say it's unethical to sell water to the poor, and corruption runs rampant. It takes a long time for these entrepreneurs to overcome those barriers, to iterate, fail, and start again. When Acumen Fund started, we thought we needed five- to seven-year capital, but as we've grown up and listened to the market, it is more like seven- to fifteen-year capital. As we see it, if we deploy the appropriate funds, provide a lot of management assistance, and insist on not only the financial returns but also social impact, we'll see models that can ultimately scale either to the capital markets (in cases of agricultural investments) or through government (in cases of primary health care and clean water delivery).

I'd like to share with you a few stories about the extraordinary entrepreneurs we've had the privilege of working with. In 2002 I met an incredible entrepreneur named Amitabha Sadangi from India, who'd been working for twenty years with some of the poorest farmers on the planet. He was expressing his frustration that the aid market had bypassed low-income farmers altogether, despite the fact that millions of farmers in India alone make under a dollar a day. They were either creating subsidies for large farms, or they were giving inputs to the farmers that they thought they should use, rather than that the farmers wanted to use.

At the same time, Amitabha was obsessed with a drip irrigation technology that had been invented in Israel. It was a way of bringing small amounts of water directly to the stalk of the plant. It could transform swaths of desert land into fields of emerald green. But the market also had bypassed low-income farmers because these systems were too expensive and were constructed for fields that were too large. The average small village farmer works on two acres or less.

So Amitabha decided that he would take that innovation and would redesign it from the perspective of the poor farmers themselves, because he spent so many years listening to what they needed, not what he thought that they should have.

He used three fundamental principles. The first one was miniaturization. The drip irrigation system had to be small enough that a farmer had to risk only a quarter acre, even if he had two, because it was too frightening, given all that he had at stake. Second, it had to be extremely affordable. In other words, that risk on the quarter acre needed to be repaid in a single harvest, or else the farmer wouldn't take the risk. And third, it had to be what Amitabha calls *infinitely expandable*. That means that with the profits from the first quarter acre, the farmer could buy a second, and a third, and a fourth.

As of today, IDE India, Amitabha's organization, has sold these systems to more than 300,000 farmers and has seen their yields and incomes double or triple, on average. But this didn't happen overnight. In fact, when you go back to the beginning, there were no private investors who were willing to take a risk on building a new technology for a market class who made under a dollar a day, who were known to be some of the most risk-averse people on the planet, and who were working in one of the riskiest sectors, agriculture.

So we needed grants. Amitabha used significant grants to research, experiment, fail, innovate, and try again. When he had a prototype and had a better understanding of how to market to farmers, that's when patient capital could come in. We helped him build a for-profit company that would build on IDE's knowledge, start looking at sales and exports, and be able to tap into other kinds of capital.

Now, including the farmers' family members, roughly 2 million people are benefiting from higher income levels—for some, $5 to $6 a day, instead of $1 to $2. By all measures, that is the kind of return on investment we need to see in a world with more than 2 billion people living in poverty.

Acumen has been on this incredible journey with entrepreneurs like Amitabha who recognize that the impossible really is possible, and, if we bring the right combination of capital, innovation, and a lot of determination, we can see tremendous change. To date, Acumen Fund has invested about $60 million in fifty-seven companies. We've seen follow-on investments of about $200 million, and more than 35,000 jobs have been created. But, perhaps most important, we have seen models for change that governments can take and make their own.

How do we do this work? How do these transformations begin? The gating factor for any potential Acumen Fund investment is our understanding of its potential impact on the lives of the poor. Our goal with any investment is to have transformational positive impact on the lives of millions of poor people, and we rigorously assess and map out our social impact thesis as part of the core of our diligence and investment approval process. A priori, we invest only in companies whose products and services address a critical, material need for the poor. In addition, and as important, we look for clear evidence that the poor demand the product or service, there is evidence of customer acceptance, and the management team's core focus is to understand and address the needs of low-income customers. Finally, and most important, we look for clear, well-documented evidence that the proposed product or intervention has a material impact on the lives of the poor. This could be in the form of increased income or economic activity, decreased spending, direct impact in terms of better health outcomes, higher safety and security, jobs created, decreased carbon emissions; decreased environmental impact, and follow-on effects of increased economic activity as a result of the success of the company.

For example, when analyzing d.light design, some of the potential impacts that we studied and continue to monitor closely include

- *Need:* the overall need, mentioned in the preceding pages, represented by a lack of access to electricity (1.5 billion people) or unreliable electricity (1 billion people).
- *Potential health impacts from decrease in kerosene use:* Burning 1 liter of kerosene emits 51 micrograms (mcg) of $PM_{10}$[1] per hour, which is above the World Health Organization's (WHO's) twenty-four-hour mean standard of 50 $mcg/m^3$. Burning a kerosene lantern for just four hours in a typical base-of-the-economic-pyramid household can result in concentrations of toxic particles several times the WHO standard.[2] A study from India reports that the average daily $PM_{10}$ concentration in households using solid fuel can sometimes exceed 2,000 $mcg/m^3$.[3]
- *Potential health impacts from reduced indoor household pollution:* Nearly 2 million people die each year from diseases associated with indoor air pollution from household use of solid fuels,[4] and in India alone 2.5 million people suffer severe burns from kerosene lamps each year.[5]
- *Increased hours of study and educational results:* A study in India found that portable solar lighting raised students' average study hours from

1.5 to 2.7 hours, with corresponding effect on school performance.[6] Furthermore, new World Bank research and field research from d.light are beginning to demonstrate that access to bright solar light significantly improves educational outcomes for children.[7] Finally, in a d.light pilot in India, 100 percent of 275 students surveyed said they regularly studied with the d.light S1, and all of them experienced benefits, including increased productivity, cleaner air inside the home, and reduced risk of fire.

- *Decreased spending:* Low-income households in Africa spend 10 to 25 percent of monthly income on fuels for lighting, a substantial cost burden. Even in India, where kerosene is heavily subsidized, households spend from three to five days' worth of income on kerosene each month, meaning that a household that replaces a kerosene lantern with a d.light solar lantern could expect a 10 to 15 percent increase in disposable income.[8]

- *Decreased $CO_2$ emissions:* Total consumption of kerosene worldwide is estimated to be 440 million barrels of oil per year, releasing 190 million tons of $CO_2$ annually, equivalent to the emissions of 30 million cars. Use of kerosene for lighting likely accounts for well over half of these emissions, with poor households in Africa alone accounting for about 20 million tons, or 12 percent of global kerosene emissions.[9]

I've recently been asked to be talk about the future of capitalism. Too often the question posed is, "Is capitalism broken? Do we need to change it?" This strikes me as a very odd question in a lot of ways, because if we look at the last twenty years of our global history, capitalism has moved 500 million people out of poverty. That's more movement out of poverty than ever in human history, but it has also left us at a point in our history where 2 percent of us own 50 percent of the wealth in the world, and 50 percent own less than 1 percent of the wealth. Though these numbers aren't terribly skewed from what we've seen historically; the difference today is that people all around the world can see each other—everything is transparent. As human beings, we don't compare ourselves to what we made last year, we compare ourselves to what *you* made last year and what I am making this year, and that is where so much instability exists. Fortunately, that is also where possibility exists.

We need to start reframing the questions so the conversation is not only about how we fix capitalism. We do need to think about how to extend capitalism, but, more important, we must think about the kind of ethical and moral leaders we need who will use capitalism to change the world. How do we, in our business schools and in our own organizations, build leaders who don't use the law as an excuse for what they do but who do the right thing because it's the right thing to do? We need leaders who will think about their actions and decisions based on the question, "How am I making the world better?"

At Acumen Fund, we run a global fellows program because we believe it is our responsibility to invest in leaders as well as companies. Typically we receive several hundred applications from sixty-five countries for just ten spots. We place them in factories that make bednets and with community power systems that transform rice husks into electricity; but we also spend six weeks training them in operational skills, financial skills, and what we call *moral imagination*, the idea that if you can put yourself into another person's shoes and build solutions from that perspective, we would do a lot better as a world. We ask them to read the writings of Aristotle, Plato, Nelson Mandela, and Martin Luther King Jr.; talk about their deepest values and how to integrate them into the way we think about business; and discuss how public policy needs to interact with business.

In our 2010 class of fellows, I met an extraordinary young man named Josephat Byaruhanga, a farmer from Uganda. Acumen Fund placed him with a company called Western Seed, which now sells hybrids seeds to more than 200,000 farmers in Western Kenya. The company is essentially busting the Kenyan government's monopoly on seed, a monopoly that has been the only game in town for the last fifty years. It is opening up opportunities for small-holder farmers; it is increasing crop yields and aims to reach 800,000 farming households by 2014. It reached 150,000 in 2010 and 300,000 by the end of 2011; it's on track to reach 800,000 households by the end of 2014.

When Josephat returned from the field, he said, "I thought that as an African farmer I would be really good at convincing African farmers to buy seeds that would increase their productivity, but I was humbled by how hard it was. I made so many cultural mistakes. What I learned is that, for me, leadership is like a panicle of rice. At the height of the season, rice is green, it's beautiful, and it reaches up toward the heavens and feeds the earth, but, right before the harvest, it bends over with great humility and touches the ground with gratitude, thanks, and appreciation."

Our leaders today need to walk with that sense of audacity, the confidence that they can change the problems that we face as a world, but also with a sense of humility and gratitude that we still have much to learn. I have seen humility best performed through the skill of listening. We need to do a better job of listening. That is where the opportunity really arises and where future leaders with moral imagination to navigate this highly complex world will earn the greatest respect.

Seamus Heaney once said that there are moments when "hope and history rhyme," and though we live in a time of great chaos, of great frustration, of great fear, I look out and see young people who want to change the world and want to use the skills they have to the take on the toughest, most intellectually challenging issues we face as a world.[10] That is hope. Hope and history are rhyming, because we've never had better access to resources, knowledge, and skills to solve our problems.

I'd like to leave you with some lines from one of my favorite poets, Mary Oliver:

> *Doesn't everything die at last, and too soon?*
> *Tell me, what is it you plan to do*
> *with your one wild and precious life?*[11]

## Notes

1. Particulate matter with an aerodynamic diameter of less than 10 microns; widely believed to pose the greatest health problems.

2. World Bank (2008), *The Welfare Impact of Electrification*.

3. Smith (2000), "National Burden of Disease in India from Indoor Air Pollution."

4. World Health Organization (2009), *The Energy Access Situation in Developing Countries*.

5. Solar Electric Light Fund (2011).

6. Agoramoorthy and Hsu (2009).

7. In Sudan, the World Bank found that pass rates nearly doubled, from 57 percent in 2007 to 97 percent in 2008, after students used solar lighting for one year. The pass rate reached a full 100 percent in 2009 and was maintained in 2010 (Social Edge, 2011).

8. Pena, 2010.

9. Solar Electric Light Fund (2010–2011).

10. Seamus Heaney, *The Cure at Troy: A Version of Sophocles' Philoctetes* (New York: Farrar, Straus and Giroux, 1991).

11. Oliver (1992).

# FUNDERS AND INVESTORS

## A Conversation

Shapiro: One of the characteristics that's often cited about social entrepreneurship is that it blurs the demarcation between profit and nonprofit. I wonder if you could speak to whether or not business acumen skills or even profit-making aspects are integral to being a social entrepreneur.

Osberg: I think the skills are imperative. You have to be disciplined, you have to be focused, you have to know what you're doing, you have to build a venture, you have to run it responsibly, and you have to be accountable; no question about that. Whether that's a business skill or just plain strategic focus and smarts, I couldn't really tell you. We at the Skoll Foundation see social enterprise, which is the term that's usually used to describe a profit-making concern that has a social objective, as a subset of social entrepreneurship and not the other way around. So for us, the model that serves the mission is what's relevant here. I don't want to confuse the model for the imperative. The goal here is to create social value—to crack the code on a problem to make a difference for humanity. If you have to do that with a nonprofit venture, fine, do it with a nonprofit venture. If it makes sense to do it as a business venture, do it as a business venture. We have the means—capital across the spectrum of all the assets we have to invest—and have built the strategies to put that capital to work. The driver for us is the potential for impact, regardless of whether the venture is organized as a for-profit or a not-for-profit. It's really the goal that matters—the focus, the discipline, the drive, the ability to stay with something. That's what distinguishes the social entrepreneur regardless of whether it's a for-profit or nonprofit venture.

Novogratz: I think the biggest and the most legitimate criticism is that our language makes it sound like the markets alone will change the face of poverty. They won't. I try really hard to be a voice that says, "Look, we know that charity alone is not going to change poverty, and we know that the markets alone will not change poverty, but there is a really powerful model by using the tools and the ethos of business with the ethos of the nonprofit humanitarian movement." It's in that melding that we'll create change. By using the market as a listening device, so that we're really hearing how customers respond at any price level, in some ways we have a much more honest dialogue with them. We can learn both where the market works and where the market is limited. There is a real and valid criticism that people fear that what many hear is that all we need is the market. I think that's the biggest piece.

The second piece, as we're seeing this kind of nascent industry froth and build, is that there are lots of new groups coming in and making promises that I don't think they'll be able to fulfill. "We're going to be able to solve problems of poverty, too, and we're going to give you a 20 percent financial return." We're not seeing that in the for-profit sector. Traditional classic venture capital firms with no constraints, over the last ten years, have an annualized return rate of about 3 percent, on average. So if the guys who are hard-core going after the money are coming in at 3 percent, it is unrealistic, and it's irresponsible to be promising 20 percent, but it sounds a lot sexier than Acumen's pitch, which is, "Look, if we make anywhere from –20 to +10, and we transform industries"—and then we give examples of where we have—"that's a pretty great return on your philanthropic dollar." But we often get back, "Well, that sounds like it's fuzzy investing. Maybe if you had used our business skills, you would do a better job." That's one of our challenges.

In this interconnected world in which we live, we don't really have the option anymore of being able to say, "I'm just going to go and make money any way I can." If you're starting what looks to be a mainstream traditional company, you have no option but to do it with ethics and do it with integrity and think about the people that you're employing as real stakeholders in what you're doing. I don't think the consumers are going to want to buy from you otherwise, long term. We're seeing that our natural resources really are limited in the world, so your responsibilities as an entrepreneur, as an employer, have to extend there, as well. There's almost arrogance in saying, "*Here*'s the social entrepreneur side, and *these* are just the normal entrepreneurs." I think what we are seeing, and what is really exciting, is a convergence, but it's about holding each other accountable to a different standard that recognizes that we need a stakeholder model. We need to redefine what profit is in a way that really does internalize the resources that we use and the change that we make. We need to redefine business.

Shapiro: Matt, when Omidyar Network invests in for-profit entities, what kinds of returns are you looking for; and is it across the board, or do you have certain parameters you're looking for?

Bannick: Our process in doing for-profit investments is that we look first for companies that drive significant positive social impact; that's the screen. There is a range of the positive social impact that any company will deliver. We tend to only invest in companies that we think can have a fabulous positive social impact. Then we would apply the typical, standard, financial analysis that you would to determine whether a business is going to be successful. Our experience is that, in almost all of these businesses, there are people who are socially motivated but also very much motivated to scale the businesses up. That means, in part, generating the returns that will help them get the capital to help them grow bigger and faster and have a bigger impact.

Shapiro: There is a great focus on scale within the discourse and within programming goals. I have found throughout these conversations that there is a difference between scale and systemic change. Would you say there is a difference between them? If so, what is that? And are you looking for scale, or are you looking for systemic change?

Bannick: Both. Back up a little bit, and say we look for impact, right? How we think about impact is how many people you reach and the depth of change you are able to help create in their lives. So we say, "Reach $x$ engagement": the number of people, times the level of engagement, equals impact. That is how we think about it. Scale is one element, right? Scale is reach, and then we look at the depth of an impact. So whether somebody is getting the impact of education with Bridge, or a light with d.light, those are different types of impact that you need to think about a little bit differently.

Now, in terms of systemic change, that is critically important. Our approach is to find the social entrepreneurs who are working in areas in which we're interested, who we think have that opportunity to have that impact—reach $x$-times engagement—but we're also looking at creating a network of these entrepreneurs—hence the name, right, the Omidyar *Network*. The notion isn't just investing in individual entrepreneurs, but then bringing them together as a network, so that the whole is much more impactful than simply the sum. So to create that network, we're also looking at how you create that systemic change within that network. A lot of times that's investing behind yet another social entrepreneur. And a lot of times that's investing in specific elements of what we'd call infrastructure to move the whole sector forward.

We're looking for very big, large social impact, well-run entrepreneurs. We do take, probably, more risk than other investors would probably take. For example, Bridge Academy is doing fabulously well now; we invested at a very, very early stage and at 5 percent, not to get to technical, but the risk-free rate on government bonds in Kenya must be 30 to 50 percent. So we aren't going in expecting a 100 or 200 percent return on Bridge. It's not realistic. If you were to ask a typical venture capitalist what the required rate would be for going into the slums of Nairobi to build schools—well, first of all, they wouldn't look at it, right? Second of all, if they did look at it, and looked at the numbers we're looking at, it's not clear that they would invest. So we have a high risk tolerance: social impact, disciplined financial analysis, but also with a high tolerance for risk in terms of what we're willing to take to have that positive social impact.

We are in an era now where there is more experimentation with things such as impact investing. I think we should be more open to looking at the solutions that are working. We're close to the Valley here in San Francisco, and one of the hallmarks of having success in the Valley is to try a lot of things and figure out which ones don't work and shut them down. Figure out which ones *do* work and put more resources behind them. We're now in an era of a lot more experimentation. Sometimes the social sector is not so disciplined in shutting down experiments that don't work, and for good reason. There are frequently lives that are dependent on those programs. But we have to have a more disciplined approach and lots of experimentation, shut down the things that don't work, and really find out a way to scale up the things that do work.

Osberg: For the Skoll Foundation, the question of scale is not registered in an organization's size or budget but through the scale of its impact: its ability to transform systems, right injustices, and demonstrate that it can solve even the most intractable problems. This isn't to say that social entrepreneurs shouldn't grow their organizations but that how big you are is in no way a measure of how good you are at driving change. In effect, we see impact at scale as defined by systems, behavioral, and policy change.

Let me offer a couple of examples of what results at scale look like. International Development Enterprises in India, founded by Amitabha Sadangi, has reached more than one million smallholder farmers with its treadle pumps and customizable KB Drip irrigation units, helping its clients turn from subsistence to income-generating production. In fewer than twenty years, IDE-India's work has resulted in more than $1 billion in new wealth generated, with that wealth translating into significant increases in health, education, and dignity for rural producers. But the data get even better when one factors in India's depleted groundwater supply and growing desertification. IDE-India's data demonstrates that its products are 50 to 70 percent more efficient in their water use, while boosting crop yields by 50 percent. They are doing for rural producers what Grameen did for poor borrowers: literally design building the field of micro-irrigation. Is there any wonder why the Gates Foundation invested $27 million in IDE-India so that the organization could do the same in Africa?

Partners in Health, cofounded by Paul Farmer, Thomas White, and Todd McCormack in 1987, stopped an epidemic outbreak of multiple drug-resistant tuberculosis (MDR-TB) in northern Lima with its community-based treatment model. They achieved one of the highest cure rates for MDR-TB ever reported: 83 percent. Armed with this evidence, PIH challenged public health orthodoxy, which considered treatment of MDR-TB "impractical and unaffordable," though it kills more than 2 million a year. By 2006, the World Health Organization and others involved in the fight against TB, including the U.S. Centers for Disease Control, released new guidelines sanctioning treatment of MDR-TB in poor communities, effectively adopting the PIH model. The new guidelines included increasing the number of MDR-TB patients receiving treatment worldwide from 16,000 in 2006 to 800,000 in 2016.

Those are just two examples of what impact at scale looks like, with metrics to prove that social value is indeed being delivered and that social change is being advanced.

Shapiro: Willy, where are you and Root Capital on the profit–nonprofit continuum?

Foote: Root Capital is now housed within a 501(c)(3), and we have a spread business within us. That is our social bank, if you will, where over time we will spin out for-profit funds or for-profit banks in-country. But given the depth of the market failure that we've chosen to address and the need to raise philanthropic first-loss capital and cover operating deficits in the early years, as we try to prove the business case for lending to these otherwise unbankable businesses, we felt that it was important to start, to not potentially hit the wall if we set up as a for-profit. We haven't been able to throw off the profits that we didn't need in time, and we didn't want to abandon the mission. So we're a 501(c)(3). It's all mushed together, and yet we're pretty darn good at making sure that we separate the wheat from the chaff, and we don't have co-mingling of funds, et cetera. But I'll repeat: Over time, the view is that we will spin out for-profit entities for the lending. Lastly, for the public goods that we deliver—in other words, financial training, financial literacy training, and the field building—we have the think tank within us, the mouthpiece for building the industry, that will most likely forever be philanthropically funded and stay within the NGO.

Shapiro: Are there particular characteristics that really stand out for you that are absolutely necessary to be a successful social entrepreneur? The unwillingness to cede defeat, for example?

Osberg: I would say that it's more about not being willing to cede defeat, and I'll give you just one example. I mentioned Victoria Hale and OneWorld Health. You know, Victoria's really a remarkable social entrepreneur, but OneWorld Health ended up going through some tough times, and she ended up leaving. Well, she could have gone back into her corner and blamed whoever for the collapse of the organization and the institution that she was building, but she didn't. She's on to her next venture, and she's found new investors. She's smarter, she's wiser, she's more resilient, and she's going to do more extraordinary work. I'll bet on her any day. She cares too much about this work as a pharmaceutical scientist herself. She can't accept the fact that there are readily available drugs in the developed world and treatable diseases in the developing world, that children still die of diarrhea; she's going to do something about it. So in answer to your question, I would say it is about dealing with and pushing back against failure. Social entrepreneurs can look failure in the face, and they can keep going. She's a wonderful example and a real inspiration.

Novogratz: I think that entrepreneurs are stubborn and have a certain degree of fearlessness in them. So they go after the vision that they think is important, and then they let the work teach them. They don't let failure stop them. I think entrepreneurs, in some ways, start off as kids. By the time I was ten, I was running businesses. I think that there is almost an entrepreneurial personality. There are as many routes to entrepreneurship as to almost any other kind of endeavor. I was an accidental banker. I learned a lot, and I think I represent using big institutions as launching pads for the kind of gadfly-turned-innovator approach to getting things done. I have been saying it from the beginning, but I really think it's about knowing who you are and building the skills along the lines that will help you get there, but it's been really interesting. Entrepreneurs are driven to create things that haven't existed before. That's what will drive whether you do it or not.

Shapiro: I would like to ask you about the notion of measurement and return on investment. What are your strategies when it comes to measurement?

Osberg: It's not always possible to draw as straight a line from the innovations led by social entrepreneurs to key performance indicators, though one of the defining characteristics of social entrepreneurs is their accountability for results. Discipline and accountability are at the heart of the system we've developed to prove our hypothesis that social entrepreneurs and their innovations serve as catalysts of change. First, we look for indicators of impact in three defined categories: policy change, behavioral change, and infrastructure change. We're focused on social entrepreneurs solving the world's most pressing problems, so we have also distilled seven targets or "desired states" from our issue framework.

Environmental sustainability, for example, is part of our overall issue framework, while reducing the rate of deforestation in the Amazon is a desired state target. Our measurement system then rolls up metrics from the innovations led by social entrepreneurs to assess impact at the desired state level. In the case of Imazon, for example, we know that the organization's satellite monitoring system has been critical to Brazil's commitments to reducing its emissions from deforestation: That's policy change, which in our model demonstrates large-scale change. In the health area, we measure the rate of increased access to quality health care. In the Gambia, where Riders for Health is providing 100 percent coverage for community health workers, the country's 2 million citizens now have access to clinics, to vaccines, and to bednets. Key performance metrics we look at here include those drawn from available data—for example, decreases in mortality rates from Malaria.

Social entrepreneurs are themselves market oriented and disciplined in gathering the market feedback that tells them if they are succeeding or not. They take the lead in defining metrics that demonstrate the efficacy of their innovations. We see ourselves as their partners and share accountability for capturing and tracking evidence that matters.

Bannick: First off, I'd like to start off by saying a lot of the foundations have done a much better job on measurement than they're given credit for. Fundamentally it's really difficult to measure the outcomes of some of the things that they do, and given that they've actually done quite a nice job. The way we think of measurement is somewhat different in the private sector, with our for-profit investments and our not-for-profit investments. The similarity between both of them is that we try to come back to this notion of reach and engagement. So whether it is nonprofit or for-profit, it's how many lives did you impact or reach? What was the depth of that impact? We use that framework for both for-profit and not-for-profit investments. For the for-profit investments, you have the additional metrics for financial return. It's interesting; most of the for-profits in which we invest are already capturing the metrics that we care about from a social impact perspective. So, use eBay as an example: In terms of financial success, you can look at the returns there; but, having been inside eBay, I know that the critical part is the notion of how many people are active on the platform. How many sellers are there? How successful have the sellers been? A typical well-run business will have a number of metrics that are not just financial metrics but that give the business a sense of how positive an impact they're having on the lives of their customers.

Novogratz: Acumen Fund's culture has always been data driven in order to help us understand what works, what doesn't, and how we can work with our entrepreneurs to help them drive growth in their businesses. One of the early challenges that we faced was that our learnings were largely insular; we had good data for our portfolio of investments, but with the lack of industry standard metrics, we had no way of comparing our portfolio's data with that of our peers. We had no way of knowing if we were doing "well" relative to the larger industry of peer funds and their businesses. As a result, we sought to benchmark our own performance against a set of standard metric definitions or to aggregate impact beyond our businesses to that of the sector. None of this was possible several years ago.

Foote: We're developing a knowledge management platform where Latin American and African investment officers and monitors can trade best practices. We've developed an obligor scorecard and a credit-risk rating system that is quite sophisticated—it looks and feels like what a bank would want to see—and training them to use all those tools is part of it. We are members of the Global Impact Investing Network, which provides standard metrics for social investing. Comparability of metrics I think is super important. No single organization can do it itself, and you can't really tap into scaled impact investment dollars unless you behave like an efficient market. How can you quickly size up who's doing what, who's good, who's bad, and how this fits together? And that happens through industry alliances, infrastructure, standards and metrics, and collaboration.

Shapiro: Can you address what are some of your greatest challenges?

Novogratz: I would say talent is a really big issue for us, ironically. On the one hand, we see a talent tsunami. We have 4,000 applications on file at Acumen, but the skills we need are often incredibly specific. Right now, some of our companies are looking for human resource directors, and they're scaling. Our 128 Ambulances is hiring 2,500 people this year, so they need someone with serious HR experience. We are looking for an India country director with at least ten years of venture capital investing who also understands the emerging markets and is comfortable with our whole investment philosophy, which means they're not going to make a lot of money. So we're looking for extremely precise and special individuals.

Foote: You hit upon one of the greatest challenges. Starting out with Root Capital, you think that you're so brilliant because you've identified the problem and you've come up with a potential solution. Well, the easy thing is identifying the problem; harder is coming up with a solution; hardest by far is building the organization and finding the talent. It's kind of cheeky, but our core company value is multilingual on boardrooms and back roads and beat-up buses. To find that talent that not only has the hard skills, the MBA skills, but also has deep social and environmental commitments is not easy.

Osberg: It is hard not to be overwhelmed by the scale and complexity of the challenges confronting us all, whether it's geopolitical instability, climate change, resource depletion, food security, disease, and the deep misery of poverty. These are truly formidable challenges that affect us all. So when I think about the efforts of social entrepreneurs and the magnitude of these challenges—well, it's all pretty daunting!

That said, I also know that we work with many social entrepreneurs whose innovations have extraordinary potential to make real headway. What they need are what all entrepreneurs need: talented teams, great partners, serious investment, and supportive policies.

SECTION 3

# THE THINKERS

Profoundly New Ideas Create New Paradigms
for Change

# A COMMUNITY COMMITTED TO SOCIAL ENTREPRENEURSHIP

Christopher Gergen, Founder and CEO, Forward Ventures

As the world's challenges become more complex, how can we drive positive change through innovative problem solving? This question has been an undercurrent through much of my work over the last twenty years—as an entrepreneur, educator, author, and now community organizer. On my path, I've had the fortune of learning from a number of really smart people and have accumulated a set of experiences (often learned the hard way). This chapter is for people who are driven by the same question as me. It's got urgency to it because we can't wait. If we're serious about leaving the world a better place than we found it, we need breakthrough solutions emerging from communities that are intentionally harnessing this entrepreneurial spirit.

This chapter will start with important characteristics for individual change-makers and social entrepreneurs. We'll then explore how cities can unleash the entrepreneurial spirit through intentional community building. Along the way, I will hold up a couple of my personal experiments as examples of what these ideas look like in real life.

There is a pattern, a flow, in the process of putting a bold new idea into action. These patterns aren't necessarily relegated to a business or a nonprofit organization; rather they are expressions of the mind-set of the change-makers themselves, people who are doing truly extraordinary things in their lives, no matter what their field. They could be ballet dancers, artists, "intraprenuers"—anyone with a creative spirit. One way or another, these are people who ultimately had taken a very intentional and purposeful path. These stories need to be told and shared not only with people who are going to become entrepreneurs but also with all people who are in the process of figuring out how they themselves can live a more purposeful life. In this spirit, my good friend Gregg Vanourek and I collaborated on a book called *Life Entrepreneurs: Ordinary People Creating Extraordinary Lives* to help share these stories. We interviewed fifty-five people who we thought had really created extraordinary lives for themselves, and we tried to uncover the key lessons that we could learn from their experiences. Working from more than 1,000 pages of transcript, we distilled what we thought were really important components of the entrepreneurial life path.

We found that the people who are life entrepreneurs, people who are leading truly extraordinary and intentional lives, have many things in common. First, *they have a very clear understanding of who they are as people.* They have a deep sense of what their core identity is. Second, *they are awake to the opportunities that are around them.* As Carlos Castaneda shares, there are "cubic centimeters of chance" around us all the time, but you have to be a warrior to have the speed and the prowess to pick up on these. Life entrepreneurs have that. Third, *they must be able to take advantage of those opportunities by creating a vision of what the future should look like.* Entrepreneurs believe that the future is malleable, to quote Netscape founder Marc Andreessen, that we have the ability to look out on the horizon and create a new future for ourselves, for our communities, and for our world. In fact, our world is dependent on this entrepreneurial spirit. But, to create change, you have to be able to see the gaps and create a vision for where you want to go. Fourth, *you have to be able to develop the set of goals and strategies to get there.* Entrepreneurs pull that off in small ways, taking small risks, getting those early wins, gaining confidence, and building momentum. Fifth, *the only way you're going to be able to build that momentum is if you have a strong support network.* There are three characteristics that make for a really healthy support network. One is deep trust: You need to be engaged with people whom you are confident opening up to and sharing your vulnerabilities and questions with—particularly during tough times. Two is diversity: When you face a tough challenge, it helps to talk to people from a wide range of backgrounds who might be able to offer different sets of perspectives. Three is reciprocity: Pay it forward, helping each other out along the way. With deep trust among a diverse set of mentors, friends, and family members who are all looking out from one another, we can create our "personal board of directors" to hold us accountable, challenge us, and pick us up when we fall down.

Another thing that is really important in living a life of entrepreneurial purpose is that ultimately you have to be willing to assume an element of risk. Departing from the status quo and going from living a life to *leading* a life is ultimately illogical—or, to quote George Bernard Shaw, "unreasonable."[1] One of the things that business schools are struggling with right now is that entrepreneurship is ultimately illogical. You have to depart from something that is safe and secure to follow something that you ultimately feel deep down is the right path for you to go down. A lot of people, most people, are really scared of failure. So we asked the same question of the fifty-five people whom we interviewed: "What are you most scared of?" The thing they were most scared of was regret. That's a pretty interesting alternative: fear of regret versus fear of failure. When you transition from fear of failure to fear of regret, the world opens up because you look at things in a very, very different way. Finally, there's the idea of embracing renewal and reinvention, recognizing the fact that you've got to pick up your head frequently, daily, to be able to get those moments of reflection and to figure out, "Am I on the right path?"

The research for our book helped lead me to a couple of my current affiliations with Duke University, as an adjunct faculty member and a fellow within the Center for the Advancement of Social Entrepreneurship (CASE) and Fuqua's School of Business, and the Center for Creative Leadership as their innovator in residence. Within both institutions our aim is to harness the young, energetic talent who want to go take on the world and make it a better place and to give them the skills, support, networks, and mentorship to help them accomplish this. Through this work, I've come to realize that just focusing on creating really good, entrepreneurial seeds is not enough. We've also got to start paying attention to the fertile ground in which to plant these seeds. If these seeds end up in arid, rocky ground, if they end up in cities or communities that don't embrace that entrepreneurial spirit, they will blow away or wither, and we won't get the full benefit of their potential. We can't afford to squander this talent—especially in place like North Carolina, where we are on the cusp of positioning the state as a true entrepreneurial destination.

Let me provide some context about North Carolina. Fifty years ago we were almost totally dependent on three industries: tobacco, textiles, and furniture. The state leaders at the time—the business and political leaders—had the great foresight to see that they were on a dead-end road with these three industries. They took bold action. They quietly bought up 5,000 acres of pine brush because it was located between three universities—Duke, University of North Carolina, and North Carolina State—and they called it the Research Triangle Park. It was that vision and that fortitude and a little bit of cash that were able to start attracting the likes of IBM and a number of other research and development activities. The result is that the Research Triangle Park now houses more than 170 companies, employs 40,000 people, and creates a multitude of patents. It's become one of the biggest engines of growth for our state.

Inspired by the example of RTP, a group of leaders in Durham began thinking about new growth engines for a city that had fallen on hard times following the collapse of tobacco. Durham has an impressive history of entrepreneurship, including "Black Wall Street," which produced some of the leading African-American–led enterprises in the country, including the first African-American insurance company and bank. It also has a strong talent pool with Duke and North Carolina Central Universities, as well as over 2 million square feet of old tobacco warehouses that are being converted into beautiful mixed-use housing, retail, and office space. The cost of living and doing business is low, while the quality of life is high—leading to an emerging creative class. Now the question became: How can tap into all of this potential and connect the dots in a very intentional, growth-oriented way? Specifically, how can we create a new model of urban development that helps foster, develop, and scale the next generation of change-makers?

This work is important because there is a lot of entrepreneurial energy out there. We've seen that firms that are less than five years old create two-thirds, if not more, of net new jobs. This is the future of our economy, and, as we look at our country, we know that we cannot borrow our way forward; we can't spend our way forward; we ultimately have to innovate our way forward. We need to recognize the fact that entrepreneurship is going to be one of our major growth engines, and we need to continue to innovate to stay ahead of the game. Further, if channeled in the right way, this entrepreneurial, innovative spirit can also help us tackle some of our toughest challenges in education, health care, environmental impact, poverty, and so on.

So how do we do that? How do we create the intentional environment? This is how Bull City Forward (BCF), where I serve as executive director, came into being. In response to these questions, we set out to create a comprehensive ecosystem focused on social innovation. In other words, we applied the key entrepreneurial characteristics of our BCF team to create an engine for other entrepreneurs. This is the kind of project that has exponential potential! With an exciting idea in hand, we did two different things to assess the field. First, we mapped all of the assets we had in our community and did a gap analysis. Second, we looked at best practices around the world, ranging from Helsinki to Pittsburgh, Indianapolis, San Francisco, Austin, Seattle, and Providence— thirteen cities in total. We also looked at the research and work of Living Cities, the Surdna Foundation, the Annie E. Casey Foundation, Ashoka, Social Venture Partners, New Profit Inc., and the Brookings Institute, among others. We tried to learn as much as we possibly could from efforts to harness that entrepreneurial energy.

We came to realize that there were a lot of really good ideas out there. Some communities, like Indianapolis, were doing a great job developing and recruiting a strong pipeline of entrepreneurial talent. Others, like New Orleans, Pittsburgh, and London, had built out robust entrepreneurial support systems. Some, such as San Francisco, Toronto, and Boston, had created model incubator or accelerator spaces. And others, like Providence and Pittsburgh, were smartly tapping into their universities for talent, research, and a new venture pipeline. Throughout, data on impact were relatively scarce but increasingly important, and policymaking, while recognized for its importance, was often not actively directed toward promoting and supporting social enterprise development. Finally, the importance of access to capital came up again and again, though with a few exceptions (San Francisco in particular) it was relatively thin in most communities and not well organized. In short, while there was much to be learned from each community, it was quickly apparent that no community was taking a truly comprehensive approach to intentionally fostering, developing, and scaling high-impact, high-growth social enterprises.

With that conclusion, the BCF team went out and got money from key investors in our community: the Chamber of Commerce, the city, our universities, the local community foundations, the business community, and the nonprofit community. We wanted to make sure that the creation of Bull City Forward was truly a community-led effort. We also knew that if we got a few early wins, we could build critical momentum. So, as we kicked off our planning process, we also opened a 5,500-square-foot incubator/entrepreneurial hub in downtown Durham that quickly became a tangible manifestation of the community we were trying to build. We also formed eight different working groups made up of more than 150 people across the community who were charged with discussing the best-practice analysis and our community asset map and developing a set of strategic interventions to create a truly comprehensive, community-led approach. The result became Bull City Forward's road map.

BCF is guided by the conviction that by purposefully encouraging, enabling, and scaling high-impact social enterprises and socially driven entrepreneurs, Durham can foster a robust cluster of innovation that will measurably improve our communities and transform our economy. Thus, the mission of Bull City Forward is "to unleash the potential of local entrepreneurs to create enduring social and economic impact."

Bull City Forward envisions a transformation across Durham and the region, where a world-class cluster of creative minds is scaling for-profit companies and nonprofit enterprises that contribute to thousands of new jobs while improving the local and global community in meaningful and measurable ways. This continually evolving cluster is sustained by a talent pipeline of problem solvers who are homegrown locally and recruited globally. The community is defined by collaboration, sustainability, diversity, and accountability—and its success attracts millions of dollars in investment capital.

To achieve this vision, Bull City Forward is catalyzing a supportive ecosystem for entrepreneurs in Durham. We are one piece in this ecosystem, but our hope is to encourage the development of the other necessary pieces and to serve as community glue, connecting stakeholders and aligning our community around citywide priorities.

Since launching in the spring of 2010, Bull City Forward has built a membership base of 160 local social entrepreneurs, representing over 600 jobs and $110 million in revenue in every sector, including education, health care, the environment, and poverty alleviation. Forward Ventures Communities, our nonprofit arm, helps us expand our community outreach and talent development, as well as share our model with other communities. This fall, we launched Queen City Forward in Charlotte to help connect the city's two entrepreneurial communities. We are also active partners in the Fourth Sector Cluster Initiative in North Carolina—trying to stimulate social enterprise economic development across the state. And we feel our work is just beginning.

BCF sees four core components as key to achieving enduring impact through community building. The first is really *focusing in on how we homegrow talent in our community*. How do we create a pipeline of talent and how do we create on-ramps of opportunity for people who are disenfranchised traditionally from the entrepreneurial dream, specifically people who come from the poorer communities in our city? In Durham we have significant economic disparity as well as ethnic diversity. We are about 45 percent African-American, 45 percent white, and 10 percent Hispanic, and the Hispanic population is one of the fastest growing in the country. Among the more disadvantaged communities, you do see a lot of entrepreneurial activity, but little of it is focused on social entrepreneurship, because it's often about providing for one's family. But what we're seeing is that some of those small-scale entrepreneurial organizations with which we're starting to work are recognizing that if they embed a social benefit focus in their business model from the get-go, it can attract more customers, which will drive their business. Through education, appreciation, and respect, we can support lower-income populations; we can help empower them and provide them with a sense of self-efficacy and the ability to create a better future for themselves. If you look at the individuals who are part of our staff at Bull City Forward or who are collaborating with us, we are extremely inclusive and have high levels of diversity built into our operating model. To develop homegrown talent, we have partnered with the Durham Public Schools and Durham's Office of Economic and Workforce Development. Additionally, BCF works in partnership with Duke, North Carolina Central University, UNC-Chapel Hill, and Durham Tech to support their social entrepreneurship programs through hands-on programming and projects with the local social enterprise community.

As we're building that talent pipeline, home growing it and recruiting it, then what do we do in terms of the venture-enabling? How do we take organizations from seed to scale, which is what we're focused on? Our second strategic cornerstone is *building community and breaking isolation*. We have all this entrepreneurial energy, but the challenge here is that most of our entrepreneurs are not connected to one another. They're often working in isolation. But if you plant thousands of entrepreneurial seeds and create an intertwined, integrated collaborative environment, those entrepreneurs will stay, they'll flourish, they'll grow, they'll create jobs, and they'll create impact. This idea of collaboration is so powerful. We use several strategies to build connections and robust support systems, including connecting high-growth entrepreneurs through peer leadership groups, coordinating feedback sessions, and connecting social entrepreneurs with the talent, networks, discounted services, and capital relationships to help them scale. Entrepreneurs also need access to cheap and flexible space to work from, have meetings, host events, and so on. You don't want to sign a twelve-, or twenty-four-, or thirty-six-month lease; it doesn't make sense at an early stage of growth. We provide that space, which has become the cornerstone of our community building efforts. The goal is to also plug our community into the broader national and global social entrepreneurship network. This includes developing a multicity ecosystem strategy in North Carolina as well as forging partnerships with organizations like the Hub, which has coworking spaces in twenty-five cities around the world.

As we grow, it's critical to *measure our impact* in terms of economic development and social impact. As I've noted already, we've had a substantial impact on Durham since our launch in 2010, and we expect our reach to grow. We are also seeing measurable social impact of our members in the fields that they serve, whether education, health care, transportation, food and nutrition, or the like. This is the beauty of social entrepreneurship—it drives economic growth and fuels innovation for positive good in our communities.

Armed with good data, we can then *educate and advocate* on behalf of our members. Forging partnerships with the city, county, and Chamber of Commerce as they determine their economic development investments and procurement strategies is critical. Public–private partnerships between government and the social enterprise sector can increase innovative approaches to addressing our community's most pressing needs while ideally increasing accountability and ultimately improving outcomes while decreasing long-term costs. Similarly, these positive stories of entrepreneurial impact become a good source for local and national media, which in turn increase awareness (and ultimately engagement) in the broader public. Again, we focus on our policy agenda and communications strategy in very intentional ways to help achieve these results.

We have much to learn and accomplish still in the field of social entrepreneurship. While the lessons described in the preceding pages are a start, they are far from an end point. One of the things holding us back in the social enterprise conversation is *scale*. We are chipping away but only on the margins of some very big, hard, thorny questions. How do we break through that scale question? I'm not convinced that scale is going to happen at individual organizational levels. We may have a couple of breakthroughs, but even at the individual level that's really, really difficult. What's ultimately going to happen is that we have to create movements. We have to go back to what happened with civil rights, for example, where there were a few organizations that were driving it, but ultimately it became something much more than individual organizations; it became a collaboration of individual organizations driving toward collective impact. Therefore, looking ahead, I'm really interested in the conversation around how we can create collaborative networks and how we can create movements out of these collaborative networks.

One of the most significant challenges we face as we look to deepen and scale social enterprise remains funding. As a sector, we face a few tough hurdles in this regard: The funding climate is the thinnest I have seen in more than twenty years of raising funds for various entrepreneurial ventures; social entrepreneurship is still a relatively nascent field, and our ecosystem approach is completely new; therefore we don't fit neatly into anyone's funding categories; and, in my direct experience, the majority of funders tend to be more interested in funding direct-service organizations instead of support organizations.

If we're serious about developing scaled solutions to social challenges that have staying power I believe we have to create robust support networks that cultivate collaboration and collective impact. It's going to require a shift of mind-set for the individuals, community leaders, and funders. If we can overcome this hurdle, I think we have a real shot at moving the needle on a number of really important issues for our economy and for our society and change our current trajectory in a very positive way.

## Note

1. George Bernard Shaw: "The reasonable man adapts himself to the conditions that surround him . . . The unreasonable man adapts surrounding conditions to himself . . . All progress depends on the unreasonable man" (From *Maxims for Revolutionists,* originally published 1903).

# SOCIAL ENTREPRENEURSHIP AND SOCIAL INNOVATION

## What's New, and Why Is It Important?

### Kriss Deiglmeier, Executive Director, Stanford Center for Social Innovation

I'm going to frame the evolution of social entrepreneurship and how it fits with social innovation in three parts. First, I will define each of these concepts and show their similarities and differences, which is important for the conversation going forward. Second, I will summarize a case study conducted by the Stanford Center for Social Innovation on emissions trading. By walking us through that, I will highlight some of the lessons we have learned about how contemporary social innovations have evolved and grown over the past thirty years. Finally, I will wrap up with some recommendations about what we need to think about for moving the field of social innovation into the future.

What is social entrepreneurship? Many individuals have done amazing things in this arena, such as Bill Drayton with Ashoka, Willy Foote with Root Capital, the famous Muhammad Yunus of the Grameen Bank, Mary Houghton with ShoreBank, and Matt Flannery, Jessica Jackley, and Premal Shah with Kiva. I am a big fan of Greg Dees at Duke University, who runs the Center for the Advancement of Social Entrepreneurship; I think his understanding of the fundamental characteristics of a social entrepreneur is the best out there. His research over the past twenty years has tried to highlight "what makes these individuals so unique"—because the fact is that we want more of these individuals. He says that, first and foremost, social entrepreneurs create and sustain social value. They relentlessly pursue new opportunities. They engage in a process of continuous innovation. They act boldly without being limited by resources. And they exhibit a heightened sense of accountability to the constituencies that they serve. So this is the foundational definition of a social entrepreneur that I follow.

The field of social entrepreneurship has been grounded in the *great man or woman theory,* on the individual, the leaders of the organization. It focuses on questions such as, How do we get more of these individuals? How do we think about their characteristics, and can we foster those, and can we educate for those? That's all very, very important. Building off the traditional entrepreneurship field, social entrepreneurship has also primarily focused on the start-up. That's a good thing, but there are also a lot of limitations when we're focused only on start-up organizations or new organizations launched by social entrepreneurs to drive social change. Social entrepreneurs traditionally also have focused on working within nonprofit structures. That's starting to change in the last five years, but if you really look at the people we're holding out as the great social entrepreneurs, fundamentally they're nonprofit social entrepreneurs.

Now we have a picture of the social entrepreneurs. So, what is social innovation? Social innovation is a novel solution to a social problem that is more effective, efficient, or sustainable than existing solutions and for which the value created accrues primarily to society as a whole, rather than to private individuals.

What is different about social innovation from social entrepreneurship is that the latter focuses on the ideas, the outcomes, the process, and the solutions for social value. We are looking at that bigger construct—the necessary actors, system dynamics, interactions, and evolution to drive positive social impact.

At the Stanford Center for Social Innovation a number of years ago, we undertook a study to look at contemporary social innovations over the past thirty years because we're aware that social innovations grow in the construct of the ecology that they're in at that time. We did some research with luminaries in the field and highlighted about fifteen that we felt had scaled to a level that they were having a meaningful impact that could provide valuable insights into how they developed. Examples of the ones we selected include charter schools, emissions trading, microfinance, individual development accounts, and fair trade.

One of the unique things that came up when we were doing this research was that there was a lot of debate about whether Google (that is, the innovation of search) is a social innovation. We decided that what was important for a social innovation is to have the public value first and foremost. Being based out of the business school at Stanford, we know that there are many business schools and many academic centers all trying to understand the field of *innovation* and how to drive innovation in companies. But there are very few doing good research to understand what propels' *social innovations* forward. We really thought it was important to have that distinction about public value over private value that differentiates innovations from social innovations. In sum, to be considered an innovation, a process or outcome must meet two criteria. The first is novelty; the second is improvement. There is nothing in the literature, definition, or criteria of *innovation* that even mentions public benefit, let alone claims that the innovation need serve a social or environmental "public" purpose. For myriad reasons, we believe it is important to differentiate social innovations from ordinary innovations because the world is already amply equipped to produce ordinary innovation—those like Google itself.

I anticipate that the distinctions between social entrepreneurs and social innovations are not yet fully crystalized. I hope that using a picture of a three-legged stool can help. If we think about a three legged-stool, the first leg is social entrepreneurship and those individuals who are driving the change, which we've discussed. As already mentioned, this leg of the stool is grounded in the great man or woman theory. The second leg is social capital. What has come forth in the past ten years is the question, "How does capital fit into all this?" Today we can all go to a myriad of "impact investing" conferences, where the emergence of the social capital market is in the forefront. Clearly, social capital is a necessary ingredient to drive social change. The third leg is social enterprise. Social enterprise as a construct has been grounded in the great organization theory: How do we have more social benefit organizations? The social enterprise field looks at business models. It's looking at the evolution of organizations, their structures and models. All three of these legs create social value, hence the word *social* in front of them. Using this framework as this relates to microfinance, you have Muhammad Yunus as the social entrepreneur; you have the Grameen Bank as the social enterprise; and of course the capital to fund it all. The primary question, however, that is paramount is, How do we get more microfinance—*the actual social innovation*? That's what we're really trying to grow. The individual is a piece of it, the organization is a piece, and capital is a piece of that, but how they fit together, how they interact, and when and how they evolve are really the fundamentals that we need to understand if we want to move the field of social innovation forward. So I hope that gives the broad view of the field.

With these distinctions set forth, I am going to now highlight three characteristics fundamental to the growth and evolution of social innovation. Some
of these are distinct from the other constructs we have discussed, and others
are similar. We identified these characteristics when we conducted our case
studies. First is inclusivity. As somebody who was in the field of social entrepreneurship in the early 1990s, before there was much of a "field," I observed
a sentiment circulating that "you're either in the social entrepreneurship club,
or you're out of the social entrepreneurship club." That provided some value
and momentum; specifically, it allowed the field to work hard to understand
how it is unique and what the characteristics are that underpinned successful
social entrepreneurs. However, it also created barriers in terms of growing
the field. With such a focus on the individuals who were creating their own
organizations, many important people, organizations, and entire sectors initially were not engaged. For example, in the early years of social entrepreneur
conferences, you would be hard pressed to find individuals from government
or business in attendance. In contrast, social innovation is very inclusive. For
example, in the climate change arena you've got actors ranging from Walmart
to the Environmental Defense Fund to Al Gore. Social innovation can and
does emerge from individuals, groups of people, and organizations from the
nonprofit, for-profit, and governmental sectors.

The second characteristic of a social innovation is an orientation toward solutions. Clearly this characteristic is fundamental to all of the legs of the stool:
the social entrepreneur, social capital, and social enterprise. The importance of
this characteristic is central to the long-standing debate about how social innovations differ from traditional innovations. As I mentioned, traditional innovation criteria are underpinned by novelty and improvement. Without public
benefit criteria, we can get innovations that often have serious negative social or
environmental consequences. For example, the innovation of deep-sea bottom
trawling has had a devastating negative environmental impact. Specifically, it
is estimated that 95 percent of damage to seamount ecosystems worldwide is
caused by deep-sea bottom trawling. In contrast, to be considered a social innovation, the innovation must aim to address social problems. I like to use
microfinance as an example, regardless of the challenges it's facing right now.
The fact is that there are 2.7 billion people without access to financial services.
Microfinance has served 154 million customers. There are 7,000 microfinance
institutions, and the repayment rate is somewhere between 95 and 98 percent.

This is a social innovation that's having an impact on real people in their lives, helping them to transition out of poverty. The field of social innovation is focused on trying to figure out how to create more of these opportunities.

The third element characterizing a social innovation is an emphasis on cross-sector collaboration. We live in an increasingly interconnected world, but in some cases there are more and more silos. To drive social innovations forward, it's going to be necessary to engage government, nonprofits, and businesses in new ways. As we looked at the successful social innovations, we saw that cross-sector collaboration underpinned all of them—at what stage and to what degree the interface among business, government, and nonprofit occurred varied. But in all cases, cross-sector collaborations and partnerships drove success.

So social innovations are inclusive, solution focused, and cross-sector oriented.

Now for the case study: In studying contemporary social innovations at Stanford, we've learned that using an "innovation continuum" is helpful for analyzing process and organizations. With this continuum, first you identify a problem. Second, you get people together to generate ideas for solutions, the idea-generation stage. Third, out of that idea-generation stage you settle on an innovation to pursue and move into the piloting and prototyping stage. Next you attempt to diffuse and scale it. I'll use this innovation continuum as the framework for discussing the case study.

The case concerns climate change and emissions trading, specifically what is now known as a cap-and-trade system. In cap and trade, a cap is set on which pollutants can go into the air, and a regulatory body then gives allowances to businesses and organizations for quantities they may emit. If they emit less than their allocation, they can sell those credits on the open market; if they emit more, they need to buy credits. This was a successful innovation in the United States addressing the problem of sulfur dioxide and acid rain. How did it all start?

In 1960s, nongovernmental organizations (NGOs) began raising awareness about the connection between health problems and poor air quality. This advocacy led to the Clean Air Act of 1970 (CAA) and the establishment of the Environmental Protection Agency (EPA). The launch of the EPA was a monumental event with a massive regulatory change, and it required air quality standards to be met by 1975. What happened next is interesting. In 1972, the U.S. Chamber of Commerce in conjunction with the smelting industry came up with the "bubble policy." The idea was to enable businesses to make major plant modifications and not have to comply with the strict New Source Performance Standards section of the CAA, if they offset the new emissions reductions elsewhere. But there was not a lot of traction with that idea at the time. The NGOs were against it, and the policy regulators didn't really know what to do or how to think about such a novel idea. By 1975, even with the EPA and the Clean Air Act, all states had missed their emissions requirements. It was pretty much a mess. In 1976, Jimmy Carter realized that not a lot was going on around this policy regulation and that there were many challenges. As we look at this picture, that's pretty much the idea-generation stage. There was a lot of fighting, a lack of trust, a lack of collaboration, and not a lot happening.

Starting in 1977, we moved on to the piloting and prototyping stage. Bill Drayton, the founder of Ashoka, came to the EPA and created a lot of momentum that eventually led to the cap-and-trade model for acid rain. Drayton came on as the EPA's assistant administrator, and he realized that one of the fundamental problems was that the government was acting like a regulator and not a partner. So, in 1979 he crafted another version of the bubble policy called the Alternative Emission Reduction Option, which allows banking of emission credits. Moreover, he realigned the whole staff of the EPA to partner with business, and they convened conferences together. They started working in a much more collaborative manner. This alternative emissions option was piloted. However, the NGOs would have nothing to do with it. They still didn't trust that working with business and letting them have "pollution credits" could be effective. The National Resource Defense Council (NRDC) and a number of nonprofit organizations launched a legislative battle with Chevron that held up the project. So while government and business actually were starting to work much better together, the NGOs were still playing a divisive role in terms of moving policy forward.

Next we moved on to diffusion and scaling. Remember that we started out in 1970. Twenty years later, we still had an acid rain problem arising from air pollution. President George H. W. Bush put forth the provision to deal aggressively with acid rain through new legislation. Prior to this, the NRDC had lost its legal battle against the bubble policy. Simultaneously, new organizations such as the Environmental Defense Fund were coming onto the field thinking they could work with business. A number of NGOs came to the table to write the new legislation, and, instead of being antagonistic, they accepted the direction in which things were going. The new acid rain policy was launched in 1990, and it called for the development of the first nationwide market for

emissions trading. To control sulfur dioxide emissions, air pollution regulation morphed into a market mechanism to control pollution. States and regions created their own policies. California had its own regional initiative,
which was quite effective, and the Northeastern states worked together, so
that by 1995 they had met their quotas on acid rain reduction. They had estimated that to accomplish this across the nation, it would cost $3 to $25 billion.
It came in at only $0.8 billion. By the end of the 1990s, all states had reached
100 percent compliance.

So what does this mean from a social innovation standpoint? Thinking about what I discussed earlier in terms of inclusivity, it took more than
twenty-five years for all of the right parties to come together to the table in a
spirit of trust, collaboration, and compromise. But the eventual result was legislation on which business could act, with which NGOs could work, and that
the public could applaud for helping to address a social problem in concrete
ways. There were also many changes that had to take place within the government to allow for better relations with business and NGOs. It was solution
oriented, and it was cross-sectoral in nature.

Returning to some of the other social innovations I mentioned: Charter
schools and fair trade had different trajectories but underwent the similar
processes to help them get to the next level.

What does this mean for the future? I started out mentioning some of the
social entrepreneurs in this series as individuals. But what we really want to
be talking about are their *social innovations*—new solutions. Mary Houghton's
idea at ShoreBank was about a new community banking system. The new idea
at Kiva is peer-to-peer lending. Willy Foote's idea at Root Capital is about
social investment funds. What we really need to be thinking about is how to
take these individual social entrepreneurs' ideas and scale them out as social
innovations more broadly.

Looking to the future, I have three recommendations for the field of social
innovation. One is never to mistake a clear view for a short distance. We've
seen over and over again the time frames that it takes to get social innovations
to a scale whereby they can have an impact; they're not short, and they're not
sexy. At the Stanford Center for Social Innovation, I see a lot of launch pads
and new hubs and incubators; I think those are all great, but what's really
going to make the difference is the long haul to get to scale. We've seen over
and over again that after the excitement of idea generation, piloting, and prototyping, people fall in the stagnation chasm. There are very few social inno-

vations that make it over that chasm. Why? What it takes as an organization to move from piloting and prototyping to diffusion and scaling is a different level of capital, a different level of talent, and a different level of tenacity than I think we are seeing right now. We are lacking in individuals ready to hang in there for the long haul. I think we're also lacking funders and other actors willing to go that long haul.

To give an example of the long-term perspective, look at Grameen Bank, which started in 1975. It took twenty years for it to really even make a dent in terms of reaching millions of people with loans. On the other hand, there's eBay, which exploded overnight. Everybody wants the next social innovation to evolve like eBay's innovation. But the fact is that there is no such thing when it comes to social innovation. I would say that Kiva (which facilitates peer-to-peer lending) is probably the closest to that right now. We need to focus on changing our mind-set to support that longer-term time frame. In doing so, we'll actually get social innovations to scale in a much more effective manner than if we keep jumping to the next new idea.

My second recommendation is that you find your "lever." As we've looked at different social innovations, we've seen that when we're at that piloting and prototyping stage, we're trying a bunch of different things, and that's all good. But there is usually one "lever"—one thing that helps the social innovation make it up that hill. Fair trade's lever was to focus on consumer demand—on changing consumers' awareness and buying patterns and making a product that's equal in quality to those produced without fair trade. In my talks with social entrepreneurs, I find that they usually do have a sense of their lever. But what they generally lack is the time to figure out how to make it work because they (or their funders) want change "in the next quarter." Yet sometimes it's going to take many years to see some momentum. For example, in his chapter, Willy Foote alludes to working differently with corporations when it comes to social investment funds. That might just be a new lever, as opposed to relying on nonprofit funding to make things go forward. On another front, an organization called B Lab is trying to change legislation around the country to allow companies to include a triple bottom line as they incorporate. Maybe that's the next lever for fair trade to evolve further. As legislation is changed to value more than financial returns, fair trade is poised to benefit from such changes.

My third recommendation is to internalize a cross-sector philosophy. Everyone is talking about it, but few people know how to do it. In a recent Google search I conducted, I found 129 million hits on business strategy, and

7 million on nonprofits and business partnerships. But cross-sector collaboration yielded only 509,000. This needs to be where academics, practitioners, and businesses go next. Social innovations over the past thirty years that have scaled show us that cross-sector collaboration is the key to success.

To close, as Bill Clinton said, "If we want to build a stronger, more sustainable world for future generations, one with more partners and fewer enemies, we have to work together."[1] We're all in the solution business, and the fact is that the solution business is complicated, the underlying causes are complex, and it's going to take hard work to drive those future solutions. It is going to take finding the lever. It is going to take being inclusive. I hope that books such as this one on social entrepreneurship and social innovation will motivate people to become engaged and act differently. Our future depends on it.

## Note

1. Clinton (2008).

# THE BLENDED VALUE IMPERATIVE

Jed Emerson, Founder, Blended Value

My role here is to explain my passion for social entrepreneurship and why I think differently about social entrepreneurship from some of the other contributors to this book. While thinking about this chapter, I came on a quote from Albert Einstein, who said, "Try not to become a man of success, but rather to become a man of value." As I think about social entrepreneurship, the issue for me is that too much of the conversation today focuses on the success of social entrepreneurship rather than what it is supposed to achieve in the world and what it's supposed to advance. Increasingly, I feel that, at the end of the day, what all of this is about is a question of value and value creation, and that social entrepreneurship is simply a means to an end. My fear is that in a lot of the discussions, debates, conferences, lectures, and teaching, we're basically losing our focus on the end in favor of a discussion of the means. It is important that we understand the means that we're applying, but after fifteen to twenty years of these discussions, maybe it's time we moved the conversation to another place. I think that place includes much more than simply social entrepreneurship.

When we talk about the evolution of the idea of social entrepreneurship, where it came from, and where it's heading, I think about the invention of the automobile. In the United States, if you ask the average American who invented the automobile, he or she will say, "Henry Ford." Of course, we all know that Henry Ford did not invent the automobile. He commercialized it and brought it to market and made it a part of American life, but in fact there were, around the world, literally dozens of people who were creating automobiles, creating the internal combustion engine, and figuring out different ways to work with this. So when I think of social entrepreneurship, I think of Bill Drayton from Ashoka as our Henry Ford. Bill is the one who really built Ashoka and promoted the concept of social entrepreneurship internationally, and he brought it back to the United States, where it did not actually have a base with Ashoka initially. While Bill was off "building the brand," if you will, a lot of people in the UK, the United States, Europe, and other places around the world were tinkering with ideas and were creating their own models of social entrepreneurship. As an example of this, two or three years ago I was going through some old papers, and I came upon the outline of a talk that I gave to the San Francisco Rotary Club in 1987 about our work at the Larkin Street Youth Services center. I thought that, as part of my appeal to the audience, I should speak in businesslike terms. So I described our work as a form of social entrepreneurship, without any awareness of what Bill was doing on the other side of the country and around the world or what other folks were doing.

When we talk about social entrepreneurship, there's an element of it that really does speak to a question of urgency. A lot of times when you hear people discuss social entrepreneurship, they talk about the role of business ideas, thinking, and practice being applied in a social application, and that that's what social entrepreneurship is about. I actually don't think so. When I was twenty-one and in my master's of social work administration program, we were taught from MBA textbooks. This was in the 1980s. We were taught that we had to take business management skills and use them for nonprofit management. So the idea that social entrepreneurship is simply about doing better management or something is wrong from my perspective. It doesn't really capture the passion or the potential of what social entrepreneurship really is about.

In my case, one of the reasons I left the Larkin Street Youth Services center in 1989 was that I had really become disenchanted with traditional nonprofit management, the way that human service organizations were managed, the way that philanthropy was executed, and the disconnect between the allocation of capital and the actual execution of strategy. I hope this is a little less so today than it was twenty years ago, but it felt as if traditional philanthropy was being done on the basis of politics and perception and persuasion and not on the basis of impact or value creation or change. I believed that at Larkin Street we were doing great work. We were serving kids no one else wanted to serve, and we were helping them get off the street, but at the end of the day we were being paid to serve people. We weren't really being paid to change the conditions on which they were brought to us. We weren't really incented to drive toward that goal. I think that a lot of traditional nonprofit management is really just that: It is management. It's not what I would consider to be more innovative, challenging, pathbreaking work because that's not what nonprofits really want to do. They want to serve people.

So I left Larkin Street and through a number of very humorous and amusing stories that I'll spare you here, I ended up working for George Roberts and Lyman Casey. Lyman was running a philanthropic consulting group, and George was a client. I really owe everything of the last twenty years of my career to George Roberts because basically here was a business guy who said, "I appreciate philanthropy, I appreciate charity, I appreciate the nonprofit sector, but the way this is done is not compelling for me as a business person. What I'm interested in is exploring how you could take more of an investment approach to philanthropy, as opposed to viewing it as a drive-by philanthropic act, where you simply write checks and get reports a year later." His challenge to come up with a different way to think about philanthropy opened up a whole exploration for me of different ways of thinking about how to engage in philanthropy and nonprofit work.

As part of that process, I began a six-month research initiative in the second half of 1989. Basically, I knew enough to know that the idea of taking a businesslike approach to social work or to philanthropy was not a new idea, that there was already community economic development, there were community change agencies in the 1960s; there were a whole bunch of existing models. So the question for me was not so much, "How do you think about this?" but, rather, how had other people thought about it, and how could we take some of these ideas and move them to another level without replicating the failures that other people had experienced in the past? I interviewed about 125 people, all of them experts in economic development, job training with homeless people, and a whole array of related things. At the same time that I was doing that metawork, I was also spending more and more time in other communities around the Bay Area. My background was with homeless youth, and I had had some exposure to homeless adults, the homeless job-training network, and that kind of thing. but I really spent time looking for folks who were doing more than providing services and who were really trying to look at a different vehicle for providing those services. One of my "a-ha!" moments came when I was interviewing a senior program officer with a major foundation that is not west of the Mississippi. I get in trouble every time I critique traditional philan-thropy because I always get zinged by somebody who reacts with, "You don't understand all this stuff." Anyway, this was a big foundation with lots of ex-perience and expertise. I was interviewing this guy, telling him what we were looking to do. Early on in the conversation, I can still remember him saying, "If there's one thing we know about nonprofits after thirty years of practice and experimentation, it's that they cannot run business enterprises. So don't put your money into this whole idea. Focus on job-training programs, because that's really where the action is if you want to have an impact on homeless people's lives." It was just really interesting, because I thought, "Wow, it must be really nice to be so confident"—especially in the context of homelessness in the 1980s, where it was pretty clear that we did not know anything. There was still, as there are today, numerous challenges. The strategies were not effective, and the idea that this person sitting in his nice office in a large glass complex could lecture me on ignoring this whole other idea was just intriguing.

At that point I was far enough into the research to have met a whole num-ber of people who had said, "Nobody is employing our clients, so we have to create opportunities for them. When they fail, we have to ensure that they're not going to fail back to the street, but that they fail back to the coun-seling room or whatever the program intervention is. That's what we have the possibility to do here." I was really struck by the fact that these people who understood the big picture were not the majority of the people in the homeless-services network. They were not quite marginalized within that net-work, but they weren't really viewed as central to the strategy of how to ad-dress homelessness. Again, most of the focus at that time was on job-training programs, and they were based on the Job Training Partnership Act (JTPA). Basically the JTPA strategy was that we put someone into a classroom, we taught that person about a new job, and he or she graduated in about thirty days and got a job. The problem, as one of our investees described it, is that we had thirty-day training programs but a thirty-month need. For formerly homeless folks, it wasn't so much the job that they needed, it was supported employment, mental health training and support, substance abuse support, reconnection with family, and learning how to reengage on a personal basis with people. It was about rebuilding the entire space of what somebody's life was about. The job was simply a means to that end.

What struck me as the "a-ha!" point was that here was a segment of the employment market that the mainstream market didn't see and grossly undervalued. From the traditional businessperson's perspective, you could see how that would be, because as far as he or she was concerned, the homeless person had no value; that person didn't show up to work on time, he or she had too many barriers to employment, we had to do too many things to keep that person engaged in the work setting. From a business perspective, perhaps he or she had no value; but from a social entrepreneurial perspective, we could say, "Maybe that work environment didn't fit his or her potential and skill level, but what are the possibilities for that person to actually contribute to the creation of value in an enterprise context? What might it look like if we had the right kind of business structure to plug him or her into?" So we began experimenting with this. We basically spent about four years in what was in essence an R&D position, in which we did not do any publicity around what we were doing. We had no press conferences. When George and Leanne first endorsed this initiative, they made an $8 million commitment, and my response, again, coming out of the previous reality of how to promote our work, was to say, "We need to have a press conference about this, because this is a big deal." I knew enough to know that this idea of creating businesses to employ formerly homeless folks was not necessarily top-of-the-mark for a lot of folks. George's response was, "Instead of telling people what we're going to do, why don't we execute, and then we can show people what we've done? That's the point at which you would engage folks."

One of the problems with how social entrepreneurship has evolved is that too many people on both sides of the checkbook promote strategies that actually have not been tested, have not really proven themselves; and they're more vaporware than actually demonstrated, effective, impactful approaches to working with communities in need or to creating change. We went through that whole process and then realized that we did have a different way to think about this. We realized that we couldn't engage in traditional philanthropy. We couldn't make a grant on the basis of a proposal and come back six or twelve months later to assess performance against that proposal because they didn't know what they were doing and we didn't know what we were expecting. We didn't have that option to follow a traditional grant-making approach. So early on we began to hold monthly meetings with the executive directors and the business managers of the enterprises into which we were putting money. We began creating a learning circle among the people in whom we were investing. We would invest in business strategies, but then we would allow for modification on literally a weekly basis, based on what the actual experience was in executing the strategy. For almost all of the enter-prises—whether it was Rubicon, Juma, or any of the other organizations that we funded—where we ended up was just not where we thought we were going to be when we started. We had to have a different way to engage.

The other piece to this is that I had no formal training in philanthropy. I would hear these other program officers talking about the board meetings, and they would basically spend months writing the dockets that would go be-fore the board; everything would stop at the foundation while the staff wrote up everything, and then they would take these things to the board. You would have literally a thirty-page write-up that none of the board members would have read. They would just look at the paragraph summary, listen to the pre-sentation of the program officer, and give a *yay* or a *nay*. In my first meeting with George, I basically did that. I walked in with a notebook with maybe forty or fifty grants that I wanted us to make, and I think we got through three or four. He stopped me and said, "I really appreciate all the work you've done." He gave me all these nice little compliments so I wouldn't be com-pletely crushed, and then he said, "But you know, honestly, I have no idea if this group should get $50,000 or $500,000. As far as I'm concerned, this is an investment fund, and you're my fund manager. I'm going to put money in this account on a regular basis, and it's your job to make the allocations in the investments. Then I'll hold you accountable for performance over time. We'll meet three times a year, and you'll tell me how we're doing, and we'll have a discussion about what's not working and what's working, and then we'll go from there." So in the monthly meetings that I would have with the execu-tive directors, we would have made an initial seed investment, and then when stuff came up—and stuff always comes up; something breaks, or we need to hire one more support person, or whatever it is—I would literally pull out this humongous leather-bound checkbook, open up this thing, and write the checks in the meeting. I would just say, "Here's $10,000. Go deal with that." "Here's $50,000. Let's do that." It just worked. It was much more dynamic. It was much more engaged. It put us, as investors, in the middle of the process, and it also communicated to the investees that we were not going to sit back and watch them spin. Again, at the risk of being really snooty or snarky, I have to stress that a lot of philanthropy has got this "let a thousand flowers wither" approach. So we'd rather make a lot of grants, because we can go into a room, everybody wants to talk to us, and it's all very exciting. Instead, we were shift-ing the conversation to say, "I think these six flowers over here should die, and we shouldn't have anything to do with them, and these over here aren't ready to go anywhere yet, but, boy, this set right here, let's put a ton of focus and emphasis on really trying to make them go somewhere." We had spent four years working with forty to fifty organizations in the greater Bay Area around these issues in a variety of ways. We weeded out the majority, selected maybe ten, and we made bigger grants to those organizations. Our minimum grant was in the neighborhood of $150,000, and then we would augment that with capital investments for different parts of the business strategies in which we were involved. We scaled for depth. We did not say that we were going to be in five cities in five years. We didn't do that kind of scaling up and out because we were interested in scaling down for deeper value and impact with the groups in which we really believed within this area. I think that, again, that was a kind of "a-ha!" shift because it took us out of the conversation of competition with international foundations and going to the council or foundation meeting and trying to impress everybody with the quality of our work; we just did not care because they were not relevant to what we were doing. It gave us a level of freedom to "fail forward" in our processes that I don't think we would have had if we had had a big press announcement talking about what we've done and how great it is or any number of other things that you see now in traditional philanthropy.

The other part of it that was really different was that we made a real investment with intellectual capital. Basically, George's attitude was, "It's okay if you come back and something didn't work, but I need to understand *why* it didn't work, and you need to be able to enunciate for me what the take-away was. Because if you blew $150,000 on whatever, we have got to get something for that. At least, give me something." So when we published our first book on social entrepreneurship in 1996, the best part of the book was these short cases on each of the investees, and the last page had "10 Things I Really Wish I'd Known Before I Blew This Cash." It was fun. It wasn't flip; it was a genuine and open inquiry. It really shifted how we thought about what we were doing because I wasn't in the position of having to defend my grant making. I was in the position of being involved in a process of investing in change, and change is dynamic; you get things other than what you thought you were going to get. This open conversation puts you in a position to speak truth to power, both upward and downward. With our grantees, I was able to have a fundamentally different relationship with them, to talk about and explore the nature of the work that they were doing and how we were engaged with them. It opened up a whole new level of deeper, better relationships with those investees, and it also positioned us in a much different way to speak to other foundations about what we were doing.

Today a lot of these ideas are commonplace, but when we started pushing the envelope on metrics and performance measurement, at the time, foundations would say, "We invest for social returns." I would say, "Wow, that's really great. What's the methodology? How do you actually track that?" They would say, "Oh, no, no; it's a metaphor." So we actually took that as a very serious issue, and we created one of the first formalized methodologies around social return on investment; we really invested financially in building the information-system capacity of the groups to be able to track performance and impact, so that, as an investor, we could look at that and use it as a baseline to measure the performance of our capital. This set off a whole series of explorations in this intersection, kind of the muddy middle, and brought me onto this other side of the same conversation with groups that were for-profit organizations.

Around this same time, in the late 1980s and in the 1990s, more and more social venture network-type businesses were being launched, organizations that were for-profit but wanted to pursue profit with purpose. I began spending more time with those folks, and, as I was in those discussions, I realized that, at the end of the day, all of these people were talking about what was to my mind fundamentally the same thing. They were talking about understanding value as not an *either-or*, but rather a *both-and*. When they were thinking about value, they weren't limiting themselves by thinking that, because they were in a for-profit, they couldn't or shouldn't consider social or environmental factors. Or, if they were in a nonprofit structure, they were thinking about the performance that they were trying to achieve in terms of some level of economic performance and responsibility and discipline, and they were integrating these things intuitively. These organizations were finding that there were shortfalls in institutional structures—how we think about the corporate structure of a for-profit versus a nonprofit. They were trying to transcend that, and they were finding limitations to this categorization. It was at that point that I began looking at blended value as a concept. At the end of the day, I'm really agnostic in terms of the delivery vehicle. I don't care if it's a nonprofit or a for-profit or a hybrid or cooperative structure, because that's just a shell game. You can have nonprofits with a wholly owned for-profit subsidiary, for-profits with support organizations; you can do all kinds of things. Especially today, you can do a lot more than you could do years ago. The point isn't so much whether you are nonprofit or for-profit but rather how you manage for maximum value and impact as a leader. How do we create organizations that can capture as much of their value potential as possible? How do we assess extra financial value and performance as part of the process of running an organization, and how do we drive that assessment into decision-making within the firm—whether, again, it's a nonprofit or for-profit? How do we think about capital structure? How do we think about capital as a continuum from zero-interest, zero-return philanthropic capital to concessionary-rate, below-market capital to commercial-market, market-rate-and-above capital? How do we think about the enabling environment that's required, the infra-structure of the organizations, the regulations, the policies, the law, to really make this whole ecosystem thrive, as opposed to this artificial bifurcation that forces us to either "do good or do well" as opposed to simply maximizing the value of the organizations that we're with?

As I think about social entrepreneurship, I believe that there really is no single definition of social entrepreneurship. It is simply a flow across a matrix of a variety of different forms and themes and manifestations, if you will. That goes from social enterprise to civic innovations. It goes across nonprofit to for-profit to hybrid mixes. It goes through a variety of different capital and equity structures in which, for example, people now are doing a convertible form of a private return investment. We can take a below-market-rate loan from a foundation, and we put it into an organization. If it performs and hits certain benchmarks, it flips to equity. On the backside, if it doesn't, we write it off as a grant. That's a pretty innovative kind of structure. There is a variety of ways to think about social entrepreneurship. We really limit ourselves by drawing the boundaries too firmly and spending so much time debating how many social entrepreneurs can dance on the head of a pin. It really doesn't matter, because it's just not the question.

Another thing that I've really become aware of, especially in the last three to five years as a lot of the social networking platforms have started to really come into their own, is that social entrepreneurship is fundamentally a "glo-cal" activity. It is a global phenomenon that manifests itself locally around the world. It looks different in East Africa from East Harlem, and that's okay. The idea that somehow we have to come up with one definition that fits everybody hasn't been my experience. I have spent a lot of time writing papers on, "What is social entrepreneurship?" Nobody pays any attention. They go and do what-ever they want because they're entrepreneurs, right? Recently Muhammad

Yunus made a call for standardizing social entrepreneurship. He wants to put a salary cap on what social entrepreneurs are paid. He wants to have standards of performance for who can call him- or herself a social entrepreneur. I have no idea how he thinks he's going to enforce any of this. But it's striking to me because it simply reflects his perspective and his normative or moral posture with regard to who we should be as social entrepreneurs. I think that Muhammad is going to be really disappointed because it just doesn't work that way. I also think that we've got this whole issue of the millennial promise where we've got these twenty-somethings who are kind of bubbling up, and much as I hate to say it as an early-fifties person, I look around and I'm bemused at how ossified our networks, our thinking, our structures have become as we've aged. It's just really funny because I see them bumping up against the stuff that we created to be entrepreneurial and innovative. Guess what, kids? We're not so entrepreneurial and innovative anymore. We're managing big budgets; we have mortgages and kids to put through college. We want some consistency and regularity in our life; twenty-somethings, not so much. I think the impact of their leadership coming up is going to be very profound.

What it all boils down to is that there's a lot of conversation around the blurring of the sectors. It's like we're in a car, and the car is social entrepreneurship, and we're bombing down the road; we look out, and everything's blurry going by us. We think the only reason it is blurry is because we're not wearing the right glasses. But it's because we're in the wrong car. If we get out of the car, and we stand on the bluff and look at the traffic, it's not blurry. We can really see who's moving, what lanes they're in, and where they're going. It's a very different perspective.

I'll end where we began, with my own version of Albert Einstein's comment: Try not to become a person of success, but rather, try to become a person of deep impact and blended value. Ultimately that's what we're trying to do. We can call it whatever we want, we can teach it however we like, but it's got to be broad and comprehensive and a big-tent vision about what it is that we're doing, because it is simply the means to an end, and it's the end that matters.

## THE THINKERS

### A Conversation

Shapiro: There are several themes that have surfaced over the course of the chapters and discussions: the blurring of the demarcation between profit and nonprofit, the notion of scale and how it brings about social change and innovation, and measurement and efficacy. I would like to focus on these in our discussion. With terms such as *social enterprise, social innovation,* and *social entrepreneurship,* there is quite a bit of variation in thinking about the role of money and profit. Can you help us to think this through?

Gergen: Money is important, and ultimately I think that we are moving in a direction where you are finding more and more companies become socially responsible and more and more nonprofit organizations recognizing the fact that earned income is a critical path to sustainability and ultimately to scale. We've got to get to a point where we can't rely on philanthropy; we have to rely on market-based solutions for a number of different things. I'm going to be fascinated to see if there are increasing relationships and partnerships between for-profit companies and nonprofit organizations, almost to the point of a merger or acquisition. For example, if you are a for-profit company that wants to dramatically increase your social impact in a particular area, does it make sense to take on a nonprofit, or consolidate a number of nonprofit organizations, and begin to invest in that and figure out a way that it can begin to generate revenues back? It's a model that I haven't seen yet, but I think it's coming down the pike.

The other thing that really needs to happen is that much more rigor needs to be put into place in a lot of nonprofit organizations with which we work, and they need better strategies for earned income. All of that said, that access to capital is critical. That's the reason I was talking about the social innovation fund; there is a big valley of death between the friends-and-family round, where you go hit up everybody to get a little bit of cash to start your organization, and getting any traditional financing. We've got to solve that valley. We've got to put a couple of oases into the mix.

Deiglmeier: It really depends on the need you are addressing and the type of intervention that would most likely work. Let's take a look at companies that have base-of-the-pyramid products. I think that in the field right now, sometimes there's a debate that I find somewhat paternalistic, as if, "We're just selling things to poor people." Why should I be able to have something and somebody not who is at a lower income level? So I don't want to get into the moral debate around consumerism at the base of the pyramid, but they are a constituency that wants to move out of poverty. Commerce is going to play a piece of that, and I think we can leverage that. An example right now is Unilever, the woman who runs its soap division. If you can get people at the base of the pyramid to wash their hands more, you're having a major impact on health in those communities. I believe from what I've read that the for-profit model for that particular intervention is the best strategy versus a nonprofit model. Again, nonprofits can do things around an education piece, but actually getting the product to the people at the right price that is affordable—Unilever is in a good position to do that. There can be social innovations at the base of the pyramid that can really improve people's lives.

I think that we're at the early stages of figuring out these new models. For-profit social-purpose businesses still have a lot to learn, and we're going to try some things, and then we'll also have some failures along the way. Specifically answering your question, I think that first, you really need to look at your mission, and you need to prioritize what is important in terms of the earned-income stream versus your social mission. For example, when we were at Juma Ventures, we were a nonprofit and had these for-profit subsidiaries. Some of those subsidiary businesses had earned-income streams, but the mission was such that some of those businesses lost money, and we were okay with that. We never could have existed as a for-profit entity because we made a decision that the social mission would always be first. So you've got to look at the mission, and then you've got to look at what your capital requirements are. Jump ahead to think past that idea generation of how you would scale your organization or scale your idea. That might lead you to a different decision. For us at Juma it made the most sense to be a nonprofit with these for-profit subsidiaries.

I think we're starting to learn more about these structures, but, as it is right now, they're very individually based. Looking at your mission, what are you trying to achieve? Who are you going to serve? Where are you going to get capital? What are your opportunities for scaling? On a personal level, I definitely believe wholeheartedly that we have to engage business differently and that for-profit social purpose businesses are important and can be of huge value to address social problems. I also believe in really strong, traditional nonprofits, and not everything should be for-profit. We need all of those as part of the solution.

Shapiro: Jed, is that "blended value"?

Emerson: We have to go back continually to the touchstone of what it is that we're really trying to do. I think that there are very few people who, at the point of death, are going to look back over the trajectory of their life and say, "Wow, look at how much money I made." They're not going to say that. Money is almost always a means to an end, even for people who just use it as a marker for social success and dominance in the business community. It's a social vehicle, a social construct. Currency is a social construct. So the idea that somehow there's this objective econometric world and then there's this social namby-pamby environmental world is just wrong. We know this, but what happens is that, the older we get, the more we get tracked, and we're forced to decide. You either go into business, or you go into the nonprofit or public service sectors, and there you go. You're just off to the races. I really don't care what the real language is as long as the point is that the purpose of organizations is to try to maximize the value that they have the potential to create. The purpose of capital is basically to drive value through organizations and in markets. The nature of capital itself is fundamentally whole. It is nondivisible. It is not triple bottom line, which is a great way to track as you go, but, ultimately, if you don't reintegrate the value proposition into a whole, you're left with the finance people looking at the numbers and the nonprofit people looking at your sustainability report. That's just the wrong way to go. We need to think about all of this on a more integrated, holistic basis. That's blended value.

Shapiro: Can you give us an example of a business or project that epitomizes "blended value"?

Emerson: Not to punt, but I'm not sure that there is a truly comprehensive example. I think that a lot of different people are grappling with different parts. I still don't see the whole, and I don't see the execution at the level I'd want to see. Having said that, I think of Patagonia, which basically says, "We're going to innovate in terms of sourcing and supply-chain management, and we're going to create products that actually are recycled Coke bottles, and we're going to sell that to consumers. And guess what? We're actually going to go put a cap on our profit targets because we don't want to grow endlessly. That's cancer. That's not success." For Patagonia, they're saying, "We want to grow in a certain way. We want to be a sustainable corporation." So they're practicing in that way. I would just hold them out; I'm just looking for a company that treats its people well in a demonstrative way that they can report out on, that sources in an ethical way. I'm looking for some broader sense of a vision around what the firm should be. I think about, for example, Pioneer Human Services in Seattle, which runs maybe $40 to $50 million a year in billings with Boeing and a whole host of other companies, and it provides supported housing to formerly homeless folks in the greater Seattle area and supported employment. It's a nonprofit, but it's got all kinds of economic value that it's capturing, and it's creating a true and deep social impact for a community of people basically nobody was paying attention to twenty years ago—or, in their case, maybe forty years ago. I think there are different examples we could explore, but I think this is part of the point, that the triple bottom line helps you analyze performance toward an end, but I don't know that you ever attain the end because, if you attain the end, then you do that in death. Does that make sense? So when I die, I will fully be so whole, and I will transcend to the blended-value heaven.

Shapiro: Kriss, is that what you think about in terms of social innovation and the role of the corporation?

Deiglmeier: When we're looking at the companies, some of them are doing traditional corporate responsibility efforts, but I do think Walmart provides us with a helpful example. Through its supply chain, it is really driving social innovations forward, working with NGOs and partners and using technology in new, innovative ways that have really reduced their carbon footprint. I think in particular with Walmart, as it's going deeper into the supply chain, it's starting to work with governments in countries. It has a robust experience of working with NGOs. You need to include those as you're thinking. What are some other companies? I think there's Nike, which is doing some really innovative work around cradle-to-cradle thinking for all of its products.

Shapiro: By "cradle-to-cradle," you are referring to the concept of total recycling of materials so that no waste is created, yes?

Deiglemeir: Yes, Nike has been working on it for ten years. It's at step one; it's still in its idea-generation phase. But if a company such as Nike can start thinking differently—like every shoe would be recycled, and they'll go back into playgrounds and start working with NGOs differently—there's huge opportunity for social innovation through those companies.

I have just returned from China. Going there, one realizes that the role of business is too large to not aggressively work in a collaborative manner to solve the social problems. They *have* to be a partner. I fundamentally believe there's no other choice. There's a huge role for NGOs, and that's critically important, too; but we've got to move past this stage of "the NGOs are good, and business is bad" to think about how we pull together these entities differently?

Shapiro: Christopher, what is the difference between a social entrepreneurial organization and just an effectively and well-managed nonprofit organization?

Gergen: I think the key differentiator tends to be that of innovation. If you look at Greg Dees's definition of social entrepreneurship, first and foremost you have to be focused on creating social value. Two, you have to be relentless about pursuing new innovative solutions to be able to take on some of the hardest challenges. I think that if it is an effective, well-managed organization, there are quibbles about whether you're innovative or not; if you're relentless in pursuing that, then, yes, you're a social entrepreneur. I'm not precluding, by the way, that there are some very well-established 100-year-old social entrepreneurial organizations or organizations that could become more socially entrepreneurial. You also are operating in resource-constrained environments, and you don't mind going for it if you feel like you don't have the cash to be able to pull it off. Then, finally, you are holding yourself accountable for results, and you've got very clear assessments along the way. So if that effective, well-managed nonprofit organization is doing all of those things, then they're social entrepreneurs.

Shapiro: Kriss, would you say that the next social innovation is when the social change becomes a new paradigm or has brought about systemic change?

Deiglmeier: I think social innovation has the potential to lead to systemic change, but we need to differentiate between incremental and radical social innovation. I also don't want to leave the incremental social innovation not getting resources and discussion, too. Yes, the ultimate goal is systemic change, and we should all shoot for that, but sometimes you need incremental social innovation on the route to get there. For Sally Osberg and Skoll's definition of social entrepreneurship, the whole ecology changes. There are not too many examples of this. At some level you do a disservice to set the bar too high; that is too unrealistic. So I think you set the vision and the goal out there, but, along the way, it may come in blocks, it may ebb and flow, and we want to be inclusive of that, also.

Emerson: Every once in a while there's somebody that's truly revolutionary, but that once in a while is like every forty years or something. So most business strategies are incremental improvements, they're not blinding innovations that just scream success. So find people in business who have already built the kind of enterprise that you're trying to create, and co-opt them into your process, and nine times out of ten—because you're just a little start-up or something like that—they won't even take you seriously anyway, so you don't need to worry that they're going to rip off your great idea or go make millions at your expense.

One thing that has struck me over the years is that a lot of businesspeople just slave away to build their enterprise and their company, and hardly anybody ever asks them anything about their experience, what they've learned, or any of this kind of stuff. You'd be shocked at what some of these folks will tell you about how to be successful in their business. I've been floored by that. Getting those people into social ventures and for-profits with a mission is really critical, I think, not only to the success of the enterprise, but to building the broader space, which is, again, what we should be focused on. All of these enterprises, all of these investments, all these strategies—I'm happy that everybody's figuring out ways to do well and to do good, but, ultimately, we have to take care of each other, and we have to be more committed to building the commons as opposed to the garden. That's really what a lot of what I'm trying to say is about. I also think it's important to just step back and recognize the things that have been learned before and try to bring those forward and position yourself in a way so you can hear what people are discovering today. We can put these together into creating whatever it is that's yet to come.

Shapiro: Do you feel that measurement and the metrics around social change and innovation have evolved? What else needs to happen in thinking about success and efficacy?

Emerson: When I talk to certain practitioners, I think, "Wow, I can't believe we're having these conversations, and we've come so far." When I read *The Chronicle of Philanthropy*, I'm phenomenally depressed. There was recently an op-ed piece about how we should just give up on this whole metrics and measurements thing because it's just a failure, and we should just fund from the heart. I was thinking to myself and actually posted a comment to the guy who wrote it: Look, it's not a question that, gosh, metrics are bad or having no metrics is good; it's a question of *appropriate* metrics, it's a question of applying them well in the right situations. It's a question of understanding the domain in which you're applying those metrics and what the relative bar is for what we know about how to measure stuff. It's a question of understanding the difference between measuring an intervention strategy and tracking the performance and the fidelity to the execution of that strategy as you go to scale.

We really owe it to ourselves to stop wrapping ourselves in this cloak of righteousness and basically saying, "We're here for the kids, so there must be some good somewhere." Too many people confuse intent with impact. They think that because they mean well something must be working somewhere here, and we're all good people, so of course it's working. If you want to spend fifty years of your life in that kind of game, great. You have a really good annual report and another great picture of a kid on the cover, but at the end of the day—I'm sorry if I'm cynical—that's just not enough. Getting a smiling face or a hug from a child is great, but if I've got like 20,000 kids who die every day of preventable diseases in this world, one picture isn't going to cut it. We've got to raise the bar and be more aggressive, and we've got to hold ourselves accountable to raise the conversation to a better level. Discussions that simply say, "It's bad" or "It's good" do nothing to advance the conversation. It's shameless that people are still allowed to bring it down to this level, when in fact after twenty or thirty years of pretty deep exploration and discussion, we know so much more about how to be effective in the application of metrics than these discussions would reference.

Deiglmeier: At the Center for Social Innovation, we definitely care about this work, and what we have found is that there's traditional measurement on your nonprofit, and your impact has to be tailored. Are you in health? Are you in education? What I think is important is that you need to align the measurement with the stage of your organization. So if you're in the idea-generation stage, pick a couple things you're going to measure. Don't kill yourself on some huge evaluation methodology of interviews, because what you think is going to be your intervention is likely going to change. You need to do your best guess, your hypothesis, do it quickly, and then through your idea-generation stage you get to piloting and prototyping; you need to move to be a little bit more rigorous and start thinking in a more systemic and deep manner around measurement. Then, if you're really going to go to diffusion and scaling, you had better be investing heavily in measurement.

What I get frustrated with is that nobody differentiates the stage of innovation aligned with measurement. I shouldn't say *no one*; I should say a number of foundations and investments put everybody together, and that does a disservice for what they're requesting in terms of impact. It really does a disservice to the organizations both from a resource allocation standpoint and the ability to innovate and continually improve. So we can hope that response will be to align your measurement with the stage at which you are as an organization.

Shapiro: Jed, throughout this series and in a lot of the literature and when we think about social entrepreneurs, it's almost this Lone Ranger out there with his or her idea, changing the world. The entrepreneurs, however, often take issue with this metaphor. Louise Packard, for example, argues that you must embed yourself in the community and work with all of the groups that are already in the community. What are your positions on this?

Emerson: Again, it's not going to surprise you. We've fallen into this deification of the individual in a way that's really destructive because what you do is celebrate the social entrepreneur; you don't celebrate the team, you don't celebrate the organization, you don't celebrate capacity building, you don't celebrate a whole host of things that are critical to execution. For me, personally, I went through a period where I had been here in the Bay Area working and doing all this work. I ended up moving to rural Colorado and doing a lot of my work from there. There was this point—and I can't remember exactly what set it off—when I suddenly realized that the pinnacle of my career had led me to live by myself in the woods. I thought, "Something's wrong here." I went off-track. I'm really thinking more and more that it's less about innovative ideas and thinking and more about effective execution and management of total resources toward an end, and that that's the fundamental challenge and issue that people have. The trick is that for years we were thinking the wrong way about what that end was. Now we've got too many people with too many great ideas. They're going to change everything. I don't know how many of you were in the Bay Area in the late 1990s leading up to the Internet bubble, but there was the concept of vaporware, where basically companies had raised a first round and spent it down, so they had to go out and raise it again. One of the ways they did it was to say, "We've got this great second version coming out, and this is why you should give us the venture money for the second round," but there really wasn't anything. There were a bunch of engineers just sitting there, typing away. I think we kind of have some of that, where we've got these individuals with the pressure to be perceived as innovative, and we end up with people rebranding concepts and ideas and practices that ten years ago were already being used and put into effect, but for some reason that concept is not as snappy or something. Blended value, integrated value, now shared value: same fundamental ideas but just marketed and packaged in a different way for a different audience for a different end. I think we need to just kind of pause, and, yes, we're all very talented and innovative.

I don't believe any of these people who stand up and say, "Wow, our strategy is so good," like, "Look at what we've done." I'm thinking, "What about the other 2 billion people who are not touched by your 300-person outreach program?" We are so focused on what success looks like, and I understand that. We have got to do that—keep people excited. But, at the end of the day, many of these issues are still going to be here, and, if we make incremental progress, I'll be pretty happy. If we can just save a couple of polar bears, I'll be pleased. Let's just say that right now. We're all very proud of ourselves. Let's just get back to work and execute, because that's really the tough part.

Deiglmeier: If I'm stranded on an island, I want to be with the social entrepreneurs because they're so resourceful. But as we look at the structure of the world now—I'm not saying this is a social innovation but rather an example of why you need to work with existing organizations—Walmart has done more for sustainability via its supply chain than many social entrepreneurs I know in the environmental field. So to move the social innovations forward, we have to work with those existing organizations and pockets because they have the footprint, they've got the resources, and usually they've got the strength to move things forward more quickly than that start-up organization.

Gergen: I do think that everyone has the capability of being a change-maker. If I didn't believe that I wouldn't be doing the things that I'm doing now. I'm working actively to try to awaken young people to the possibility of being problem solvers in their communities and trying to take things on. Now, does that mean that everyone needs to be an entrepreneur? I don't think so. We don't need another 1,100 nonprofit organizations. We need really sharp, innovative, awakened, resourceful, accountable individuals out there trying to make the world better.

Shapiro: Kriss, there's a lot of energy around social entrepreneurship and social innovation now. As an individual who's going to go make a difference in the world, if you say it's going to take thirty years, and people may or may not know that you were the cog in the wheel that moved this forward, what does that do for the energy and the appeal to primarily young people to move into the field—your students, for example?

Deiglmeier: It's hard to say, "Be a cog in the wheel, woo hoo!" Especially when you're in Silicon Valley. But there's also the importance to talk about the truth and the reality. I think people are starting to question a little bit about the heroic social entrepreneur now, and I think that's okay to do, and it's okay to think about systems and about execution as the driver for social innovation. The bigger question or solution is, Can somebody make that sexy? I sometimes feel like the challenge we all face is that everybody wants sexy and new, but, solving social problems, we haven't had those successes in the past. There's not that sexy or new thing. It takes a different mind-set, a different toolbox to do that. So, to answer your question, I would say I don't necessarily know the answer. Students, young people—you can move them to act, and if they want to do it in a social entrepreneurial way, that's great; they're adding value. At the Center, we were very deliberate in picking social innovation. It was funny, because when I got there people were saying, "You should be the Center on Social Entrepreneurship." I pushed back and said, "No, we are the Center on Social Innovation, and here's how they're different." If we can raise the awareness of the value that social innovation provides and raise awareness of the benefit of working within organizations, and you can see that impact, we can hope that will be just as sexy as the social entrepreneur. I do know of those individual cases of the woman who thought, "Should I be a social entrepreneur, or should I go into the soap division at Unilever?" She literally looked at the calculation and said, "I have the potential to have a much bigger impact as an individual working within this large corporation." So it doesn't always have to be new. If we can raise the importance of the impact piece, raise the importance of the level of community and multiple individuals, I hope we can get more people to do that just as much as they want to do the new thing.

# SECTION 4

# THE CHAMPIONS

Elevating the Discourse to Global Dimensions

# COLLABORATIVE ENTREPRENEURSHIP

The Way to the "Everyone a Change-Maker" Society

Bill Drayton, Founder, Chairman, and CEO, Ashoka

I want to make a request: Please give your imagination a stretch, because we're going to go on quite a fast trip, and you're going to need those imaginations. This is not a trip to an imaginary place; this is a trip to our future, which is coming very, very fast. It's going to change what all of us do—and the skills we need. Whatever institution you're a part of will have to be managed and led and organized differently. The main thing that I hope we can do together now is journey into that future. However, first let me share with you a little bit about Ashoka and the learning process we've been through. It will help you understand the larger picture.

Start by imagining a nineteen-year-old young American in India. That person was not made by God for football and thought that Latin and math were tortures with no redeeming charm or utility, but he rather liked starting things and had been affected by the U.S. civil rights movement. There in India, ideas became realities; statistics became people and friends. There was a 100-to-1 difference in average per capita income between America and India at that point. What would you do about that? That was the question that I had, and that's where Ashoka came from.

What is the most powerful force in the world? It's pretty clear: It's a big, pattern-change idea, but only if it's in the hands of an entrepreneur. It is that combination that moves the world.

With that insight, Ashoka was born. Its first and core objective is to help more entrepreneurs dealing with the world's problems get started and succeed and come together in a powerful community of mutual help and collaboration. It turns out that that is an extraordinarily good investment.

There's a moment in the lifecycle of social entrepreneurs when they know what the next step is. They don't know exactly how they're going to get there or how all the pieces will fit together. It may take years, but they know where they want to go—and that they *will* get there.

But the established order asks: Who are they? What is this idea? The more important the idea, the less it fits the existing structures. If you intervene at that moment and help that person have the freedom to fly—to work with, refine, and demonstrate his or her idea—a very small investment can have a very big impact. Then build a community of those people, and that impact becomes far more important.

That's the core Ashoka idea we launched in India thirty years ago.

We now have 3,000 leading social entrepreneur Ashoka fellows in this community. We have fellows virtually everywhere in the world. There are a few places where we can't elect fellows, like Burma or Belarus, but fellows from other parts of the world work in those countries. There are very few places we don't touch.

We do an evaluation every year to evaluate the impact of those fellows. More than half of them have changed national policy within five years, and more than three-quarters have changed the pattern in their field at the national level within the same five years. This is a very, very powerful group of people who have a strong sense of where the world is going.

In addition to helping support those key people and ideas, we've always been focused on building institutions in this field. We've helped more than 300 groups join in this effort around the world. Some of them you know very well: AVINA, Echoing Green, Skoll, Schwab, New Profit, and hundreds of others. This is hugely important: We now have a field.

When we first got started, there wasn't even a word; we had to invent one. People tended to go glassy-eyed when we said "social entrepreneur," and some smart ones annoyingly would say it's an oxymoron.

In the last couple of years, we have discovered something far more powerful still than the top entrepreneur or big idea and the community that unites them: *collaborative entrepreneurship*. This has never been done before in the world. It's bringing together hundreds of the world's best entrepreneurs in a field from every continent to figure out together where the world has to go and then to *entrepreneur* together to tip the world. This is Ashoka 3.0. We will discuss this most powerful force more fully shortly. However, we must first provide necessary framing.

As the field and Ashoka have grown, matured, and learned, we have moved from the individual to the community to the global team of teams entrepreneuring together in these collaborative entrepreneurships. These three levels are not only a progression from powerful to more powerful to extraordinarily powerful, but they also each multiply the power of the others.

Obviously, the social entrepreneurs are the foundation. Their ideas do change the world. Moreover, they each recruit, empower, and support hundreds—usually thousands—of local change-makers. They do not seek, as business does, to capture a market and dig a moat; the social entrepreneur's goal *is* to change the world. It is not realistic for them to run all the schools or institutions or government agencies in an issue area. However, if they can persuade local people to go for the opportunity, those people become local change-makers. They in turn will be role models for others; they will recruit others; and some of them will become the next generation of big pattern-change entrepreneurs. This is a key, if little-appreciated, energy source underlying the acceleration of the rate of change and of the coming of the new "everyone a change-maker" world.

The community of leading social entrepreneurs and our chief allies and—most especially—the global teams of teams of leading social entrepreneurs that are entrepreneuring fundamental pattern changes together are among the most important reasons that the rate of change is still accelerating exponentially. So is the number of change-makers and, more important, the ever-expanding richly interconnecting combinations of change-makers. It is this now-dramatic and steeply exponentially increasing rate of change that is the driving historical force of our era.

This force is quickly rendering obsolete the world of small elites, of hierarchies where a few people direct masses of others engaged in repetitive functioning, whether it is on the farm, the assembly line, or the law firm. These hierarchies of repetition are characterized by high, fixed walls. They have little capacity to collaborate across their maze of walls. In another ten or fifteen years, given the acceleration of this underlying historical force, every human grouping is going to be surrounded on all sides by fast-moving and richly interconnected change. The opportunity to contribute value will be in contributing to this surrounding change. The old hierarchies simply cannot do this.

They are being replaced right in front of our eyes by teams of teams and by ecosystems (such as Silicon Valley) of teams of teams. In this new environment, to add value each group must spot and understand change processes to which it can contribute and then pull together the team of teams (from within and without) best suited to contribute to each opportunity. As a change process moves forward, the contributing teams will have to keep changing as well.

In this new team-of-teams world, everyone will have to have the skills to be a change-maker. One does not have a team unless everyone on it is a player, and, in a world defined by change, one must be able to contribute to change to be a player.

We have been building up to this moment of transition for several hundred years. Now we are approaching the tipping point, a transition that is as important as the agricultural revolution. However, it will take barely one percent of the time that the agricultural revolution did; the tipping years just before us will be barely a flash.

The transition will not be easy, though thoroughly wonderful and leading to a far, far better future. When everyone is a change-maker, there is no possibility that the problems will outrun the solutions. When everyone has the power to express love and respect in action significantly, the inequities of the world where only a few people were powerful in large part become a bad memory.

During the transition and after, the role of social entrepreneurs becomes only more important. Historically we have been able to assume that the basic systems are stable, at least from the perspective of a human life. That will no longer be the case.

What is the mechanism that will keep the constant changing of the basic architecture from spinning off in harmful directions as interests and forces come to bear in unpredictable ways?

For example, right now privacy is sinking fast. There are three reasons. First, we have an objective need for preventive surveillance that is only going to grow. Second, Moore's Law (that the cost of processing information declines by 30 percent a year) has reached the point where connecting the infinitude of dots has become almost costless. Third, the business entrepreneur's dominant formula for profit in terms of news and knowledge now is to provide some useful service, obtain information as a result, and to profit by selling that information. This is but one current example.

As each of the world's systems evolves faster and faster, how are we systemically to ensure that it evolves in the interests of society as a whole?

That is why social entrepreneurs are becoming more and more centrally critical. They are "entrepreneurs"—that is, focused on changing the systems. And they are "*social* entrepreneurs" because, to their core, they are committed to the good of all.

They are, in other words, the chief built-in force constantly pulling all the systems in the direction of serving the world as a whole.

We need to increase their numbers and to make them as powerful as possible. This is the job of the field of social entrepreneurship and, most especially, collaborative entrepreneurship, which allows the world's best social entrepreneurs in every field, as it ripens, to come together and entrepreneur to tip the world in the right direction globally.

And it is very much the central reason to help the world make the transition to its "everyone a change-maker" future, a future where people will be increasingly committed at the core of their personalities to the good of all.

Aided by this road map of the extraordinary historical forces at work, let me introduce you very concretely to a few of the social entrepreneurs who are so central to both this history and our future. As I introduce you to these few individuals, try to figure out what are the common elements. What makes a really great social entrepreneur?

One thing that is clearly not required is astrophysics. If you gave yourself permission to see the issue and then to imagine possible solutions, you could have conceived all these ideas. And you could have refined them and made them fly.

Let me introduce you first to Mary Gordon. A Canadian, she grew up in Newfoundland and sounds like a Caledonian Mary Poppins. She faced a challenge in her Toronto classroom: More and more kids were coming who could respond only with aggression when another child made them uncomfortable. Of course, that invites aggression back. With each repetition of that cycle, it gets deeper. She said to herself, "Solving this problem is more important than the formal curriculum." She gave herself permission to change the system and created her now award-winning Roots of Empathy program. Now, there are 15,000 classrooms in a half-dozen countries that have adopted her approach. Bullying rates come down and stay down after this intervention.

What does she do? She asks for a couple hours a month from the schools— that's all—for a year. The program then finds volunteer parents who will bring in their infant, less than one year old, into elementary classrooms. The baby wears a little T-shirt saying "the professor." The students, not the teacher, then sit and try to figure out what the professor is saying and then feeling. They're also watching the deep empathy between the parent and the child. They quickly grasp empathy through a limbic learning process. Throughout the school year, they develop a connection and relationship with the baby, and, through this, empathy grows.

This is profoundly, profoundly important. Any child today, anywhere in the world, who does not master a highly sophisticated level of empathy will be marginalized. As the rate of change escalates, the rules cover less and less. They're always changing; they're in conflict; they haven't been invented yet. It is no longer possible to be a good person just by following the rules. The skill of empathy now is essential.

How many elementary school principals in San Francisco, or for that matter, anywhere in the world, know that they're failing if they have one second grader who has not grasped empathy? It isn't even in the discussion. But Mary saw a need for this, and she created a program that has had an incredible impact on now close to 400,000 children worldwide.

Here is the story of another Ashoka fellow, in this case from San Francisco: Jill Vialet. She set to work to restore recess because she believes in play, partly because, when she was eleven, someone allowed her to play boys' games on the playground. Now, what she does is introduce group play so recess no longer leads to conflict and becomes highly educative. What is group play? That's how kids learn to play together. It is one of the most critical ways of practicing and enriching the skill of empathy. She created Playworks as a comprehensive program to create safe and inclusive environments for play and physical activity both within and beyond the school day. Through Playworks, she collaborates with school staff to orchestrate lunchtime and recess activities and to reintroduce physical education in and after school. Principals and teachers now cite Playworks as one of the most indispensable programs in their schools.

In Boston, Ashoka Fellow Eric Dawson is redesigning the classroom experience to foster empathetic skills. His program engages children in peacemaking and conflict resolution. His Peace Games initiative brings together students, teachers, and volunteers to collectively change the status quo and build the skills that crowd out violence.

In Charlotte, North Carolina, Molly Barker focuses on fifth- to eighth-grade girls, a time when previously flourishing and energetic girls suffer a loss of confidence that is all too often reflected in the "mean girl"—the opposite of empathetic—syndrome. To help these girls get out of what she calls "the girl box," she created Girls on the Run, a nationwide grassroots movement of girls and concerned adults. It has more than 80,000 volunteers. Girls aged eight to thirteen enroll in a twelve-week training program for a fun, noncompetitive 5K event in which the girls can walk, run, or roll (in wheelchairs), as long as they keep moving forward. The program encourages the positive emotional, social, spiritual, intellectual, and physical development of young girls. Most important, it challenges girls to stay true to themselves in the face of pressures to conform.

What are the common elements among these four examples? First, each fellow gave him- or herself permission to change the world, and then each persisted and persisted. It's very simple. Ultimately, failure to do these two things is the fatal barrier that holds people back.

Ashoka is very clear about what it is looking for when it seeks out the next generation of top social entrepreneurs. It has a rigorous five-step process. There are different people at each step.

The criteria are very simple: creativity, entrepreneurial quality, the social impact of the new idea, and ethical fiber.

The creativity test is straightforward. However, we look for two separate, necessary elements: goal setting and problem-solving creativity.

The most challenging criterion is entrepreneurial quality. We do not mean getting things done, managing, or leading. Millions of people can do that. The core to understanding entrepreneurs is that they can't be happy human beings, they can't stop, until their idea has become the new pattern in society. They're married to the idea, and there's no negotiating about reaching that goal. To start, they can't possibly know how to get there. Their path is one of experimenting, learning, changing; but they're going to get there.

That means they're focused on the how-to questions as well as the goal. How am I going to solve this problem, seize that opportunity? How are the pieces going to fit together in five or ten years? It's a very understandable, easily recognized mind-set. We therefore ask how-to questions. All the idealists can do is tell you what Xanadu looks like again. They don't engage with the how-to issues. The entrepreneurs, by contrast, may be surprised that someone is asking, but they quickly engage and are with you. Also, they're very good listeners. They're not closed ideologues. They have to hear if something isn't working. They want to hear. That's part of their learning and iterative building process.

The third criterion focuses on the idea, not the person. Once the idea has been demonstrated in one place, assume that the entrepreneur disappears. Will people in that field look at the demonstration and decide that it is sufficiently new, attractive, and feasible that they will copy it? Does the idea have legs—and, if so, how far will it spread, and how beneficial will it be?

The fourth criterion, ethical fiber, is extraordinarily important. Entrepreneurs are always asking people to do things that are unreasonable, things they have never done before and that are probably going to be very hard to explain to the boss and others around them. Yet most people do what entrepreneurs ask them to do. They do not do so because of the words. The basic transaction begins as soon as the entrepreneur walks into the room. People know that this is a good person. They trust him or her. That's absolutely essential. Second, they know that this person and this idea are married. They're one. Therefore, they can trust the idea. That's the heart of the transaction. Any entrepreneur who's not a really good person, who's not seeking to express love and respect in action for the good of all, isn't going to succeed.

In any case, Ashoka cannot afford to have anyone in its community who is not deeply trustworthy. One untrustworthy person in a room means that there will not be a conversation; there will not be a fellowship.

Ashoka's judgmental challenge is not an easy one. It seeks out people before they have succeeded and are famous. It has to make its choice very commonly before even the entrepreneur can fully explain the idea. This is much harder than the Nobel Committee's job.

And yet, year after year, more than half of the Ashoka fellows have changed national policy within five years. Ashoka's clarity about its criteria and its tough and rigorously enforced selection process work.

In a world where too often people and institutions are afraid of judgment and therefore rely too much on numbers and ratios, the success of the Ashoka process demonstrates that the disciplined application of judgment works.

The stories of Mary, Jill, Eric, and Molly fit together. Each has a complementary approach to ensuring that every child masters empathy, that she or he practices and practices a high level of empathetic skill. (And they are but four of the 700 Ashoka fellows worldwide working for children and young people.)

That's the foundation for going on to becoming adults who are able to engage in teamwork, leadership, and change-making, which in turn is what everyone must master if he or she is going to be a real contributor to society.

The Ashoka fellows sketched on the preceding pages are leading the fellows and partners in North America in actively entrepreneuring this critical change for the continent. This team increasingly is mirrored on the other continents. These teams together constitute a global team of teams that has the power in fact to ensure that soon every young person *will* be a practiced change-maker before he or she passes the age of twenty-one. We will come back to this extraordinary new power of collaborative entrepreneurship shortly.

First, let me clarify that there are many other types of fellows. The giant African rat is not a fellow but is a critical partner to an East African fellow. It turns out that this African rat is pretty smart and has an extremely good sense of smell. With a little training it can become highly effective in detecting land mines. Moreover, it has the great advantage over dogs and people of being very light: The rat isn't blown up if it makes a false step in a minefield. The rat also turns out to be very good at identifying tuberculosis from spit samples. If you don't have a lab in a village, this is a very useful thing.

I could give you almost 3,000 examples. They have certain things in common. Each of these people gave themselves permission to cause a big change, to change the whole system—and they're doing it. Everyone reading this book could have solved these problems. There's no rocket science in any of these answers, but these men and women gave themselves permission.

Their confidence, power, and happiness exemplify the world we're trying to get to, an "everyone a change-maker" world. If you don't think of yourself as a change-maker, you don't have this confidence, so why on earth would you want to see a problem? All you're going to do is feel badly about yourself. On the other hand, if you know you are a change-maker, you're always looking for an unsolved problem: "Aha! Here's an opportunity for me to contribute importantly"—that is, to express love and respect in action, which is what people most want to do. You know you can do it, and other people know that they can do it. And you all know how to come together to do it. That's a world where there's no way that the problems can outrun the solutions. That's the world to which we must get quickly.

After five years, 97 percent of the Ashoka fellows are continuing full time. (A few people get ill; a few go into government.) Eighty-eight percent have had independent institutions copy them. As I've explained, more than half have changed national policy, and three-quarters have changed the patterns in their field nationally within five years of their launch. (No one is making this up. These statistics come from nine years of evaluations, most recently by the Corporate Executive Board.) Social entrepreneurs are really, really powerful. You can be as well—if you give yourself permission. Please do!

Ashoka's job is to help build an "everyone a change-maker" world. The foundation is supporting the most critical actors, the entrepreneurs bringing major system change and whose lives are committed to the good of all—that is, the world's top social entrepreneurs, the Ashoka Fellows. That is the essential foundation.

Ashoka's second task is to build them into a community. This is incredibly powerful. Let me illustrate. Iwan Nusyirwan is an Indonesian Ashoka fellow. He figured out how to create a whole new crop without land: The farmer puts mushroom seeds on soft wood chips and floats them on rice paddies. This idea is valuable in a large part of the world, but Iwan didn't want to be Johnny Mushroomseed for the rest of his life. So he works with other fellows. Their work—for example, in rural development—benefits, and Iwan benefits. Each leverages the other with the scale of impact that only top entrepreneurs bring. Here is another example: Because Pakistan is a very dangerous place right now, Ashoka has built a highly encrypted system that fellows in especially high-risk areas can use to communicate and work together.

Ashoka's newest level of high leverage impact, Ashoka 3.0, is the most powerful. It transforms social entrepreneurship from a world only of solo practitioners into one that draws together a global team of teams of top social entrepreneurs in a field when it is ripe for major change to define where the world must go in a field and then to transform the world accordingly. This is *collaborative entrepreneurship.*

It is very hard for business entrepreneurs to join together because their challenge is to capture a market and, if possible, to dig a moat to protect it. They also must deal with antitrust regulation. Social entrepreneurs aren't in that game. Our game is, "How can we change the world?" We have already discussed how social entrepreneurs spread their innovations chiefly by building movements of local change-makers. They make their ideas as accessible and user friendly as possible. They recruit and support local change-makers, who in turn recruit many others. This process of multiplying local change-makers is critical to building the coming "everyone a change-maker" world. For example, the Canadian fellow described above, Mary Gordon, is not running thousands of schools. That would never happen. But she can get people on the Isle of Man, in New Zealand, and in Winnipeg, to say, "This is really important; I want the kids, including my kids, in this community to have this. We're going to organize and make that happen."

Collaborative entrepreneurship, Ashoka's most important innovation and its third dimension, works for the same reason that leading social entrepreneurs build team-of-team movements of local change-makers: They can collaborate with one another happily and effectively to tip the world for the good.

However, it has taken Ashoka years to learn how to make this work. Simply putting social entrepreneurs together in a room does not do it.

The last five years have brought key breakthroughs.

In our first phase of learning, during much of the 1990s and the first half of the first decade of this century, our objective was to identify the most useful cross-cutting patterns among the fellows' many ideas in a field. This "mosaic" work was very fruitful because indeed it is far easier to spread a pattern than the hundreds of partial answers that constitute it.

However, it turns out that that's only an intermediate step because the patterns one sees are what's practical, what's feasible now. What one really must do is see what the new paradigm is going to be, the new S-curve. It is only when one sees where one must journey that the full, purposive entrepreneurial drive can come alive.

The most important element of bridging between today's pattern and tomorrow's new paradigm is grasping the questions the new patterns are trying to address. Plus there's a great deal of patient, iterative work!

Here's an extremely important example. I very intentionally introduced you to fellows dealing with young children. The old paradigm of growing up was: Learn knowledge and rules, and you'll be fine. Well, in a static world, that's probably true. But in the world we're in, let alone the world that a fifteen-year-old today will be in when she's thirty, that is not fine. It is absolutely inadequate.

We have to redefine what success in growing up is. That redefinition is the new paradigm: By twenty-one, one must be a *practiced* change-maker. One must master the necessary underlying skills the only way one can, which is by actually doing it. You start in first grade; you grasp empathy; you practice it; you practice it; you practice it through group play and other things. From ages twelve through twenty, you have to be practicing empathy, teamwork, leadership, and change-making—mastering four complicated, *learned* skills. You don't do that by reading a book. It's not simple. It's like learning language.

The challenge is, in fact, very similar to that of achieving universal literacy. We're going to understand in five years that any young person who does not have these social skills is socially illiterate. Without these critical skills, she or he is not going to be able to express love and respect in action, to be a contributor, to be a team member. This is the worst thing we can do to anyone and to any society.

Any society that doesn't change what it does with its children and young people right now is going to be in serious trouble in fifteen years. It won't take fifty years. If the United States doesn't have a population of change-makers—if Poland, or South Africa, or India, or any country for that matter doesn't have a population of change-makers—the country will slip quickly toward failure. They won't be able to compete in the new world toward which we are headed, one in which success is defined by what proportion of the people are change-makers, at what level, and how well they work together. This is the new prerequisite for success for any human group.

If you're a parent, what would you do if your fifteen-year-old daughter was failing at math? You'd hire a tutor, perhaps because you're not so confident of your own math skills. But you certainly know that you have to do something, and you have a mental list of options ready. Now, if I asked you, "What would you do if she was not practicing change-making?" Would you notice? Would you know what to do? What you need to do is actually pretty simple. Teenagers give themselves permission to see things that are messed up, and they tell you. So why don't you say, "Why don't you go and fix the way immigrant kids are being treated in school if you think what's happening now is wrong?" "Who, me?" "Yes, why not you? And besides, this is really important. If you're going to grow up and be successful, this is a set of skills you've got to have." Any parent can do that; anyone can do that for a young person they care about. Beyond your own parenting, you can also help change the schools and get the principal to focus on this topic.

This is only one example of the power you have once you see the new paradigm. We can't get to an "everyone a change-maker" company, city, society, or world if we don't change how young people grow up. So that is what we're setting out to do, ideally with your help. We want to make sure that, five years from now, every principal knows that the children in his or her school must master empathy and that his or her teens have to be practicing it and, indeed, all four of the skills now needed for success.

How does collaborative entrepreneurship work once it spots the new paradigm? How does this new collaborative approach propose in fact to tip the world?

There are two necessary elements.

First, in each of the ten big influential parts of the planet (such as India, Brazil, the United States, or German-speaking Europe) that must tip if the world is to tip, a team of top social entrepreneurs and supporting staff and partners must commit very seriously to lead the effort. The four North American fellows I have already described are, for example, key leaders for the Every Child Must Master Empathy collaborative entrepreneurship effort there. They are in turn a part of the global team of teams of their peers from the other key areas. They know the field and its people. They love to entrepreneur, and here they have the chance to do so in their area of passion at a level far beyond anything they could imagine before. Moreover, engaging here both helps them and makes their own work more important.

Second, as with any major entrepreneurial change, there must be a jujitsu point of leverage. No entrepreneur has the capacity to force a society to change by direct brute force. Instead, the entrepreneur or, here, the *team* of entrepreneurs must set in motion a self-multiplying jujitsu force that will be able to move society to disentangle a million relationships to allow a new pattern to take hold. Competition, opinion influencers, and the active intervention of an interested class of agents are examples of common ingredients.

In the case of Every Child Must Master Empathy, the jujitsu leverage will come from the interplay of two key sets of actors.

First, in the United States and each of the other priority areas, we need to identify a representative 5 percent of the influential elementary schools and help them use what we know to develop their own ways of reaching the goal. Here we are, once again, creating a team of teams. Several years hence, they will have succeeded and be eager to lead.

Second, we need, in each major country, to help thirty or so of the most serious and respected "maven" publishers, writers, and other top intellectual intermediaries "get" "everyone a change-maker" and why Every Child Must Master Empathy is absolutely a prerequisite for any society arriving there. As they connect with the school leaders who are on fire because they know what needs to be done and have experienced what success means, they all will feed one another's understanding, confidence, and commitment. Soon thereafter, whether a school is excellent in empathy will become an important determinant of competitive success, further widening public awareness, and thereby further speeding change.

There are many other examples of emerging collaborative entrepreneurship thrusts that are also key parts of this era's jump to an "everyone a change-maker" future—for example, having the law serving everyone, and business and society working together in profoundly new ways. Individually, and even more together, there is no more powerful—let alone beneficial—force in the world today.

What does all this mean for you? If you have a young person you care about, you now have a new agenda. If you care about an institution, ask yourself: Is that institution successfully making the transition to be a team of teams, or is it still a hierarchy? In every industry, there's going to be one company that figures out how to be a thoroughgoing team of teams, and it is going to demolish the competition very quickly. If you're a leader of an institution, whether it's a company, a church, or a citizen group, that's a strategic problem you have right now.

We as a society have an opportunity to help everyone see this change in the strategic environment and what it means for them. Nothing will do more to speed the change. If you are a writer or know one, or if you lead an organization, it's very easy to do this; and it's very important. At this moment of profound transition, we need you.

# BUILDING SOCIAL BUSINESS

## Muhammad Yunus, Founder, Grameen Bank

We have before us extraordinary challenges, such as poverty alleviation, so-cial inequity, and poor quality of life. I believe that business can provide solu-tions to many of these challenges that we face today. Business has often been thought of as part of the problem, but our experience at Grameen Bank shows that it can also be a major tool in solving these problems. I want to explain why social business is an idea that the world needs now. But, before that, it is important to explain the evolution of Grameen Bank, first in Bangladesh and now around the world, including in the United States.

I began Grameen Bank in 1974, during the famine in Bangladesh. I could not convince the local bank on our campus to lend money to the poor women in our village, who were being forced to go to loan sharks, putting their liveli-hoods and their families at risk. The bank told me in a very harsh way that it could not be done because poor people are not credit worthy. So I made a loan of $27 to a group of forty-two families. It is a very small amount of money for a bank, but was a significant amount for the poor women.

This is the simple story of how microcredit came about. We didn't sit and think and say, "Well, let's think about something that will give credit to the women." That's not how we did it. We actually said, "I don't know if anything will happen or not, but let me try." So I tried it, and it worked.

People said, "Well, he can do it in one village, but it will never work in two villages because it's too big and it will collapse."

I said, "Let me try again." We did it in two villages, and it worked.

The bank manager, who was waiting to have the whole thing collapse, said, "Maybe you should try it in five villages; because one village and two villages are the same thing, they aren't big enough." So I did it in five villages, and even then I didn't know if it would work out, but it did. That's how it grew.

Ever since, Grameen Bank has been expanding in Bangladesh and around the world. Within Bangladesh, we have more than 8 million borrowers now, 97 percent of whom are women. The bank is owned by the borrowers, as usual. The bank makes a profit; the profit goes back to the borrowers as a dividend, so it's a complete circle; nothing goes outside.

Also, it's a complete circle from another sense: We don't take any money from outside. We don't borrow from anybody; we don't take money from the government or from international agencies. We lend out more than $100 million a month in tiny loans, averaging less than $200 each, to more than 8 million borrowers. It's a lot of work, a lot of bookkeeping, a lot of checking, and so on. But the fact is, where does of all this money come from—$100 million per month, more than $1 billion per year?

We have more than 2,600 branches more than 27,000 staff. Each branch is responsible for finding its own money; it is not as if one lucky branch supports ten branches. Every branch has to be self-sustaining. It's a very simple system: We take deposits from people and lend the money to the poor people. It works out very well. We tell each branch, "It's your money; it's your poor people around your neighborhood. Your task is to mobilize this deposit, lend the money to the poor women, and become self-sustainable yourself so that you won't be losing money in the branch." That's their task, and they perform it well.

The concept has grown outside of Bangladesh as well. At first, people said, "Well, it may happen in Bangladesh; Bangladesh is a funny country anyway. It could never happen in another country." But then Malaysia started, and I said, "Look, another country is doing it." They said, "Oh, it must be something about Muslim countries." See, they always find something to argue with. Then came the Philippines. This is not a predominantly Muslim country; it's a Catholic country, but the naysayers said, "It's because it's an Asian country."

But then came Arkansas. We started there all the way back in 1987, at the invitation of the then-governor of Arkansas, Bill Clinton. Governor Clinton saw the possibilities for community banking to positively affect the economy. He invited Grameen along with ShoreBank of Chicago to come to Arkansas, and together we started the Southern Development Bank Corporation in Arkansas, a bank that is still thriving today.

From Arkansas it spread to Chicago, then to South Dakota, and to many other places. But still, people would say, "It will not work here in the United States because it's not sustainable." So that debate went on. I put forward a challenge and said, "Look, it simply is a question of doing it right. If you do it right, everything's possible." A friend of mine took the challenge and said, "I'll provide the money, and you can show us." So we started doing it New York City. In 2008, we started Grameen America in Queens. It is working beautifully. Repayment is good, the interest rate is low, and we are moving toward self-sustainability. So this is one successful location, and now we are moving to other places. The second branch opened in Brooklyn and became equally successful. We just opened up a third branch in Manhattan, in Harlem, so we now have three branches working in New York. After seeing the exciting impact we have made in Jackson Heights, someone invited us to do it in Omaha, Nebraska. So we started in Omaha about eight months ago. It is working very well, and later on this year we will open fifth and sixth branches, one in San Francisco and another in Washington, D.C. A journalist asked me recently why we are doing Grameen America. I told him that though we are beginning with tiny loans in a few branches, we hope that one day, everybody will have access to microcredit.

Within Grameen Bank, not only do we give loans to the poor people, but we also make sure that children in Grameen families go to school. This is part of our mission because the majority of the parents in those 8 million families to which we lend are totally illiterate. To make certain that their children do not repeat the cycles of poverty, illiteracy, and disease that have been going on for centuries, we promote our plan for education and make it attractive to our borrowers. Our borrowers are mothers, so they understand this issue very clearly and have supported it enthusiastically. Their support has fostered an enormous amount of effort to take these children to school and keep them in school. The first generation of students is now at the college level. Right now, the ones who are in medical school, engineering school, and other higher-education programs number about 52,000. There are also those who have graduated and are already in their professions, and so on; many have completed their PhDs. Up to high school, it's easy in Bangladesh because their entire education is free, provided by the government. But the moment you come to higher education, things become very expensive, and many young people stop studying. We said, "No, no way. You continue with your education as far as you can go, and Grameen Bank will give you all the money for education." This plan has become very popular; kids love it because now they can continue, and parents love it because they have no money to pay for them.

When I sit down with young people, I want to hear what they are thinking, what their worries are, what they want to do in the future. They always ask me the same question: "Grameen Bank has helped us get an education, and we are grateful, but what about jobs? Bangladesh doesn't have many jobs for us. So once we graduate, what do we do? How do we find jobs? Can you help us?" After listening to that question many times, I came up with a response. Whenever that question arises now, I say, "Look, you are a very special kind of young person; you are very privileged, because your mother owns a bank. So you have no shortage of money. Your mother would love to give all of this money to you so that you can move forward with your life. So money is not your problem. Why should you be looking for a job? Why can't you think of something else? Why don't you think this way and follow it. Repeat this as a pledge in your life, every morning you get up and repeat this to yourself: 'I'm not a job seeker. I'm a job giver. This is my job. My mission is to create jobs for others.'" I said, "*That*'s what you should be doing rather than everybody chasing one single job. One gets it, and everyone else is rejected. That's not a good prospect for a young person. A young person should be looking forward. Create a new world for yourself rather than wasting yourself in chasing one tiny little job here and one tiny little job there."

In the beginning, they were really scared. This was a radical concept for them. They would ask, "How can I create jobs when I don't have a job myself?" It feels contradictory to them. Seeing that, I start telling them that when they get disheartened and lose spirit and don't know what to do, they should look at their own mother and what she has done. She started her life with Grameen Bank some fifteen or twenty years back. When she took her first loan, it was probably $30 or $35. She was scared to death taking this $35 loan. She was shaking. She couldn't hold herself still because such an enormous amount of money was being put into her hand, and she was so nervous about it. But she assembled her courage, fought for it, and made it a success. She paid back the first loan all with her money, and since then her loans have become bigger and bigger. In the meantime, you were born, she sent you to school, and she made sure you stayed in school. Today, you are in medical school; today, you are in engineering school. What good is your education if you are not better than your illiterate mother? She did not choose to be an illiterate village woman, and yet she succeeded. Your education should have given you a much broader perspective to take on life's challenges in a much broader way. You are talking about ideas. How did she get her ideas? If you are looking for examples, you have examples right in your home: Your mother is an example. So why can't you create a business ten times bigger than what your mother does today, because you have an education? So gradually, many students are taking out loans and starting their own enterprises. I tell them to start a small enterprise; it doesn't have to be big, and, by the time you finish your education, you already have a small business that you can work on and grow because you have gone through the start-up phase. You're ready for the whole thing.

This thinking is beginning to really help them, and they are taking it seriously. I feel happy when I talk about them because they are not as nervous as they used to be. This is another way to look forward, to create something that they see they are capable of doing. When I talk to these young people, it's an amazing feeling. I speak to many student groups in universities everywhere—India, Europe, and many other countries—and I see no difference between the average student and these young people who come from extremely poor families. When I talk to them, they have the same kind of feelings about their future and so on; they just happen to come from extremely poor families. Looking at them, we can know that poverty is not really created by those individuals. Neither has their mother created it; it is created by somebody else and by external factors. I try to explain that poverty is created by the system. Unfortunately, we have a system that tells half the population of the world that if they are poor, it is their fault, and they are no good.

This brings up an important question: Who is credit worthy? Is it people without collateral who pay back their loans, or those with lots of collateral who are not paying back? During the recent credit and financial crisis, we revisited this question many times with many different organizations, companies, and people. When we opened Grameen America, we had no idea that, at the same time we were starting our microfinance efforts in New York, something cataclysmic was happening in the financial sector. We found ourselves in a strange situation: Grameen programs were flourishing in New York City, with customers borrowing and paying back 100 percent without collateral, without guarantees, and without any lawyers. Meanwhile, just down the road, the big banks, with lots of collateral and lots of powerful lawyers, were just melting away. This juxtaposition illustrates one of the key points Grameen has been trying to make since we started: The definition of *credit-worthy* does not depend on collateral or capital but on integrity and motivation.

Throughout the crisis—in New York City, in Bangladesh, and around the world—microcredit programs have remained robust. In Grameen Bank in Bangladesh, we don't even know that there is a crisis going on because our work goes on so smoothly. Many people ask me why this is the case. I say that one reason I see right away is that microcredit and Grameen Bank are much closer to the real economy. When we give a loan of $100 or $200, there are some chickens, there are some baskets, there are some cattle—things that equal the value of that $100 or $200. It's a one-to-one relationship. As long as the banking relationship remains rooted in solid ground with real people, real businesses, real valuations, we cannot go wrong. The big banks started to go wrong because they moved away from the real economy. They made decisions and loans based on speculation and castles in the air. Once one piece of this beautiful edifice of speculation fell apart, the whole thing fell apart. That's the danger, when you move away from the real economy to an artificially constructed system.

Our experience raises fundamental questions about the structure and rules of banking. The structure that we have now, the architecture of the financial system and the entire economic system, is grossly flawed. We must not just gloss over and move on as if nothing happened. We'll make a big mistake if we do that. We have to look at it very carefully and redesign the system before we move on into the future. If we leave things untouched, even if we create a "normal" situation, that normalcy will not last long. It will be following the same track and end up in disaster again, maybe even a bigger one than we have right now. This crisis powerfully shows the numerous weaknesses of the international and local banking systems.

In addition, the financial crisis is not an isolated crisis; it's a combination of many crises. Other crises are not on the front page of the newspaper because it's not exciting news for many. The food crisis is still on. In 2008, if you recollect, the food crisis hit the whole world: Three governments fell, and there were street fights because of food shortages. Most of the food exporting countries closed their doors, saying that they were not going to sell their food anymore because they were worried that their own people would go hungry. Food importing countries got into terrible shape because they could not buy from anywhere. All their lives, they had been buying food and concentrating their business in other sectors, but suddenly exporting countries said, "No, we're not going to sell." What do you do in a situation like that? That crisis has not disappeared. It's still on, and it will show its ugly face any time in a way that will shake the whole world.

The energy crisis: Again, in 2008, if you recollect, oil prices went up to $150 a barrel. That energy crisis didn't disappear. It simply went down for a while, but it will come up because it's a fundamental issue of an energy shortage. And of course there is the environmental crisis, which we have not done very much on yet. There is also the social crisis—poverty, diseases, and so on. It is an amalgam of all these crises. It tells us one thing very clearly: We have not designed our life and our system in which we perform our daily chores properly. Something is wrong in that.

I repeatedly point out that this crisis and megacrisis that we have is just a great opportunity to undo the system and redesign it because, when things work, you don't want to touch it because it's working. Because it's not working, this is a good time to really address it, so that we go to a new normalcy, which will take us to a new path where we will not have all the problems that we created in the past.

This brings me back to the notion of microcredit and social businesses and the role these innovations might play in creating a new structure and system to solve our problems. Though the word *microcredit* has become popular around the world—everybody knows about it, and there's a great respect for this ideal—the concept that we created in the Grameen Bank hasn't taken off like it should because governments are not creating new laws to regulate microfinance banks so that they can take deposits and lend money to the poor people.

There is also a new phenomenon within microfinance that is quite worrisome. New microfinance lenders are raising money, and private foundations are putting more money into many of these new lenders. Recently, investment firms also started investing money. I got very worried when investment firms starting coming to lend money to microfinance organizations. I believe strongly that poor people should not be presented as an opportunity for rich people to make money. When we created microcredit, we didn't do it to make money for ourselves. We created it to fight the loan sharks and to give loans to poor women so that they can change their lives. That was the purpose; that's what microcredit is all about. Microcredit is not something that should be taken as an opportunity for making money for somebody else. If it does that, then you move into the direction of the loan shark, not in the direction of helping the poor.

It is important to understand that, throughout the world, in capitalist systems, the concept is that business has one goal: profit maximization. I feel uncomfortable with pronouncements that generalize about all human beings, their motivations, and their behaviors, such as, "All they want to do in their business lives is make money, nothing else." This presents human beings in such a narrow way, as if humans are one-dimensional beings. I believe that human beings are multidimensional, even if economists do not have theories that explain our multidimensionality. They took one piece of a human being and built a whole theory out of it. Thus we have created a system and systemic problems on a premise that is faulty. It excludes much of what makes a human *human*. Economists built business on the basis of selfishness. In that business, everything's for me, nothing's for others. It is true that selfishness is a basic human trait; it comes from our necessity to protect ourselves. Similarly, there is one other equally important basic human trait: selflessness. When we see somebody in distress, we jump in; we try to help. Let's look at the example of Haiti. When the Haitian earthquake happened, there was hardly anyone who didn't want to help. People wrote checks, gave cash. Students raised money. We don't know who the Haitians are who were affected—we have never met them—but our human response to help other people comes out. When the Asian tsunami happened in 2004, the whole world was involved in helping those affected. This is part of us. I'm not saying there aren't some selfish people. But every single human being has both of these elements of selfishness and selflessness at the same time.

With Grameen Bank, I realized that we could behave differently and build businesses around selflessness as well as on selfishness. We can do both. We can do business to make money, and we can use the money to change the world. So recently I have started promoting this idea, the creation of another kind of business based on selflessness. I'm not saying conventional businesses should be closed down. Let conventional business flourish. We can fix them a little bit whenever we see something wrong with them, but, basically, let them function, and let them grow. At the same time, we open another door. If you want to address a particular problem, we can create a business to solve the problem. So it's a problem-solving business, not a moneymaking business. In that business, I invest for the cause in which I believe so that I can eliminate the problem forever using a business model. I am calling this model "social business."

Today, this is done through philanthropy. The distinction between philanthropy and social business is that, in philanthropy, you give the money and achieve the goal—which is an important goal—but the money never comes back because that was not the intention of it. If we can design a business to address the same issue, the same problem, then the money comes back. The same money will recycle again and again and again and achieve so much. You will have created an institution, which is subject now to improvements and enhancements and through which learning and opportunities open up.

In the beginning, people didn't pay much attention to the idea of a social business, but nonetheless we started on a small scale in Bangladesh. But there was a large public response when we announced a social business joint venture with a big company Danone (known as Dannon in United States). The reaction was loud and swift. "What are you doing?" they asked. "Why should Danone be doing this? Are they crazy? We know this guy's crazy, so let him do it; but why Danone?"

Together, we created a social business in Bangladesh by creating a company called Grameen-Danone Company. We produce yogurt. Danone is very good at producing yogurt, but this is a very special kind of yogurt. Grameen-Danone is dedicated to addressing malnutrition among children. Bangladesh has a very young population. We have a total population of 150 million, and 50 percent of our children are malnourished. Most of them are severely malnourished. When a child is malnourished, you don't have a future for the nation because malnourishment stunts a child's physical and mental growth. That's not good news for a nation that needs creative young people to build its future. Over the years, lots of efforts have been made to address this problem, but nothing really has worked, certainly not enough to make an overall impact. So we thought, "Why don't we try to set up a social business?" We put micronutrients into the yogurt—vitamins, iron, zinc—and started selling this yogurt at very inexpensive prices. The children love it. A child who eats two cups of this yogurt within a week and continues to do so for eight or nine months gets all the micronutrients she needs. The child becomes a healthy, playful child. A little child who had been just sitting there, crying and doing nothing, now is an active, lively child. It is an amazing difference.

This is the purpose of the company. The owners of the company can take back their investment money, but they will never take any profit out because this is dedicated to the cause. We have created a number of these kinds of cause-driven companies with many other companies that have come forward to do social businesses as joint ventures with us. We see enormous possibilities. Young people are taking a lot of interest.

Many universities are creating institutes and chairs of social business so it can be studied and taught as part of the curriculum The California State University Channel Islands has created an institute of social business. So I see a good response both from the business area and also from young people around the world. We also have an enormous amount of technological innovation in the world today. If we can bring together our creative minds, utilize businesses in a constructive way, and use this technology, all of the problems we have piled up over the years will disappear in no time. So that's a challenge that we all face: how to bring out the creativity in each individual, each one of us, rather than waiting for the government to solve everything, rather than waiting for the international agencies to solve the problems of the world. We are much better as individuals. We can create much more dynamic and much more creative things to solve problems that were never solved before. That's what social business empowers us to do.

## THE CHAMPIONS

### A Conversation

Shapiro: Within this field of social entrepreneurship, there's a lot of talk about the morphing between profitable enterprises and nonprofit enterprises. And there is the focus that is implied by the word *entrepreneurship* on bringing business rigor into the equation. Some people have very strict definitions about this term, and some do not. Where do you see the field moving in terms of private sector initiative versus nonprofit, and what would be a good outcome in this regard?

Drayton: First of all, the idea that business is doing better is highly suspect. We know, for example, that privately held companies consistently do better than publicly held companies because they don't have the quarterly focus on finance-only measures. Do we really want to have quarterly measures and those sorts of things? I don't think so. I'm from McKinsey; I like analysis, but that's not the point. There are a lot of things for which you need judgment. Social entrepreneurs have a new idea; there's no comparison. How do you do a comparative analysis for Mary Gordon when she's getting started with Roots of Empathy? You have to use judgment—discipline and judgment. We're afraid of judgment. Bureaucracies can't do it. Twenty-four-year-old financial analysts don't do it. This is not a good model. When you think about a global team of teams, having this division between business and society is incredibly destructive. It's a leftover from history. Business was the first "everyone a change-maker" sector; around 1700, it said, "Everyone with a better idea: If you implement it, we're going to make you really happy, and we're going to copy you." That set in motion the history of progress and change. The social half of the world got stuck for 300 years, for a variety of reasons. It remained small, fragmented, and unproductive, so you had these two worlds that didn't talk, wore different clothing, and didn't like one another. In 1980 a citizen sector broke free from that and became entrepreneurial and competitive in exactly the same sense as business. People can enter, and, if you do better, you gain market share and resources and élan. That's why we set up Ashoka in 1980; we saw the historical moment. Since then, there has been an explosive catch-up growth in productivity in product, and scale, and now globalization. So you actually have two sectors that have the same architecture and have closed most of the productivity gap.

Just one measure of that is that the citizen sector has employment growth at 2.5 to 3 times that of the rest of the OECD economies, because we're catching up in productivity so much. Now, we have an incredible strategic opportunity to end the division, and one of the other areas of collaborative entrepreneurship that we've been working on for the last four or five years is to do precisely that. We have 500 of the fellows working on ensuring that every human being can be a full player in the economy. One of the first things they figured out is how to tear down this barrier and create an entirely new production and distribution system that takes the best of the citizen sector and the best of the business sector. This is not moving a product through existing systems. This is completely changing the system. To sell this, we figured we had to demonstrate it in three different industries on four continents. We have now done this in six of these cases.

I'll give you just one example. We started fourteen months ago in India. India has a shortage of 24.7 million housing units for informal-sector workers inside the cities, according to the government. That's before the 700 million arrive that are about to come into the cities. The current system didn't work for these people—total market failure. Builders and developers and finance people couldn't deal with informal-sector workers—someone who sells vegetables, works every day, and has income but no paperwork. Furthermore, these sort of elite people don't know these other people. There are probably class and caste differences and political uncertainties. So it's a total failure of the market. Now, the citizen sector in the last ten years has come up and is very competent. You have big citizens' groups that know how to deal with these people; they deal with them all the time. The citizen groups are not particularly good at building or finance, but they're particularly good at dealing with the market. You put these together, and in fourteen months we have $120 million financed for more than 15,000 new units for informal-sector workers in the city. Now, if you divide 15,000 into 24.7 million, you can begin to imagine the size of the market failure that we're beginning to deal with.

The exact same thing is happening in health and irrigation. Irrigation companies in Mexico don't serve small farmers. It's not profitable. The cutoff is ten to fifty-five hectares. Well, there's a huge part of the land area of Mexico that is comprised of smaller farms that are not included in the market reach of the irrigation companies. But, if they were, the farmers would have two or three times the income and less uncertainty because they wouldn't be dependent on the rains to be conserving water. This is a really big deal. Again, it's a market failure, but in the last ten years, citizens' groups have come up all over rural Mexico serving 50,000 or 100,000 small farmers. Their cost structure is low. They understand the politics. You put these together, and all of a sudden you can actually get drip irrigation to small farmers. We're talking about hundreds of millions of small farmers across the world. For those of you who are in finance, start thinking about the size of the financing opportunities here.

This is not a small deal. This is a fundamental pattern change. Our goal, five years from now, is that anyone who is thinking about strategy in any sector is going to ask, "Where is the business–social hybrid that we can build?" That's one of the stock, strategic questions. They know the next five questions. Our strategy that I'm inviting you to join—those of you who are in the management-consulting and perhaps financial sectors—this is a whole new practice. Hystra is a French company that has just been founded to do these hybrid strategies, and it is doing very well. It's going to be keeping consultants busy for sixty years, building hybrid value chains and improving them. There's tremendous opportunity and tremendous need. But, again, you have to break the frameworks of thinking, and that's what collaborative entrepreneurship does.

Shapiro: Can these hybrid models be profitable, for for-profit companies as well?

Drayton: They are highly profitable. Just take the first example. Builders, developers, and finance companies are all making a lot of profit. They're loving this. The citizen groups are getting a 30 or 40 percent markup. Think about what that means for the citizen sector. You don't have to deal with the government or the foundations anymore. You get to be independent in a couple of years if you do this. This is really very profitable. We are actually very grateful to one of the Draper funds being an investor in Healthpoint, which is the health care model. I'm sure that they thought it was going to be profitable, which it will be.

Yunus: Grameen bank and social business—one is the offshoot of the other. We started with Grameen Bank, but we got involved with many, many other companies. In the process, we created almost forty different companies with the Grameen name on it—Grameen energy, Grameen phone, Grameen IT company, Grameen solutions, Grameen textiles, you name it. Always, whenever I see a problem that I want to address, that I want to solve, I create a business. I create a company. I think creating a company can solve a problem. This makes much more sense to me because I can control how the solution is crafted and put into practice. Through that business, I can address it.

For example, when I saw that information technology is such a powerful thing happening in the world, I realized that if we could somehow bring this technology to the hands of the poor people, poor women particularly, the world would change dramatically. Poverty would take care of itself; people will overcome this poverty because now they would be the masters of their fate. So I was looking for opportunity, and that opportunity came when we created the Grameen mobile phone company. It became a very successful mobile phone company, bringing mobile phones into the villages and putting them into the hands of the poor women to run businesses with their phones. There are many other examples in addition to this one.

The idea of social business grew out of the idea that business provides solutions. I created all those companies, and people think that I am a very rich man. I have so many companies. I try to explain to them that, yes, though I created all those companies, I'm not a rich man. Then they get very puzzled. "Why do you have so many companies, but you still say you are not a rich man? Don't you own all these companies?"

I say, "No, I don't own any one of these companies."

"Then why do you create companies if you do not own them?"

I say, "It never crossed my mind that I have to own them. I created them to solve problems; I was not thinking of owning them. I don't own a single share in any of the companies that I have created." This really puzzles people!

What about Grameen Bank? Does Grameen Bank make a profit? Do the owners make money? Yes, it does, because Grameen Bank is owned by the poor people. So there needed to be a second definition of *social business*: I said, "Any business that is owned by the poor people, even if it is a profit-making company, even if they are taking dividends, that is a social business because it is collectively owned by the poor people."

Shapiro: There is now a fair amount of money being put into social investment vehicles that focus on profitable efforts to deal with a social challenge. It sounds as if what you're saying is that there are plenty of opportunities to make money and that these types of funds are going to proliferate. Is that right?

Drayton: I'd like to go a little bit further. We have two financial systems: one that has its problems but is pretty efficient and very adaptive and very competitive; and then we have government grant agencies and foundations, which are the main institutional finance for the citizen sector. The chasm between these two financial systems is very unhelpful. McKinsey did a survey that *Stanford Social Innovation Review* published about four years ago. Just the transaction costs of dealing with foundations and governments was 20 to 45 percent. For private financial and business financial institutions it was 2 to 5 percent. That's before you get to being willing to deal with long term and so on.

If you think about what a social entrepreneur needs and what these two sets of institutions institutionally are set up to do, there's an almost complete mismatch. The entrepreneur wants you to really like a new idea. Well, how does that fit into legislation and rules and regulations and branches and divisions and, for foundations, strategies? It doesn't. It's a huge pain in the neck for the program officers because they have to talk to five other people. They don't want to do that. It takes time. There's nothing in it. That doesn't work. You have to build an institution. Causing change in a democratic society is not instantaneous. It is not a one-year affair. Well, that doesn't fit their time on the horizon. The entrepreneur wants you to be loyal to him or her because this is their life. It's not a one-year project. Well, these institutions don't do that. That's judgment. How would we deal with that? Building institution is overhead. There's a complete serious structural problem here.

Now, individuals try very hard to overcome this. There are some institutions that are closer to their founders that do a really good job. But that's the exception, and it's not the structural problem. So I think we need to collapse these financial institutions. We actually have six projects designed to do that. One of them, to which I invite everyone reading this to contribute, is the social investment entrepreneur programs. We're looking for people who are entrepreneurs in social finance. There's a wave that's coming. It's wonderful. Felipe Vergara from Colombia looked at the education finance system in most of the world. It's one of the main causes of structural corruption. The government puts whatever money it has in its budget; it has no market-clearing mechanism to figure out how much is appropriate, let alone within each areas. So you have something that's hugely valuable and that they then underprice. So what on earth do you think that leads to? The nice word is *influence.* The father of a very good friend in Mumbai founded nine law colleges there. Every fifth or six dinner someone comes by late in the dinner, "Oh, you know my niece—very nice person, really smart, don't you think? Don't you think she should be a lawyer?"

"Oh, yes, why don't you have her come and see me?"

Well, that's nice influence. In Nigeria, it's just priced. It's very straightforward. All over the world, young people are entering their adult life in a corrupt system, and they know it. Everyone knows it. We don't have enough places now. So Felipe Vergara has founded a very simple way: He's creating for-profit human-capital funds. You can invest in proving undergraduates or a fund for disabled students going to college in Mexico. You don't know what any one earns, but you do know what the group will earn; very safe. Think where this is leading. You've done away with the capital shortage. You have a market-clearing mechanism. If you invest too much in veterinary students, the return will go down, and it will say "bad fund," and you've cut away the legs of corruption.

There's more to it. I could give you many examples. We're just entering a wave of change in the financial system that is part of eliminating the gap between business and society. It's really important; San Francisco is a center of financial innovation; here is a new opportunity. I love these new initiatives. They're pushing the frontier. I just caution that we need to have new financial systems all across the board, not just in the social enterprise area. That's a little caveat.

Shapiro: What can governments do to facilitate an increase in social entrepreneurship and social business?

Yunus: As far as conventional business is done, I'm sure we all know what the government is supposed to do. If it is related to what the government can do to promote social business, then yes, there are a lot of things that government can do. Government could create a social business fund, so that anyone who wants to do social business can go to the fund and say, "Here are my social business ideas. Would you give us investment money?" For example, somebody said, "Okay, I have a great idea: I'm going to create a social business. I would like to take ten people out of welfare through a social business. I create a business to take people out of welfare, and I need $X$ amount of money as an investment to do that; gradually I will pay you back because that's our business—we pay back. But, in the meantime, I will take these ten people out of welfare completely." So if this government fund is available, then it is in the government's interest to help create the business, remove people from its own budget and help alleviate poverty. It is a very leveraged investment.

Shapiro: Does that fund exist anywhere?

Yunus: Not yet, but it will come. Any new idea like this needs a little time. Funds like these are beginning to be created by individuals and soon by governments. What about government assistance in the international arena of development, foreign aid? Foreign aid money goes to the government and goes to the agencies and so on. But if you think about it, if governments set up social business funds instead of giving money to government agencies, they would be much more productive. If you take 10 percent of that money, separate out what you are giving as foreign assistance and use it to create a social business fund so that people in the country and outside the country can come and create social businesses to address health care—health care is an excellent social business idea; you can solve the problems of health care by creating social businesses— or forestry or education or environment or renewable energy; these are social businesses. This fund can be used, and it becomes bigger and bigger because it doesn't disappear. Each year, you are putting more money in, and it becomes bigger. The money that you give comes back again. Foreign aid that goes and then never comes back, at the end of the day, it becomes zero. So you have to start all over again with a fresh fund. This is better. You are taking only 10 percent of the money. If you think this is doing good work, you can gradually make an even bigger one. State governments or city governments can do the same and create social business funds and encourage their citizens to participate in solving the problem. To take drug addicts off drugs could be done as a social business. Taking care of the disabled people could be a social business. We can help and invest and do that. Foundations can do that. These are the kind of ways one can come forward and support that.

Shapiro: Dr. Yunus, you are a Nobel Laureate and rather well known. Please think back to the time you were convincing people to support your ideas. Could you discuss some of the challenges you faced and how you overcame them?

Yunus: Opposition comes from an entrenched mind-set. People love to believe what they believe. They don't want to see something different. They reject something new right away, and they keep on arguing that it's not right. It takes a lot of time to change minds. Our mind-sets are created in our educational institutions. That's where we develop our mind-sets. This is why educational institutions are so critical. Can the students remain open minded to absorb new ideas? Creating students with a rigid mind-set, I think, is a damaging thing to do because then you are sealing it off; it cannot take any other fresh ideas. We live in a world today [where] new ideas are generated continuously. As a society, we have to learn how to absorb new ideas. Otherwise, we will be damaging ourselves and our society.

Shapiro: What are the characteristics of a person who is going to bring about social change or start a social business?

Yunus: I guess others will have to find out; I cannot tell. If I see a problem, my instinct is: I can solve that problem. At least I can try, so I start trying, and usually I try it in a business way. If it is a health care problem, I create health insurance, health systems. If it doesn't work, I find out the existing thing that I used is the wrong thing. For example, now we are creating social business in health care starting with the diagnostic services. We want to bring diagnostic services to every home in the villages so that we don't have to send people to clinics for diagnostic services. We saw that existing equipment doesn't allow us to do that. It was too heavy, too bulky, and too expensive. We realized that the equipment was not meeting the challenge of village-centered health care. We have all this bulky, expensive equipment just to make sure you can write a big bill to your patients so that they can pay you more and they are impressed that you have a big machine. So why don't we go back to the chips; the simple diagnostic tools are as efficient as any other bulky machine that you have in your clinics and hospitals. So we are designing that, and we are collaborating with manufacturers who are doing that.

We are bringing equipment to the villages. For example, for pregnancy, General Electric designed, in consultation with us, a simple ultrasound that a girl could carry from house to house with the pregnant mothers and take images. The doctors are over in another place, and all those images will be transmitted to the doctors in the big city who will be sitting in front of the screen. All of these images will transfer through the mobile phones into their screen. You have an expert watching you, and you are talking to the experts with the mobile phone; so that distance has not created a problem for us. This can become a very inexpensive way of providing health services. If you can bring the diagnostic services, the bulk of your problem will dissolve. In our case, with the way we have designed our health care program, we say keeping healthy people healthy is our major objective. Wellness and prevention and all those things become second nature. Then women become our highest priority, and children become our second priority; adolescent girls become the third priority. People ask why we always go for women, and I always try to explain to them that this is the most difficult segment of the population to reach. Once you can reach these people, then reaching other people is so easy; it's no problem at all.

Drayton: If a child doesn't master empathy, you can forget the rest of it. They must be able to watch themselves understanding what is happening to other people, now and into the future, as individuals and in complex institutions— and then to guide themselves to contribute to the good and not be hurtful. We have whole communities where that is not happening because the parents don't have the skill, and the community doesn't have the skill. It's not part of the street culture. The schools don't realize it's an issue. Now, in that picture, where are the children supposed to get that skill? How on earth can we imagine them being social entrepreneurs if they can't function in society? You can't do teamwork or leadership or change-making if you don't have that basic skill. We have a large part of our population, a large part of the world's population, that doesn't have that skill.

How many middle and high schools in this country have a youth culture where it is normal for kids to take the initiative and set up organizations and solve problems? In most of our youth culture, the adults are in charge of everything and, "Please don't get in our way, because we do it better faster, and besides, we're rather nervous about you irresponsible people." If you treat people that way, they don't like it; they resent it; they have a negative peer culture. In fact, you don't have a culture. Consider the best elite high schools. I visited Phillips Academy Andover recently; there's a student organization for every nine students. The students are absolutely in charge. Well, guess what? The kids coming out of that school know they have this skill, and they've been practicing it a lot. The whole peer culture says, "Yes," and the adults have gotten used to it and actually rather like it. Consider some other high schools in this country. Leominster High School went from zero student organizations to almost forty in four years. This is not an elite high school. Just that one person said, "We don't want everyone moving out of this place. If we can get people to be change-makers, okay, they won't leave; they won't have to." I think he's right. Now, we could do that anywhere, but we have to get 100,000 young Americans every year to do this. That's a big change. If we do that, those communities will change very quickly. If the kids are doing it, the adults will learn. The best way for adults to get this is to get them to understand that it's really important for their kids, and all of a sudden they begin to realize, "Oh my god, these are the skills that I'd better have, too." Companies can help with this.

Think about your employees. Why not give a challenge to your employees? Nominate any young person you know, in your family or not, and if he or she has a dream and is willing to build a team, we'll help with the seed money. This is what Ashoka's youth venture does. We'll be happy to work with a company to do that. Well, that's a very powerful message to help the company begin to make the journey that it needs these skills. The parents help the kids; the parents learn as much as the kids. There are very simple things we can do, but if we don't do them, we're going to be a society more divided, and we might not make the cut in fifteen years.

Might not make the cut? Let me explain what I mean. The level of these skills that you need every year is going up because of that exponential curve. What was enough skill in 1960 isn't enough now. If we've got 20, 25, 30 percent of our population that hasn't even started on empathy, they're getting further and further behind. The hole is getting deeper. This is a tragedy.

Shapiro: Dr. Yunus, your tenure with Grameen Bank has concluded since writing your chapter. What are you doing now?

Yunus: Since resigning from my post as managing director of Grameen Bank in May 2011, I have continued to travel the world promoting the concept of social business and launching social businesses at home and abroad. You can find out more about my activities at www.yunuscentre.org.

Shapiro: In today's world, it is rather easy to be pessimistic, but you both seem extraordinarily optimistic.

Drayton: Let me use a metaphor, and I apologize to any biologists in the room. If you think about an "everyone a change-maker" world, analogize each person to a really smart white blood cell—that is, they live their life so that whenever they see anything that's stuck, they not only go and destroy it, but they know how to make it better. Now, that is a world in which there's no way the problems can outrun the solutions. If anyone is able to do that, she or he is going to be a happy, whole person, because what makes people happy is contributing. We have this ballet of everyone with really strong empathetic skills moving quickly; it's a very exciting world. The transition is a bit tricky, but we'll get there.

Yunus: I see the possibility that all of today's challenges can be overcome. People as human beings have enormous capacities; they are packed with unlimited capacity. It's a question of unleashing this capacity. We did some stupid things; we did some wrong things that created all these problems. It's not that it is something unalterable—something as if it comes from the heavens and you cannot change it. We created this mess; we can clean up this mess. We have the capacity to clean up this mess. I feel good about it.

# THE NEW THINKING ABOUT SOCIAL ENTREPRENUERSHIP

The United States has been philosophically disposed to charitable giving and activities since our founding as a bastion of tolerance, freedom, and equal opportunity. In 1917, only four years after putting in place income taxes for Americans, Congress passed legislation allowing deductions for gifts to charity.[1] The tax exemptions both for contributors and for the nonprofit itself were based on a belief that the purpose of the organization was to work toward societal improvement and not to amass any kinds of profit for the owners. In fact, the tax law takes ownership out of the equation. Since 1917, this model has worked very well—so well that today 83 percent of Americans donate to charities.[2] For most of the twentieth century, the American model for supporting nonprofit organizations, their management, and their funding remained somewhat static. Nonprofits relied on charitable contributions to do their work, and the unspoken corollary was that nonprofit organizations and their management teams did not need to focus as much on the bottom line. Though there have been excellently run organizations, nonprofits did not have to bear the scrutiny of an invested shareholder base or the rigor of maintaining a profitable bottom line. However, over the past twenty-five years, a number of changes have entered into the mind-sets of those involved with charities and charitable giving.

The first wave of change began to take place in the 1980s and 1990s along three important and linked dimensions: the motivations and capacity of the nonprofit leadership, the expectations and strategies of the funders, and an increased attention to organizational effectiveness. Much of this change in mind-set can be attributed to the introduction of ideas that fall under the umbrella term of *social entrepreneurship*.

The first shift in thinking, related to the new kind of nonprofit leader, can be linked to Bill Drayton's realization that the person motivated to take on a social challenge is the most critical piece of the social change puzzle. With the founding of Ashoka: Innovators for the Public in 1981, followed by the creation of the Echoing Green Foundation in 1985, a new definition of a nonprofit leader emerged. To be sure, not all nonprofit leaders met Ashoka's rather stringent requirements that, to be a true public sector or social entrepreneur, a person had to have a truly innovative idea, a concrete strategy for implementing it, and a significant chance of effecting regional or national change. But increasingly this kind of drive and passion is what we began to look for in an effective nonprofit leader.

One of the central tenets running through this book is the centrality of the social entrepreneur him- or herself. Where does that spark come from? That determination, entrepreneurial passion, and zeal? Among our contributors, there are a number of eloquent descriptions of what is involved in being a social entrepreneur. In Chapter 16, Bill Drayton said, "There's a moment in the lifecycle of social entrepreneurs when they know what the next step is. They don't know exactly how they're going to get there or how all the pieces will fit together. It may take years, but they know where they want to go—and that they will get there." In Chapter 7, Sally Osberg said, "Social entrepreneurs see and seize opportunities just as entrepreneurs do, but they must plan each step forward without financial services or venture capitalists to back them."

Louise Packard, Jacqueline Novogratz, and Premal Shah each spoke powerfully about their drive, determination, and the pivotal realization that they could solve a problem. "I had really no option but to act," explained Conchy Bretos in Chapter 3. Echoing Green believes that all social entrepreneurs have "moments of obligation," meaning that life-changing events that create unwavering commitment to social change. Despite this strong will and determination, early spiritual, intellectual, and financial support are key to giving them the extra edge they need to bushwhack through uncharted terrain and overcome the much larger number of people who come up with reasons why this project, this idea, or this intervention won't work.

The social entrepreneur must find people who say, "Yes, you can do this, and I will help you." Though this book has highlighted those times that got to

"Yes, you can," and "Yes, I can," there are numerous examples of hearing "no" and facing multiple disappointments. The successful social entrepreneur has to believe, based on faith, according to Louise Packard, or based on the belief that there really is no other choice, according to Jacqueline Novogratz, that taking "no" for answer is just not an acceptable outcome.

The second important trend that began in this wave of change was the strengthening of the social and financial infrastructure to support social entrepreneurs in their work. Even today, with a growing understanding of and support for social entrepreneurship, there are only a handful of places where one can go to get first-round financing, in addition to friends and family. Ashoka was an early pioneer in this arena and continues to be an incredible go-to place for social entrepreneurs around the world. Bill Drayton and his team over the years have built up an ability to identify truly outstanding individuals and provide them the personal financial security they need to follow their hearts and minds. Echoing Green followed shortly after Ashoka and has now been providing start-up funding to social entrepreneurs for twenty-five years. Bill Draper, though relatively new to the field, has created the Draper Richards Kaplan Foundation, which provides angel investments for a three-year period to promising social entrepreneurs. Christopher Gergen called the space between family and friends and outside financing "the Valley of Death."[3] Angel investment is absolutely critical. It signals to a somewhat skeptical world that someone does believe in you so much so that they are ready and willing to put money on the line for you to make your vision into a reality.

The third change that has taken place has to do with increased attention to organizational efficacy. According to a 2001 McKinsey & Company report for Venture Philanthropy Partners,

> There is . . . precious little information about what works and what does not in building organizational capacity in nonprofits. This is largely due to the sector's historic inattention to capacity building, which has not been adequately supported by funders and has been of secondary importance to nonprofit managers trying to deliver programs and services to people who need them. This situation is changing, and more funders are dedicating attention and financial support to organizational capacity.[4]

As the McKinsey study claims, there has been increasing rigor on the part of funders. In 1997, three Harvard researchers—Chris Letts, William Ryan, and Allen Grossman—shook the philanthropic community with a *Harvard*

*Business Review* article chronicling the rise and virtues of what was to become known as venture philanthropy: the notion that philanthropists should use similar tools and strategies for funding nonprofit organizations that venture capitalists do for profit-making investments.[5] That is to say: Fund several organizations for a longer period of time and get involved with the management and strategy of the endeavor. Venture philanthropy, like venture capital, has strong ties to Silicon Valley. A report by the Morino Institute claims,

> A sea change in philanthropic giving, an unprecedented creation of wealth in the New Economy, and an Internet-enabled transformation in organizational effectiveness are converging to create an extraordinary opportunity to work in new and different ways to meet society's most vexing and long-standing social problems.[6]

This new thinking of the 1980s and 1990s introduced a number of previously underutilized tools and strategies into the realm of nonprofit work. Venture philanthropists demanded a return for their social investments, grounded in a philosophical approach based on finding return on investment. Nonprofit management had to show impact and efficacy. New tools and management techniques began to be promoted and employed, especially those using the power of the Internet to share information. Finding the right set of metrics with which to evaluate social return is an important but difficult task. Organizations focused on this have included Grantmakers for Effective Organizations (GEO), founded in 1997, and the Center for Effective Philanthropy, created in 2000. Both of these organizations realize that efficacy is strengthened when the inputs and outputs are both robust. For nonprofit organizations to accomplish measurable, meaningful change, they must be well managed and have great leadership with transparent financial oversight. GEO, for example, helps grant makers improve their practices in four primary areas that they have identified as critical to nonprofit success: learning for improvement, leadership development, money, and stakeholder engagement.[7]

Guidestar, established in 1996, is another example of a new resource, providing financial and programmatic information on nonprofit organizations online. Guidestar, backed by several private foundations, posts tax returns of nonprofit organizations so that would-be donors can see how an organization uses its funding. In 2000, Bain Consulting created the Bridgespan Group, itself a 501(c)(3) nonprofit that helps nonprofit and philanthropic leaders in the hard work of developing strategies and building organizations that inspire and accelerate social change. These examples illustrate well the attention to organizational efficacy and sound management and financial practices that has entered into the nonprofit arena. These concepts, though still relatively new on the scene, have called into question numerous previously held assumptions of social service. With these changes, the question of how traditional business concepts, strategies, and goals can be used to improve society began to be discussed and tested broadly.

By listing out the proliferation of organizations focusing on organizational management and efficacy in the 1990s, one gets the sense of how much these initiatives resonated with funders and recipients alike, who realized the great need and in that, the great opportunity. "It's not a question that metrics are bad or having no metrics is good," said Jed Emerson, "It's a question of appropriate metrics."

## The New Thinking 2.0: The Business of Social Good

We are now into a second wave of new thinking about social entrepreneurship, growing out of the changes outlined in the previous paragraphs but in some cases now pushing the envelope even further. As mentioned in the introduction to this book, social entrepreneurship is changing the way social change is viewed, taken on, and supported. In that introduction, I wrote that social entrepreneurship is changing the way social change is being viewed and carried out in three important dimensions: through blurring of the demarcation between for-profit and nonprofit activities; through a continued emphasis on measuring impact; and through a focus on scale, finding successful innovations and causing them to proliferate widely. All of our contributors have expressed views on these subjects as well as several others that need to be mentioned.

The most significant new shift in thinking is the questioning of the role of profit in addressing social challenges. Throughout the book, one cannot help but be struck by two noteworthy themes: There is support and enthusiasm for the application of business models to addressing a social need or challenge, and there is no shared consensus about the best ways to achieve that end.

Muhammad Yunus was the most explicit when he said in our conversation in Chapter 18, "Whenever I see a problem . . . I create a business." The idea that a business is the solution to a social problem isn't radical; after all, the washing machine was an extraordinary liberator for those women with access to one. Yet no one would argue that the washing machine was put on the market to achieve a social bottom line. It was and remains a very profitable product.

Willy Foote and Mary Houghton described their realizations that the market was not meeting the needs of poor farmers in Latin America and Africa and lower-income minorities on Chicago's South Side, and both of them crafted business solutions to address those needs. For Yunus, Foote, and Houghton, the solution was clear. The tricky part is that, when the goal is social change, a business cannot always pay its bills, let alone be profitable. Bill Drayton speaks eloquently of the hybrid approach. Yes, he assures us, these can be profitable. "Our goal," says Drayton in our conversation in Chapter 18, "five years from now, is that anyone who is thinking about strategy in any sector is going to ask, 'Where is the business–social hybrid that we can build?'" In our conversation in Chapter 11, Jacqueline Novogratz calls for using the "tools and the ethos of business with the ethos of the nonprofit humanitarian movement." Matt Bannick talks about the complementarity of grants and investments. Bannick argues that different processes and organizational frameworks are necessary to deal with different issues. The bottom line for him is that the organization has significant social impact. The question then becomes, Is it always clear which one to use where and when? Sally Osberg tells us that the Skoll Foundation is agnostic about whether an enterprise is a nonprofit or profit-making, as long as it meets the criteria necessary to achieve large impact: legions of empowered stakeholders, well-designed and effectively deployed models, evidence-based systems that track results, aligned resource engines, strategic partnerships that scale and leverage their impact, and organizations build to last. Sally Osberg explains,

> The goal here is to create social value to crack the code on a problem to make a difference for humanity. If you have to do that with a nonprofit venture, fine, do it with a nonprofit venture. If it makes sense to do it as a business venture, do it as a business venture. It's really the goal that matters—the focus, the discipline, the drive, and the ability to stay with something. That's what distinguishes the social entrepreneur, regardless of whether it's a for-profit or nonprofit venture.[8]

Premal Shah echoed this thinking in our conversation in Chapter 6: "You know, what I love about social entrepreneurship is that people are really focusing on what works, and they're bringing a business rigor to it, no matter what your tax status is."

In recent years, there have been efforts to categorize models. John Elkington and Pamela Hartigan define three categories of social enterprise structures: leveraged nonprofit, hybrid nonprofit, and social business.[9] According to their definitions, a leveraged nonprofit is a more traditional nonprofit relying on outside philanthropy to maintain financial support. A hybrid nonprofit allows for revenue to be derived from the sale of goods and services and can accept mainstream capital investment. In a social business, all profits are put back into the enterprise for the good of the targeted market or population.

One of the interesting aspects of the willingness to test models and approaches is the number of permutations that can be developed. There is a growing awareness and acceptance of the mechanisms along the continuum between profit and nonprofit. It is clearly not an *either-or*. A number of examples of this surfaced during the series.

In the past two years, Muhammad Yunus and Grameen Bank have entered into a number of social businesses. In his chapter, Dr. Yunus explains the motivations behind creating social business joint venture with Danone (vitamin-fortified yogurt). He has also created similar ventures with Intel (maternal and child health monitoring systems), and Veolia (water), among others. It is clear that Dr. Yunus believes in the power of this idea, and certainly he has found some multinational firms to experiment with him. To pursue the proliferation and fine-tuning of the social business model, Dr. Yunus has set up the Grameen Creative Lab in Germany.

On the capital side, Jacqueline Novogratz and Acumen use the term *patient capital* to explain the way investments are made through Acumen. Premal Shah and Kiva have coined the term *connected capital* to describe how the Internet community can have an enormous aggregated impact on microfinance and small businesses around the world through the fostering of a sense of personalized relationships between the individual lender and the individual borrower. Mary Houghton uses the term *values-based banking*. All of these refer to investments in business enterprises without much hope for large or even medium-sized financial returns. Discussing the issue of return in our conversation in Chapter 11, Matt Bannick said,

> We're looking for very big, large social impact. And we do take, probably, more risk than other investors would probably take. . . . social impact, disciplined financial analysis, but also with a high tolerance for risk in terms of what we're willing to take to have that positive social impact.

Willy Foote describes Root Capital as a social investment fund. Root Capital invests in businesses, but it needs subsidy itself to help with overhead and transaction costs. He also talks about the imperative to continuously innovate. Toward that end, Root Capital has launched Root Lab, which puts funding into more risky and speculative ventures so that lessons can be learned and new markets entered into with a clear understanding of the challenges entailed in the venture.

Acumen is also a social investment fund, seeking patient capital to deploy across its investments. In the last few years, a new type of social investment called "impact investment" has gained much popularity. According to the Monitor Institute, impact investment funds could grow to $500 billion in the next five to ten years.[10] The Monitor Institute ends its report with a call to action, cautioning that unless clear investment criteria and outcomes are developed, much money, time, and energy could be wasted. Impact investing is in its very early days, and it remains to be seen how much one can truly do good and do well simultaneously.

Making a profit is no longer taboo, so another area of enormous potential within the social entrepreneurial space is the activities taken on by multinational corporations. As already mentioned, several multinational firms have entered into partnership with Muhammad Yunus to create what he is calling "social businesses." There is a larger phenomenon growing within multinational corporations that can be divided into two overlapping categories: efforts aligned with corporate social responsibility and/or sustainability programs and those geared toward base-of-the-pyramid products and processes.

In her chapter, Kriss Deiglmeier credits Walmart with fundamentally changing the views of those in its supply chain around sustainability and environmental issues. What Walmart has done has been nothing less than revolutionary. It says, "We know that being an efficient and profitable business and being a good steward of the environment are goals that can work together. Our broad environmental goals at Walmart are simple and straightforward: To be supplied 100 percent by renewable energy, to create zero waste, and to sell products that sustain people and the environment."[11] When one thinks about the enormous size of Walmart, it has an undeniably profound impact at the level of scale that these kinds of innovative changes can make.

Another mechanism for companies to help solve social challenges is through base- or bottom-of-the-pyramid strategies. This term, coined by C. K. Prahalad in 2006, refers to the corporate strategy of selling goods and services to the billions at the bottom of the economic pyramid rather than the top. These profitable business models are what Harvard Business School calls "capitalism at its best."[12] They entail creating solutions to social problems through the provision of a market need. An example of this type of activity is Manila Water in the Philippines. Manila Water figured out how to reduce costs, maintain the hygiene and supply of the water system, and employ numerous low-income technicians, security guards, and salespeople to increase access to clean drinking water for millions of low-income customers. When asked about making profits from the poor at a Harvard Business School conference, owner Jaime Zobel said, "Profitability has allowed us to invest heavily in the infrastructure needed to take the public utility to the 21st century. The people and communities have become great supporters, grateful to no longer be purchasing bottled water from exploitative middlemen."[13]

Jed Emerson has written a great deal about the compatibility of dual objectives of profit and social good. His blended-value philosophy states that companies must adopt a broader vision of the value proposition to do good and do well. He cites Patagonia as embodying much of what he means by blended value.

## Measurement and Results

The push toward enhanced metrics and return on investment continues to be a central tenet of the new businesslike approach to social change organizations. Those in this series and colleagues on both the funding and the recipient sides continue to face the challenge of finding ways that accurately measure social return.

Each of our contributors addressed the need to measure results and impact. The challenge is for each organization to find the right strategy to best pursue measurement, either on its own or as part of a collaborative effort. Skoll, Acumen, Root Capital, and the Omidyar Network have joined with a number of other funders and investors as part of the Global Impact Investing Network, which among other activities is developing IRIS (Impact Reporting and Investment Standards), a standardized framework for assessing social and environmental impact.[14]

Room to Read, a San Francisco–based nonprofit committed to literacy in the developing world, puts out impact statistics every quarter. They include the number of schools and libraries built, the number of books published and distributed, the number of scholarships given, and the total number of people who have benefited from Room to Read programs. These are helpful statistics, but they show clearly the challenge in measuring impact. Are these kids literate? Are their life chances improved? Have the educational systems in the countries where Room to Read is operating improved as a result of Room to Read operations there? Room to Read tries to answer these questions to the best of its ability, but, as it says, there are a number of factors that affect literacy and educational systems. Their programs cannot account for factors beyond their control.

Ashoka developed the Measuring Effectiveness program in 1997, which looks at how well Ashoka fellows bring about systemic change in addition to specific returns connected to their projects. This brings us to the question of scale. As already mentioned, there is a great emphasis on scale. Several of our contributors talked about success in terms of scale. But what does scale mean? Is there a difference between scale and systemic change?

"[Social entrepreneurs] are distinguished from other citizen sector leaders by their long-term focus on creating wide-scale change at the systemic level."[15] From the beginning, Ashoka looked for social entrepreneurs with truly innovative ideas that could have regional if not national impact, but now there is increased focus on scale. Our speakers presented differing views on scale. Sally Osberg and Matt Bannick both look for investments, whether profitable or not, that have the capacity to scale. As Bill Draper told me in an interview, "We try to encourage fast growth. The impact is just more helpful."[16]

Matt Bannick notes in Chapter 8, "We invest in and help scale up entrepreneurial ventures that each has the potential to create opportunities for hundreds of thousands if not millions of people." In Chapter 7, Sally Osberg writes that her organization's first mission was "to invest in those with the greatest potential to make lasting positive change to their communities and to the world." In an earlier article for the *Stanford Social Innovation Review,* Osberg and co-author Roger Martin write that "the real measure of social entrepreneurship is a direct action that generates a paradigm shift in the way societal need is met."[17]

A recent *New York Times* article credits actor Ashton Kutcher with having "clearly mastered the utopian lingo of Silicon Valley: 'I look for companies that solve problems in intelligent and friction-free ways and break boundaries.'"[18] How much of the new business approach in the social sector is influenced by Silicon Valley? I would argue that it's quite a bit. Like the synergy of academia and business that led to the Silicon Valley phenomenon in the first place, there are similar pieces in place for the traction of social entrepreneurship among those who have made their fortunes by betting on paradigm-shifting disruptive technologies. The influence of the last generation of Hewlett, Packard, Moore, and Gates on the philanthropic culture cannot be underestimated. The new generation of Skoll, Omidyar, and Draper, focused on social entrepreneurship explicitly, is having a profound impact. There is a great deal of traction with impact investing in Northern California. There is something magnetic about changing the world. Surely, the notion of venture philanthropy, using a venture capital approach of funding deep and over the longer term, has emanated from Silicon Valley. Bill Draper writes in his book *The Startup Game,* "We could use our venture capital skills to find and assess the best 'social entrepreneurs' in the same way we found traditional entrepreneurs who were starting a business."[19]

To be sure, these ideas are not idiosyncratic to Silicon Valley, but there is a striking resemblance to the notion of a high-tech home run. Jacqueline Novogratz said, "I'll tell people in Silicon Valley about drip irrigation and that in one harvest, we are seeing farmers get their money back plus enough profit to buy the next quarter acre of drip irrigation and we're seeing a doubling and tripling of yields. So they're like, 'Well, then it must go viral.'"[20] But Novogratz goes on to say that societal change doesn't really "go viral." It takes time. Eric Weaver, founder and CEO of the Opportunity Fund, a microfinance organization in San Jose, California, also made this point: "People are looking for the killer app to provide a fix to a social problem. Microfinance is not a silver bullet for economic hardship, but it is part of a solution. There isn't a killer app when it comes to fixing systemic problems."[21]

All the contributors have nuanced understandings and approaches to change. In our conversation in Chapter 11, Matt Bannick explained,

> So we say, "Reach *x* engagement": the number of people, times the level of engagement, equals impact. So that is how we think about it.... Our approach is to find the social entrepreneurs who are working in areas in which we're interested, who we think have that opportunity to have that impact—reach *x*-times engagement—but we're also looking at creating a network of these entrepreneurs—hence the name, right, the Omidyar *Network*. The notion isn't just investing in individual entrepreneurs, but then bringing them together as a network, so that the whole is much more impactful than simply the sum.

Kriss Deiglmeier and Jed Emerson mentioned that change takes time and is incremental. Of course, taking time and incremental change can be frustrating and, frankly, unexciting; but as Jed Emerson said in our conversation in Chapter 15, "At the end of the day, many of these issues are still going to be here, and, if we make incremental progress, I'll be pretty happy. If we can just save a couple of polar bears, I'll be pleased."

All of our contributors embraced the idea that programs need to be evaluated and impact assessed. They all also realized that, though it is possible to have the social equivalent of a home run with a particular innovation or project, systemic change takes time, determination, and drive.

Bill Drayton said, "What is the role of the entrepreneur? The entrepreneur's role is to change the system, not applications; not a new clinic, a new school, a new department store— but to change the system."[22]

## And So . . .

When I think about what I am left with at the end of this book, most notable is a sense of extraordinary opportunity and innovation. There is great excitement in crossing over boundaries, questioning borders, and creating alliances among partners, programs, and constituencies. There are two important ways that borders can be traversed. The first we have spent much time in discussing: the application of business models and strategies to solve social issues. The second is that different partners must get into the mix: business with nonprofits, governments with business, and all configurations in between.

On the profit–nonprofit continuum, Jed Emerson wraps up Chapter 14 by saying, "As I think about social entrepreneurship, I believe that there really is no single definition of social entrepreneurship. It is simply a flow across a matrix of a variety of different forms and themes and manifestations, if you will. That goes from social enterprise to civic innovations. It goes across nonprofit to for-profit to hybrid mixes."

Here it is important to make two critical corollaries to the proposition that business can be a social enterprise and a social enterprise can be a business. First, the intent has to be about social change and not profit maximization; second, the need for profit cannot trump the social impact Kriss Deiglmeier said about Juma Ventures, "We made a decision that social good would always come first."[23]

On the need to traverse constituencies, we all need to think a little more out of the box. Today's challenges are multifaceted, complex, and oftentimes regional if not global in scope. Nonprofit organizations cannot solve them on their own, and neither can governments or business. We must work together. A great lesson of social entrepreneurship is that experimentation is good— very good in fact—but it must be carried out thoughtfully, strategically. We need to work together and can best do so in by leveraging our comparative strengths and creating effective alliances.

Throughout the book, our contributors have discussed a number of ways to think about social change and capital in new, exciting ways. There is clearly a growing appetite for and interest in organizations that test boundaries and traditional delineations. Our collective experience with social entrepreneurship has only just begun.

## Notes

1. Though there are several types of tax-exempt organizations, the tax category 501(c)(3) is the term that refers to organizations engaged in delivery of social services.

2. American Giving; retrieved on September 5, 2009, from www.canonprofits.org/index.php?option=com_content&view=article&id=254&Itemid=107.

3. Gergen, speech to the Commonwealth Club on September 14, 2010.

4. McKinsey & Company, "Effective Capacity Building in Non-Profit Organizations," prepared for Venture Philanthropy Partners, 2001.

5. Christine W. Letts, William Ryan, and Alan Grossman, "Virtuous Capital: What Foundations Can Learn from Venture Philanthropists," *Harvard Business Review,* 1996.

6. Morino Institute, "Venture Philanthropy—Landscape and Expectations" (Author: Rocky River, OH, 2001).

7. "Smarter grantmaking. Stronger nonprofits. Better results"; retrieved on November 14, 2011, from www.geofunders.org/aboutgeo.aspx.

8. E-mail to Ruth Shapiro, October 17, 2011

9. John Elkington and Pamela Hartigan. *The Power of Unreasonable People: How Social Entrepreneurs Create Markets that Change the World* (Boston: Harvard Business Press, 2008).

10. Monitor Institute, 2009.

11. Sustainability; retrieved on January 10, 2011, from www.walmartstores.com/Sustainability/.

12. Business Innovations at the Base of the Pyramid. Harvard Business School Business in Society Summit, October 13, 2008; retrieved on November 14, 2011, from www.hbs.edu/centennial/businesssummit/business-society/business-innovations-at-the-base-of-the-pyramid.html, Retrieved on November 14, 2011.

13. Ibid.

14. Impact Reporting and Investment Standards (IRIS); retrieved on November 22, 2011, from www.thegiin.org/cgi-bin/iowa/home/index.html, Retrieved November 22, 2011

15. Leslie Crutchfield, Leslie, Noga Leviner, and Diana Wells, "Understanding the Impact of Social Entrepreneurs: Ashoka's Answer to the Challenge of Measuring Effectiveness"; retrieved on December 2, 2011, from www.ashoka.org/printroom.

16. Bill Draper, interview, May 9, 2011, Palo Alto, California.

17. Roger Martin and Sally Osberg, "Social Entrepreneurship: The Case for Definition," *Stanford Social Innovation Review,* Spring 2007.

18. Jenna Wortham, "An Actor Who Knows His Start-Ups," *The New York Times,* May 26, 2011.

19. William Draper III, *The Startup Game* (New York: Palgrave McMillan, 2011).

20. "Challenges in Addressing Cultural Differences in Low Income Situations"; retrieved on March 11, 2011, from www.prendismo.com/collection/viewclip/16017.

21. Eric Weaver, interview, April 25, 2011, San Jose, California.

22. Taken from Commonwealth Club talk on October 26, 2010.

23. Conversation with Ruth Shapiro, March 22, 2011.

# REFERENCE MATTER

# BIBLIOGRAPHY AND SUGGESTED RESOURCES

Agoramoorthy, Govindasamy, and Minna J. Hsu. "Lighting the Lives of the Impoverished in India's Rural and Tribal Drylands." *Human Ecology* 37 (4, 2009): 513–517.

Ashoka. www.ashoka.org.

Austin, J. E. *The Collaboration Challenge: How Nonprofits and Businesses Succeed through Strategic Alliances.* San Francisco: Jossey-Bass, 2000.

Baron, David P. "Corporate Social Responsibility and Social Entrepreneurship." *Journal of Economics and Management Strategy* 16, 2007.

Bishop, Matthew, and Michael Green. *Philantrocapitalism: How the Rich Can Save the World.* New York: Bloomsbury Press, 2008.

Bonbright, David. *Leading Social Entrepreneurs.* Arlington, VA: Ashoka, 1997.

Bornstein, David. *How to Change the World: Social Entrepreneurship and Power of New Ideas.* Oxford, UK: Oxford University Press, 2007.

Bornstein, David, and Susan Davis. *Social Entrepreneurship: What Everyone Need to Know.* Oxford, UK: Oxford University Press, 2010

Brest, Paul, and Hal Harvey. *Money Well Spent.* New York: Bloomberg Press, 2008.

Brugmann, J., and C. K. Prahalad, "Cocreating Business's New Social Compact," *Harvard Business Review,* February 2007.

Clinton, Bill. "How We Can Work Together to Build a Stronger World." Special to CNN, September 24, 2008. Retrieved on March 15, 2009, from http://articles.cnn .com/2008-09-24/us/clinton.global_1_clean-energy-global-leaders-clinton-global-initiative?_s=PM:US.

Crutchfield, Leslie, and Heather McLeod Grant. *Forces for Good.* San Francisco: Jossey Bass, 2008.

Crutchfield, Leslie, Noga Leviner, and Diana Wells. "Understanding the Impact of Social Entrepreneurs: Ashoka's Answer to the Challenge of Measuring Effectiveness," 2007. Available at www.ashoka.org/printroom.

Davis, Susan. "Social Entrepreneurship: Toward an Entrepreneurial Culture for Social and Economic Development." Ashoka Print Room, July 31, 2001; retrieved on March 1, 2010, from www.ashoka.org/files/yespaper.pdf.

Dees, J. Gregory "The Meaning of Social Entrepreneurship," reformatted and revised edition. Durham, NC: The Center for Advancement of Social Entrepreneurship, May 30, 2001. Retrieved on March 13, 2010, from www.caseatduke.org/.

Deiglmeier, Kriss. "New Paths to Social Innovation." Podcast on Stanford Social Innovation Review, recorded October 6, 2009, and downloaded on February 20, 2011, from http://itc.conversationsnetwork.org/shows/detail4257.html#.

Draper, William III. *The Startup Game* (New York: Palgrave McMillan, 2011).

Drayton, William. *The Entrepreneur's Life Cycle.* Arlington, VA: Ashoka 1996

Drucker, Peter F. *Innovation and Entrepreneurship.* New York: Harper Business Press, 1993.

Elkington, John, and Pamela Hartigan. *The Power of Unreasonable People: How Social Entrepreneurs Create Markets That Change the World.* Boston: Harvard Business School Press, 2008.

Emerson, Jed. "Blended Value Investing: Integrating Environmental Risks and Opportunities into Securities Valuation," 2007. Retrieved on December 20, 2011, from www.blendedvalue.org/media/pdf-integrating-valuation-risksecurities.pdf.

———. "The 21st Century Foundation: Building upon the Past, Creating for the Future." April 20, 2004; available at www.blendedvalue.org/media/pdf-21st-century-foundation.pdf.

Emerson, Jed, and Sheila Bonini. "Capitalism 3.0." *Values News Network,* 1(1, March 2006).

Emerson, Jed, Tim Freundlich, and Jim Fruchterman, "Nothing Ventured, Nothing Gained," Skoll Centre for Social Entrepreneurship Working Paper. Oxford, UK. Retrieved on May 18, 2011, from www.sbs.ox.ac.uk/centres/skoll/research/Documents/Nothing%20Ventured.pdf.

Fruchterman, Jim. "For Love or Lucre." *Stanford Social Innovation Review,* Spring 2011. Retrieved on September 15, 2010, from www.ssireview.org/pdf/2011SP_Feature_Fruchterman.pdf.

Gardner, John. *Self-Renewal: The Individual and the Innovative Society.* New York: Norton Press, 1981.

Gergen, Christopher, and Gregg Vanourek. *Life Entrepreneurs: Ordinary People Creating Extraordinary Lives.* San Francisco: Jossey-Bass, 2008.

Good Capital, www.goodcap.net.

Harvard Business School, Business in Society conference, October 13, 2008. Retrieved on November 14, 2011, from www.hbs.edu/centennial/businesssummit/business-society/business-innovations-at-the-base-of-the-pyramid.html.

Heaney, Seamus. *The Cure at Troy: A Version of Sophocles' Philoctetes.* New York: Farrar, Straus and Giroux, 1991.

Karani, Aneel. "Microfinance Misses Its Mark," *Stanford Social Innovation Review,* Summer 2007; retrieved on January 8, 2011, from www.ssireview.org/articles/entry/microfinance_misses_its_mark/.

Karlen, Dean, and Jacob Appel. *More Than Good Intentions: How a New Economics Is Helping to Solve Global Poverty.* Haileah, FL: Dutton Press, 2011.

Kopp, Wendy. *A Chance to Make History.* New York: Public Affairs, 2011.

———. *One Day All Children: The Unlikely Triumph of Teach for America and What I Learned Along the Way.* New York: Public Affairs, 2001.

Letts, Christine W., William Ryan, and Alan Grossman. "Virtuous Capital: What Foundations Can Learn from Venture Philanthropists," *Harvard Business Review,* 1996.

Light, Paul. *Driving Social Change.* Hoboken, NJ: Wiley & Sons, 2011.

———. *The Search for Social Entrepreneurship.* Washington, DC: Brookings Institution Press, 2008.

Maran, Meredith, with Kriss Deiglmeier, ed. *Changing Lives, Changing Times: The First Decade of Juma Ventures.* San Francisco: Juma Ventures, 2003.

Martin, Roger, and Sally Osberg. "Social Entrepreneurship: The Case for Definition," *Stanford Social Innovation Review* (Spring 2007), pp. 28–29.

McKinsey & Company. "Effective Capacity Building in Non-Profit Organizations." Prepared for Venture Philanthropy Partners, Washington DC: August, 2001; retrieved on October 20, 2011, from www.vppartners.org/.

Monitor Institute. *Investing for Social and Environmental Impact.* Boston: Monitor, 2009.

Morino Institute, "Venture Philanthropy—Landscape and Expectations." Author: Rocky River, OH, 2001.

Mortenson, Greg, and David Oliver Rein. *Three Cups of Tea.* London: Penguin Books, 2006.

Next Billion. www.nextbillion.net/.

Novogratz, Jacqueline. *The Blue Sweater: Bridging the Gap between Rich and Poor in an Interconnected World.* New York: Rodale Books, 2009.

Oliver, Mary. "The Summer Day." *New and Selected Poems.* Boston: Beacon Press, 1992.

Osberg, Sally. "Framing the Change and Changing the Frame: A New Role for Social Entrepreneurs," in *Innnovations/Skoll World Forum* 2009, p. 6.

———. "Results at Scale," from *Faith and Leadership,* March 29, 2011; retrieved on June 8, 2011, from www.faithandleadership.com/node/2096.

Pallota, Dan. *Uncharitable.* Medford, MA: Tufts University Press, 2008.

Pena, R. "Solar Lighting for the Base of the Pyramid," Lighting Africa Project of the IFC, June 10, 2010; retrieved on February 12, 2011, from www1.ifc.org/wps/wcm/connect/a68a120048fd175eb8dcbc849537832d/SolarLightingBasePyramid.pdf?MOD=AJPERES.

Phills, James Jr., Kriss Deiglmeier, and Dale Miller. "Rediscovering Social Innovation," *Stanford Social Innovation Review,* Fall 2008; retrieved on October 17, 2010, from www.ssireview.org/articles/entry/rediscovering_social_innovation/.

Prahalad, C. K. *The Fortune at the Bottom of the Pyramid.* Upper Saddle River, NJ: Wharton School Publishing, 2006.

Ralser, Tom. *ROI for Nonprofits*. Hoboken, NJ: John Wiley & Sons, 2007.

Saul, J. *Social Innovation, Inc: 5 Strategies for Driving Business Growth through Social Change*. San Francisco: Jossey-Bass, 2011.

Schumpeter, Joseph A. *Capitalism, Socialism and Democracy*. New York: Harper Perennial, 1942.

Schwartz, Beverly. *Rippling: How Social Enterpreneurs Spread Innovation throughout the World*. San Francisco: Jossey-Bass, 2012.

Skoll Centre for Social Entrepreneurship. www.sbs.ox.ac.uk/centres/skoll/Pages/default .aspx.

Smith, Kirk R. "National Burden of Disease in India From Indoor Air Pollution." PNAS 97 (24, November 21, 2000).

Social Capital Markets. http://socialcapitalmarkets.net/.

Social Edge. www.socialedge.org.

Social Edge. "d.light S1: The Little Solar Lantern That Will Do BIG Things." Retrieved in January 2011 from www.socialedge.org/blogs/let-there-d-light/d.light-s1-the-little-solar-lantern-that-will-do-big-thing/?searchterm=57.

Solar Electric Light Fund, 2010–2011. Retrieved on February 12, 2011, from www.self .org/.

Stanford Social Innovation Review. www.ssireview.org.

Taub, Richard. *Community Capitalism: The South Shore Bank's Strategy for Neighborhood Revitalization*. Boston: Harvard Business Press, 2000.

Tierney, Thomas J., and Joel L. Fleishman. *Give Smart*. New York: Public Affairs, 2011.

Wolk, Andrew, and Kelley Kreitz. *Business Planning for Enduring Social Impact*. Cambridge, MA; Root Cause Publishing, 2008.

Wei-Skillern, Jane, James Austin, Herman Leonard, and Howard Stevenson. *Entrepreneurship in the Social Sector*. Los Angeles: Sage Publications, 2007.

Wood, John. *Leaving Microsoft to Change the World: An Entrepreneur's Odyssey to Education the World's Children*. New York: Harper Business, 2006.

The World Bank. *The Welfare Impact of Rural Electrification: A Reassessment of the Costs and Benefits*. Washington DC: World Bank Publications, 2008.

World Health Organization. *The Energy Access Situation in Developing Countries*. New York: World Health Organization/UNDP Reports, 2009.

Yunus, Muhammad. *Banker to the Poor*. New York, Public Affairs, 2003.

———. *Building Social Business*. New York: Public Affairs, 2010.

———. *Creating a World without Poverty*. New York: Public Affairs, 2009.

# INDEX

Access to capital/credit, 22, 28, 42, 60, 88, 93–98, 127, 135, 152, 179
Accion Texas, 45
Acid rain, 136–38
Acumen Fund, 6, 12, 71, 99, 105–10, 112, 118, 119, 205, 206, 207
Afghanistan, 27
Africa, investing in, 26–27
African Americans: bank credit for, 38–39; enterprises of, in Durham, 126; in poverty, 43; unemployment among, 43
African rats, 171
Aging in place, 8–9, 30–37
Agricultural projects, 78, 92–97, 105–106, 115, 172, 189
AIDS, 78
Alternative Emission Reduction Option, 137
Altruism, 37
Andreessen, Marc, 124
Angel investment, 201
Ankole Coffee Producers Co-operative Union (ACPCU), 98
Annie E. Casey Foundation, 127
ApproTEC, 71
Arkansas, 178
Ashoka, 3, 14, 71, 127, 142, 163–65, 169–76, 196, 200–201, 208
Ashoka Fellows and Fellowships, 32–33, 36, 163, 170–72
Asia Business Council, 2
Asian economic crisis, 1
Asian tsunami, 184
Aspen Network of Development Entrepreneurs (ANDE), 99

Assets, leveraging of existing, 52, 57
Assisted living services, 8–9, 30–37
Astaire, Fred, 70
Atlantic Philanthropies, 32
AVINA, 163

Bain Consulting, 202
Bangladesh, 178, 185
Banking, values-based, 38–48, 205
Bannick, Matt, 11, 113–14, 204, 205, 208, 209
Barker, Molly, 168–69
Base-of-the-pyramid products, 152, 206–207
BCF. See Bull City Forward
Besser, Mitch, 78
B Lab, 139
Black Ministerial Alliance, 54
Blended value, 13, 148, 153–54, 207
Blom, Peter, 45
Bloomberg Businessweek (newspaper), 33
Bornstein, Daniel, 5
Boston, Massachusetts, 49–50, 52–58
Bostonians for Youth, 50, 56
BRAC Bank, 45, 46
Brazil, 117
Bretos, Conchy, 8–9, 60, 62–64, 66, 200
Bribes, 86
Bridge International Academies, 83–84, 114
Bridgespan Group, 202
British Broadcasting Corporation (BBC), 75
Brookings Institute, 127
Bubble policy, 136–37
Bull City Forward (BCF), 126–29

Bush, George H. W., 137
Bush, George W., 62
Business model: applied to social entrepre-
    neurship, 4–6, 63–66, 142–43, 203–204,
    207–209; themes of, 5–6. *See also* Profit-
    nonprofit continuum
Byaruhanga, Josephat, 109

California State University Channel Islands,
    185
Calvert Foundation, 45, 99
Campaign for Female Education
    (CAMFED), 78
Cantillon, Richard, 72
Cap-and-trade system, 136–38
Capital. *See* Connected capital; Intellectual
    capital; Patient capital; Social capital
Capitalism: poverty alleviation through,
    108; and social capital, 134; and social
    change, 108–109; social entrepreneur-
    ship and, 4
Capital plus, 42
Capital Plus Exchange, 41
Capricorn Investment Group, 80
Cardamom cooperative, 97
Carew, Topper, 56
Carnegie, Andrew, 77, 86
Carter, Jimmy, 137
Casey, Lyman, 143
Castaneda, Carlos, 124
CBS, 33
Cell phones. *See* Mobile phones
Center for Effective Philanthropy, 202
Center for Financial Services Innovation
    (CFSI), 39, 41
Center for Social Innovation (CSI),
    Stanford Graduate School of Business,
    13–14, 133, 138, 157, 160
Champions, 14–15
Change. *See* Incremental change; Systemic
    change
Charity, 199. *See also* Philanthropy
Charlotte, North Carolina, 128
Chicago, Illinois, 38–40
China, 155
*Chronicle of Philanthropy* (newspaper),
    156–57

Cities, entrepreneurship in, 126–30
Civic Ventures Purpose Prize. *See* Purpose
    Prize
Clean Air Act (1970), 136–37
Climate change, 136–38
Clinton, Bill, 61, 140, 178
Clinton Bush Haiti Fund, 100
Cocoa cooperative, 96–97
Coleman, Barry and Andrea, 69, 74–76, 80
Collaboration, 129, 136, 139–40
Collaborative entrepreneurship, 164–67,
    170–76
College access programs, 55
Common Cause, 71
Community building, 128–30
Community development banking
    institutions, 44
Community development banks, 9, 43
Community development credit unions, 44
Community development financial
    institutions, 44
Community development loan funds, 44
Community First Option Program, 31–32
Community Reinvestment Act, 61–62
Connected capital, 26–29
Cooperatives, 92–93
Corporations: multinational, 206; and
    social innovation, 154–55, 159; societal
    role of, 1–2
Corruption, 86, 191–92
Cotton, Anne, 78, 80
Counseling Center, Trinity Boston
    Foundation, 55
Cradle-to-cradle, 154–55
Creative destruction, 4, 72
Credit bureaus, 62
Credit worthiness, 88, 177, 181
Cross-sector collaboration, 136, 139–40
Cuba, 33–34

Danone (Dannon), 185, 205
Dawson, Eric, 168
Dearborn Middle School, Boston, 57–58
Dees, Greg, 3–4, 7, 76, 132, 155
Deiglmeier, Kriss, 13–14, 152–60, 206, 210
Diffusion of innovation, 137–38
Diversity, 124, 129

d.light, 84–85, 107–108
Draper, Bill, 201, 208, 209
Draper funds, 189
Draper Richards Kaplan Foundation, 201
Drayton, Bill, 3, 6, 14, 132, 137, 142,
    187–89, 191–92, 195–97, 200, 204, 210
Duffy, Gloria, 2
Duke University, 125, 126, 129
Durham, North Carolina, 12–13, 126–30
Durham Technical Community College, 129

eBay, 11, 20–21, 70–71, 81–82, 139
eBay Foundation, 70–71
Echoing Green Foundation, 71, 163,
    200–201
Economic development: business role in, 1;
    peace and security related to, 100
Education, 83–84, 167–69, 172–73, 179–81,
    191–92, 194
Einstein, Albert, 141
Elkington, John, 4, 205
Emerson, Jed, 13, 153–54, 156–59, 203,
    207, 210
Emissions trading, 136–38
Empathy, 167–68, 195
Energy crisis, 183
Entrepreneurs: attributes of, 169; social
    entrepreneurs compared to, 70, 111.
    See also High-tech entrepreneurs;
    Social entrepreneurs
Environmental Defense Fund, 135, 137
Environmentally oriented banks, 41, 44
Environmental Protection Agency (EPA),
    136–37
Equator Capital Partners, 41
Ethics and morality, 108–109, 112, 170
Every Child Must Master Empathy, 175
"Everyone a change-maker," 163–76, 187–88,
    196–97
Existing assets, leveraging of, 52, 57

Facebook, 25–26
Failure, 35, 116, 125, 147
Fair trade, 95, 139
Faith-based organizations, 50–52
Falk, Gene, 78
Farmer, Paul, 80, 115

Financial crisis, 181–82. See also Great
    Recession
Financial training, 98
First California Bank, 45
Fisher, Martin, 71
501(c)(3) organizations, 21, 55, 57, 66,
    115–16, 202, 211n1
Flannery, Matt, 8, 21, 23, 132
Food crisis, 182
Foote, William (Willy), 11, 115–16, 132,
    138, 139, 204, 206
Ford, Henry, 141
Foreign aid, 193
Forward Ventures Communities, 128
Fourth Sector Cluster Initiative, North
    Carolina, 128
Frei, Phil, 83–84
Frontline World (television program), 23, 76
Fruchterman, Jim, 4
Funders, 6, 10–12, 131

Gambia, 75–76, 117
Gardner, John, 71, 80, 103–4
Gates Foundation, 41, 78, 86, 89, 115
Generosity, 52, 63
Gergen, Christopher, 12–13, 151–52, 155,
    159–60, 201; Life Entrepreneurs (with
    Gregg Vanourek), 124
Girls on the Run, 168–69
Global Alliance for Banking on Values, 45
Global Impact Investing Network (GIIN),
    99, 119, 207
Glocalization, 149
Google, 133–34
Gordon, Mary, 167–68, 172
Gore, Al, 135
Government: budget concerns of, 31–33, 64;
    effectiveness of, 63; human capital crisis
    in, 36; role of, 61–63, 192–93; social and
    moral problems shunned by, 36
Grameen America, 179
Grameen Bank, 14–15, 22, 39, 45, 139,
    177–86, 190, 196, 205
Grameen Creative Lab, 205
Grameen-Danone Company, 185
Grantmakers for Effective Organizations
    (GEO), 202

Grants, 85–87
Greater Boston Interfaith Organization, 57
Great man/woman theory, 133. *See also* Social entrepreneurs: dangers of individual focus on
Great Recession, 46. *See also* Financial crisis
Great Society, 71
Green Mountain Coffee Roasters, 97
Green revolution, 86
Grossman, Allen, 201
Group play, 168
Guatemala, 97
Guidestar, 202

Haiti, 100, 184
Hale, Victoria, 116
Hamilton, Hurmon, 53–54, 57, 58
Hartigan, Pamela, 4, 205
Harvard Business School, 207
Hawken, Paul, 79
Healthpoint, 189
Health services, 194–95
Heaney, Seamus, 110
Helen Sawyer Plaza building, Miami, 35
High-tech entrepreneurs, 4–5
Home Depot, 97
Homelessness, 143–45
Houghton, Mary, 9, 59–62, 132, 138, 204, 205
Housing shortage, 188–89
Human resources. *See* Talent
Hybrid approaches, 81–91, 112, 148–49, 189, 204
Hybrid nonprofit organizations, 205
Hyde Park Bank, 38
Hystra, 189

Idea generation, 136–37, 157–58
IDE India. *See* International Development Enterprises India
Impact, 6, 77, 107–108, 112–15, 118, 157, 163, 169–70. *See also* Metrics and measurement
Impact investors and investing, 87, 134, 206, 209
Impact Reporting and Investment Standards (IRIS), 207
Inclusive finance, 42

Inclusivity, 135
Incremental change, 155–56
India, 19, 62, 65, 78, 87, 89, 105–106, 115, 163–64, 188–89
Informal-sector workers, 188–89
INJAZ al-Arab, 78
Injustice, 19–20, 34–35, 72
Innovation: defined, 134; opportunities for, 82; process of, 123; social and economic progress through, 126. *See also* Social innovation
Innovation continuum, 136, 157–58
Institution building, 163
Intellectual capital, 147, 205
International Development Enterprises India (IDEI), 78, 106, 115
Internet public goods, 66
Investors, 10–12
Iraq, 27
Irrigation, 78, 105–106, 115, 189

Jackley, Jessica, 8, 21, 132
Janaagraha, 86
Japan, 86
Jeff Skoll Group, 80
Jesus, 51–52, 58
Job creation, 31, 81–82, 126, 180–81
Job Training Partnership Act (JTPA), 144
Johnson, Lyndon, 71
John Templeton Foundation, 32
J. P. Morgan, 99
Judgment, 187
Juma Ventures, 5, 152, 210

Kenya, 83–84, 86, 109, 114
Key Bank, 46
KickStart, 71
Kimmelman, Jay, 83–84
King, Martin Luther, Jr., 29
Kiva, 8, 21–29, 64–66, 76, 138, 139
Kiva Fellows Program, 24
Knowledge service, 47
Kutcher, Ashton, 208

Larkin Street Youth Services, 142–43
Leominster High School, 195
Letts, Chris, 201

Leveraged nonprofit organizations, 205
Levers, of social innovation, 139
Libraries, 77, 86
Libya, 86
Life entrepreneurs, 124
Linklaters International Law Firm, 78
Living Cities, 127
Lloyd, Sam, 53
Loan funds, 44
Lower-income populations, social entrepreneurship in, 129
Lozano, Juan David, 55

Malaysia, 178
Malnourishment, 185
Mamola, Randy, 74
Manchester Craftsmen's Guild, 71
Manduke, Noah, 71
Manila Water, 207
Market failures, 188–89
Martin, Roger, 72, 208
May, Shannon, 83–84
McCormack, Todd, 115
McKinsey & Company, 89, 201
Medicaid, 31, 33, 64
Medicare, 31
Metrics and measurement, 6, 64, 77, 117–19, 130, 148, 156–57, 202, 203, 207–210
Mexico, 94–95, 189
Mia Consulting Group, 8–9, 30–37
Microfinance: dangers for, 183; development of, 14–15, 177–78; economic basis of, 182; and education, 179–81; hybrid approaches to, 88; impact of, 45–46; Kiva and, 8, 20–29, 64–65; and overindebtedness, 62; poverty alleviation through, 60; problems with, 88; as social innovation, 135–36; system of, 178; in United States, 45–46, 178–79
Microfinance institutions (MFIs), 22, 88
Micromortgages, 60
Missing middle, of investment finance, 94–95, 99
Mission, 152–53
Mobile phones, 28, 190
Moon, Nick, 71
Moore's Law, 166

Morality. *See* Ethics and morality
Morino Institute, 202
Mothers to Mothers (M2M), 78
Multinational corporations, 206
Multiple drug-resistant tuberculosis (MDR-TB), 115
Munuo, Shiwahiade, 92–93

National Community Investment Fund (NCIF), 39, 41
National Resource Defense Council (NRDC), 137
Networks, 114, 124, 129–31
New Profit Inc., 127, 163
New Resource Bank, 44–45
Nicaragua, 101
Nike, 154–55
Nobel Peace Prize, 15, 22, 23
Nonprofit organizations: and charity, 199; definitions of, 5; growth of, 5; and microfinance, 64–65; need for income generation by, 151–52
North Carolina, 125–30
North Carolina Central University, 126, 129
North Carolina State University, 126
Northern Michigan University, 39
Novogratz, Jacqueline, 12, 112–13, 116–19, 200–201, 204, 205, 209
Nusyirwan, Iwan, 172

Obama, Barack, 62, 73
Oberlin College, 34
Odom, Steven, 56
Office of Social Innovation, 73
Okolloh, Ory, 86
Oliver, Mary, 110
Omidyar, Pam, 82
Omidyar, Pierre, 11, 70, 81–82
Omidyar Foundation, 6
Omidyar Network, 2, 11, 27, 82–91, 113–14, 207
One California Bank, 41
OneWorld Health, 116
Opportunities: access to means for responding to, 93; crises as, 37; innovation as response to, 82; recognition and grasp of, 3, 7, 72–73, 124

Optimism, 29, 30, 79, 196–97
Organizational efficacy, 201–203
Osberg, Sally, 11, 111–12, 114–20, 155, 200, 204, 208
Overindebtedness, 62
Overseas Private Investment Corporation (OPIC), 76

Packard, Louise, 9–10, 59, 60–61, 158, 200–201
Participant Media, 80
Partnerships, 10, 36, 39, 49, 52, 56–58, 73, 130
Partners in Health, 115
Patagonia, 154, 207
Patient capital, 26–27, 104–5, 205, 206
PayPal, 20–21
Peace, 100
Peace Games, 168
Pediatric AIDS transmission, 78
Peru, 115
Philanthropy, 142–46, 184, 201–202. See also Charity
Philippines, 178, 207
Phillips Academy Andover, 195
Piloting and prototyping, 137
Pioneer Human Services, 154
Playworks, 168
Positive externalities, 85–86
Poverty: capitalism and alleviation of, 108; as external condition, 14, 181; hybrid approaches to, 112; information technology and, 190; injustice of, 19; microfinance and, 20–29; microfinance and alleviation of, 60; in rural areas, 93–94; in United States, 43. See also Lower-income populations
Prahalad, C. K., 206
Predatory home loans, 47
Privacy, 166
Pro-Credit, 46
Profit-nonprofit continuum, 5, 64–65, 81–91, 111–12, 115–16, 148–49, 151–53, 187–89, 191–92, 205, 207, 210. See also Business model; Hybrid approaches
Program-related investments (PRIs), 75
Public Broadcasting Service, 71

Public goods. See Internet public goods
Public housing, 30, 32, 35
Public libraries, 77, 86
Pulse management system, 6
Purpose Prize, 8, 32–33, 35

Queen City Forward, 128
Quinacho, 96–97

Real estate bubble, 47
Recess, 168
Reciprocity, 124
Recycling, 154–55
Refugees United, 86–87
Regret, fear of, 125
Regulation, 47, 65
Relationship building, 50–52
Research Triangle Park, North Carolina, 126
Results. See Impact; Metrics and measurement
Return on investment, 47–48, 112–13, 148, 205
Riders for Health, 69, 75–76, 117
Risk tolerance, 114, 125
Rivera, Daniel, 96
Roberts, George, 143, 145–47
Rockefeller Foundation, 86, 89
Rockhopper TV, 75
Rogers, Ginger, 70
Room to Read, 6, 207–208
Root Capital, 10, 11, 92–101, 115–16, 119, 138, 206, 207
Root Cause, 55
Roots of Empathy, 167–68
Roxbury Presbyterian Church, 53–54, 57
Rural areas, prosperity encouragement in, 92–101
Rwanda, 97, 104
Ryan, William, 201

Sadangi, Amitabha, 78, 80, 105–106, 115
Saddleback Church, 53
Salti, Soraya, 78
Save the Children, 74
Scale: community building and, 130; for depth, 147; for-profit companies and, 85;

of impact, 114–15; importance of, 6, 208; nonprofit organizations and, 66; systemic change versus, 113–14; time for increasing, 138–39

Schumpeter, Joseph, 4, 72

Schwab, 163

Selco, 47

Selfishness, 184

Selflessness, 184

Senior living, 8–9, 30–37

Sequoia Capital, 65

Sewa Bank, 46

Shackleton, Ernest, 79

Shah, Premal, 8, 60, 62, 64–66, 76, 132, 200, 204

Shapiro, Ruth, 59–61, 64, 65, 111, 113, 115–17, 151, 153–56, 158, 160, 187, 189, 191–94, 196

Shaw, George Bernard, 125

ShoreBank, 9, 38–48, 62, 138, 178

ShoreBank International, 46

ShoreBank Pacific, 45

Siegel Gale, 71

Sierra Leone, 27

Silicon Valley, 4, 114, 202, 208–209

Sisters of the Sorrowful Mother, 97

Skoll, Jeff, 11, 70–71, 74, 80, 155

Skoll Award for Social Entrepreneurship, 75

Skoll Centre for Social Entrepreneurship, Oxford University, 11, 73

Skoll Foundation, 2, 6, 11, 27, 70–80, 89, 114–15, 163, 204, 207

Skoll Global Threats Fund, 80

Skoll World Forum, 73, 76, 80

Social business, 177, 183–86, 190, 192–93, 196, 205, 206

Social capital, 134

Social Capital Markets, 43

Social Edge, 73

Social enterprise, 111, 134, 205

Social entrepreneurs, 7–10; attributes of, 2, 116–17, 124, 194, 200; challenges for, 193–94; conventional entrepreneurs compared to, 70, 111; dangers of individual focus on, 59–60, 133, 158; defining, 3–4, 6, 72, 132–33, 200; goals of, 3, 4; high-tech entrepreneurs compared

to, 4–5; lessons learned from, 79, 156; twenty-somethings as, 150

Social entrepreneurship: business model applied to, 4–6, 63–66, 142–43, 203–204, 207–209; challenges in, 119–20, 131; defining, 2, 3–6, 149, 155; evolution of, 141–42; factors enabling, 128–30; global nature of, 149–50; in lower-income populations, 129; social innovation compared to, 133–34

Social Impact Center, Roxbury Presbyterian Church, 57–58

Social innovation, 13, 133–40; characteristics of, 135–36; corporate role in, 154–55, 159; defined, 133–34; factors contributing to, 134; future of, 138–40; levers of, 139; social entrepreneurship compared to, 133–34; stagnation in, 139; and systemic change, 155–56

Social investment funds, 191, 206

Social media. *See* Facebook

Social Venture Partners, 127

Solar lamps, 84–85

South America, 96–97

Southern Development Bancorporation, 39, 178

South Shore National Bank, 39

Spiritual hunger, 52

Starbucks, 11, 93, 97

Start-up organizations, 133

Street Potential, 55–56

Strickland, Bill, 71

Student loans, 28–29

Surdna Foundation, 127

Sustainability, 5, 7, 20, 30–32, 47, 65

Systemic change, 113–14, 155–56, 163–76

Talent: attraction of, 36, 119; cultivation of, 95, 128–29

Tanseed, 99–100

Teams, 59–60, 166. *See also* Collaborative entrepreneurship

Technology, 24–25. *See also* High-tech entrepreneurs

TEEP. *See* Trinity Education for Excellence Program

Thinkers, 12–14

TIAA-CREF, 99
Tolley, Brandi, 82
"Trade not aid," 1, 15n1
Trinity Boston Foundation, 9, 49–58, 63
Trinity Church, Boston, 49, 52–54
Trinity Education for Excellence Program (TEEP), 55, 61
Triodos Bank, 41, 42, 45
Triple bottom line, 42, 139, 153, 154
Troubled Asset Relief Program (TARP), 41
Trust, 124
Tugume, Richard, 98

Uganda, 98
Unilever, 152, 160
United Nations Conference on Trade and Development, 15n1
United States: charity in, 199; microfinance in, 45–46, 178–79; poverty in, 43
University of North Carolina, 126, 129
U.S. Centers for Disease Control, 115
U.S. Chamber of Commerce, 136
Ushahidi, 86
U.S. Health and Human Services Department, 31–32
U.S. Housing and Urban Development Department, 31–32
U.S. Treasury Department, 41, 44

Vaccines, 86
Value creation, 141

Values-based banking, 38–48, 205
Vanilla growers, 94–95
Vanourek, Gregg, *Life Entrepreneurs* (with Christopher Gergen), 124
Vaporware, 159
Venture philanthropy, 202, 209
Veolia, 205
Vergara, Felipe, 191–92
Vialet, Jill, 168
Volunteers, 24

*Waiting for Superman* (documentary), 80
Walmart, 135, 154, 159, 206
Warren, Rick, 53
Weaver, Eric, 209
Western Seed, 109
White, Thomas, 115
Whole Foods, 97
Wikipedia, 24, 66
Willow Creek Church, 53
Winthrop Rockefeller Foundation, 39
W. K. Kellogg Foundation, 2
Women's World Banking, 45
World Health Organization (WHO), 115

Young Presidents' Organization, 36
Youth culture, 195–96
Youth-focused programs, 55
Yunus, Mohammad, 14–15, 22, 23, 132, 149–50, 190, 192–97, 203, 205, 206

Zobel, Jaime, 207

Made in the USA
San Bernardino, CA
23 December 2013